Predicting Earthquakes, Eruptions, and Tsunamis With Machine Learning Forecasting

Froilan D. Mobo
https://orcid.org/0000-0002-4531-8106
Philippine Merchant Marine Academy, Philippines

IGI Global Scientific Publishing
Publishing Tomorrow's Research Today

Vice President of Editorial Melissa Wagner
Director of Acquisitions Mikaela Felty
Director of Book Development Jocelynn Hessler
Production Manager Mike Brehm
Cover Design Jose Rosado

Published in the United States of America by
IGI Global Scientific Publishing
701 East Chocolate Avenue
Hershey, PA, 17033, USA
Tel: 717-533-8845 | Fax: 717-533-7115
Website: https://www.igi-global.com E-mail: cust@igi-global.com

Library of Congress Cataloging-in-Publication Data

LCCN: 2026002947 (CIP Data Pending)
ISBN13: 979-8-3373-8042-1
Isbn13Softcover: 979-8-3373-8043-8
EISBN13: 979-8-3373-8044-5
British Cataloguing in Publication Data
A Cataloguing in Publication record for this book is available from the British Library.

Table of Contents

Detailed Table of Contents

Artificial Intelligence and its Deep Learning methods are transforming how we detect and locate earthquakes and using traditional Seismological Detection methods often struggles with highly noisy datasets, small-magnitude earthquakes, and human-based feature extraction, whereas Deep Learning models (and specifically Convolutional Neural Networks) allow for the automated analysis of raw seismic waveforms so they can produce higher levels of accuracy and faster and more reliably. This Chapter examines how AI-based Phase Picking, Classifications and Multi-station Source Localisation are changing the way we view Earthquake Detection with an emphasis on how to handle various Architecture and Data Set Issues, along with Real-time Implementation and Ethical Implications. The overall theme of this Chapter is AI in Seismology presents an opportunity to improve Early Warning Systems and help improve Global Seismic Resilience.

Over the last few decades, the world has been facing critical and unprecedented environmental problems like climate change, extreme weather, and loss of biodiversity. These problems are connected to each other, and it is imperative that the growth of predictive, adaptive, and scalable solutions should be prioritized. Biodisaster management, climate and weather forecasting and biodiversity tracking and monitoring have been very useful. Nevertheless, predictive analytics has not expanded at the pace and efficiency of the computational power, combination of data, and predictive potential gaps. The chapter, Artificial Intelligence to Environmental resilience: developing Weather forecasting, Disaster prediction, and Biodiversity monitoring, introduces the opportunities of AI to revolutionize environmental resilience. It gives an in-depth account of how the AI-based models are transforming forecasting systems, enhancing disaster predictions and management, and providing scalable biodiversity surveillance.

Every year, immense losses occur during natural hazards such as earthquakes, volcanoes, landslides and floods. Advanced digital technologies such as seismic networks, Prediction systems based on unmanned area vehicles (UAV), satellite monitoring, ground based sensors, Internet of Things (IoT) generate large volumes of data. Continuous real time monitoring and prediction based on data analytics introduce numerous challenges. Multi source data collection enables the use of big data analytics through machine learning and deep learning models. Complexity may arise in terms of data velocity, quality and preprocessing cost and reliability. This chapter focuses on major big data challenges in real time geo hazard monitoring and predictive models and highlights various research issues associated with it.

Using Central Pollution Control Board historical daily AQI data (2018-2024), analysis included data preprocessing, calculation of AQI, exploratory analysis, and comparative assessment using standard error measures. Based on the findings, LSTM performed better than all other models with the least Mean Absolute Error (MAE) of 18.41 and Root Mean Square Error (RMSE) of 24.23. ARIMA followed, with an MAE of 18.58 and RMSE of 29.11. With an MAE of 34.42 and RMSE of 50.08, SVR outperformed the other machine learning models and showed the best performance among machine learning techniques. The LSTM model was used in an attempt to predict for a 60-day time frame, predicting moderately stable AQI values (150-190) for the following days. The article emphasizes the disadvantages of conventional forecasting procedures and highlights the significance of deep learning techniques on environmental monitoring systems. The findings are informative to public health authorities and environmental planners that face air pollution problems in cities.

The West Valley Fault (WVF) is a seismic hazard of the Greater Metro Manila Area. The need to have high-fidelity, real-time seismic monitoring is imminent with the suspected Big One—a 7.2-magnitude earthquake. Conventional techniques, like the Short-Term Average/Long-Term Average (STA/LTA) algorithm, tend to malfunction with urban anthropogenic noise and enormous streams of data. which adjusts to the specifics of the geology and noise of the WVF. These frameworks can be incorporated into the Philippine Institute of Volcanology and Seismology (PHIVOLCS) workflow to ensure that latency in Earthquake Early Warning Systems (EEWS) can be greatly minimized to enhance disaster preparedness in the highly urbanized seismic areas.

This study re-conceptualizes the landscape of English for Specific Purposes (ESP) in institutional English-medium instruction (EMI) for disaster-ready professionals using AI-based seismic and tsunami forecasting as a curriculum template. A narrative synthesis of seismic AI, AI-enhanced project-based learning, ESP/EMI design and disaster communication feeds into the Continuous Data Assimilation Dynamic Needs Analysis (CDADNA) cycle in which a learner performance/stakehold\- er feedback/ AI-generated earthquake data are "input streams" alongside continuously updated hazard profile for revision of tasks, language focus and assessment. An ESP-EMI prototype as well as dashboard-based projects demonstrate how seismic literacy, briefing skills and "uncertainty talk" in English can be developed in Taiwan—modifiable for other high-risk regions.

Time-Series Analysis is essential to know and predict how the Earth system will behave as a result of earthquakes, volcanic eruptions, and tsunamis. Current geophysical observation is based on the use of continuous Geophysical Sensor Data from seismic networks, GPS arrays, InSAR satellites, and ocean buoys, thus, it calls for advanced analytical approaches. This chapter provides the most important Signal Processing and Feature Engineering techniques that can be used in the Earth sciences, such as time-domain, frequency-domain, and Time–Frequency Analysis methods like wavelet transforms. Additionally, it features the concept of representation learning in Machine Learning for Earth Sciences, along with the examples of its use in Hazard Monitoring and Early Warning Systems.

This chapter explores the growing role of machine learning (ML) and deep learning (DL) in advancing earthquake prediction, detection, localization, and seismic characterization. Traditional seismological methods face challenges related to noise, limited sensor coverage, and complex wave propagation. ML and DL techniques address these limitations by enabling automated feature extraction, robust pattern recognition, and real-time processing of large-scale seismic datasets. The chapter reviews key architectures including CNNs, RNNs, Transformers, GNNs, and physics-informed models and examines their applications in seismic noise reduction, phase picking, magnitude estimation, and early warning systems. Major challenges such as data scarcity, model generalization, interpretability, and computational constraints are discussed. The chapter concludes with emerging research directions aimed at developing reliable, scalable, and AI solutions for seismic monitoring and hazard mitigation.

Volcanic seismic activity is crucial to learning about magmatic and hydrothermal activity beneath the surface, which gives early warning of possibly occurring earthquakes or eruptions. As the seismic networks grow, manual analysis is no longer feasible, and machine learning is the primary solution in the area of automated classification of the waveforms. The chapter is an overview of sophisticated methods of computing volcanic seismic signals, with a focus on deep learning algorithms, including CNNs, LSTMs, and transformers. It describes an entire methodology including preprocessing, model extraction, model validation, and model deployment in real-time. Such challenges as noise, class imbalance, generalization, and interpretability have been discussed, with future directions also being multimodal data fusion, probabilistic model, self-supervised learning, and AI-based early-warning pipelines.

Preface

OVERVIEW OF THE SUBJECT MATTER

The intersection of geophysics and computational intelligence represents one of the most significant frontiers in modern science. Historically, our understanding of the Earth's lithosphere and hydrosphere has relied upon deterministic, physics-based models. While these models have provided the foundational framework for understanding tectonic movements and fluid dynamics, they often hit a "computational ceiling" when faced with the sheer volume and non-linearity of real-time geophysical data.

Predicting Earthquakes, Eruptions, and Tsunamis With Machine Learning Forecasting explores the paradigm shift from purely mechanical observations to data-driven intelligence. This book delves into how machine learning (ML)—ranging from deep neural networks to reinforcement learning—can decode the "noise" in seismic waveforms, thermal anomalies, and oceanographic pressure changes. By treating the Earth as a massive data-generating system, this work examines how algorithms can identify precursor patterns that were previously invisible to the human eye or traditional statistical methods.

THE TOPIC IN TODAY'S GLOBAL CONTEXT

We are living in an era of unprecedented environmental volatility. As urban populations expand into high-risk coastal and tectonic zones, the human and economic stakes of natural disasters have reached a critical inflection point. The traditional "wait and see" approach to disaster management is no longer viable. In the contemporary world, "time" is the most valuable currency; even a few seconds of advanced warning for an earthquake or a few hours for a tsunami can save thousands of lives and billions in infrastructure.

This book fits into the global digital transformation of disaster risk reduction (DRR). With the proliferation of IoT sensors, high-resolution satellite imagery, and global seismic networks, we are "data rich" but often "insight poor." This publication serves as a bridge, utilizing the current revolution in Artificial Intelligence to translate this deluge of raw data into actionable, life-saving forecasts.

CHAPTER OVERVIEW

Chapter 1: AI Beneath the Surface: Deep Learning Techniques for Detecting and Locating Earthquakes

Artificial Intelligence and its Deep Learning methods are transforming how we detect and locate earthquakes and using traditional Seismological Detection methods often struggles with highly noisy datasets, small-magnitude earthquakes, and human-based feature extraction, whereas Deep Learning models (and specifically Convolutional Neural Networks) allow for the automated analysis of raw seismic waveforms so they can produce higher levels of accuracy and faster and more reliably. This Chapter examines how AI-based Phase Picking, Classifications and Multi-station Source Localisation are changing the way we view Earthquake Detection with an emphasis on how to handle various Architecture and Data Set Issues, along with Real-time Implementation and Ethical Implications. The overall theme of this Chapter is AI in Seismology presents an opportunity to improve Early Warning Systems and help improve Global Seismic Resilience.

Chapter 2: Artificial Intelligence for Environmental Resilience: Advancing Weather Forecasting, Disaster Prediction and Biodiversity Monitoring

Over the last few decades, the world has been facing critical and unprecedented environmental problems like climate change, extreme weather, and loss of biodiversity. These problems are connected to each other, and it is imperative that the growth of predictive, adaptive, and scalable solutions should be prioritized. Biodisaster management, climate and weather forecasting and biodiversity tracking and monitoring have been very useful. Nevertheless, predictive analytics has not expanded at the pace and efficiency of the computational power, combination of data, and predictive potential gaps. The chapter, Artificial Intelligence to Environmental resilience: developing Weather forecasting, Disaster prediction, and Biodiversity monitoring, introduces the opportunities of AI to revolutionize environmental resilience. It gives an in-depth account of how the AI-based models are transforming forecasting systems, enhancing disaster predictions and management, and providing scalable biodiversity surveillance.

Chapter 3: Big Data Challenges in Real-Time Geo-Hazard Monitoring and Prediction

Every year, immense losses occur during natural hazards such as earthquakes, volcanoes, landslides and floods. Advanced digital technologies such as seismic networks, Prediction systems based on unmanned area vehicles (UAV), satellite monitoring, ground based sensors, Internet of Things (IoT) generate large volumes of data. Continuous real time monitoring and prediction based on data analytics introduce numerous challenges. Multi source data collection enables the use of big data analytics through machine learning and deep learning models. Complexity may arise in terms of data velocity, quality and preprocessing cost and reliability. This chapter focuses on major big data challenges in real time geo hazard monitoring and predictive models and highlights various research issues associated with it.

Chapter 4: Comparative Analysis of Machine Learning and Time Series Models for Index Prediction: A Case Study of IGI Airport, Delhi

Using Central Pollution Control Board historical daily AQI data (2018-2024), analysis included data preprocessing, calculation of AQI, exploratory analysis, and comparative assessment using standard error measures. Based on the findings, LSTM performed better than all other models with the least Mean Absolute Error (MAE) of 18.41 and Root Mean Square Error (RMSE) of 24.23. ARIMA followed, with an MAE of 18.58 and RMSE of 29.11. With an MAE of 34.42 and RMSE of 50.08, SVR outperformed the other machine learning models and showed the best performance among machine learning techniques. The LSTM model was used in an attempt to predict for a 60-day time frame, predicting moderately stable AQI values (150-190) for the following days. The article emphasizes the disadvantages of conventional forecasting procedures and highlights the significance of deep learning techniques on environmental monitoring systems. The findings are informative to public health authorities and environmental planners that face air pollution problems in cities.

Chapter 5: Deep Convolutional Neural Networks for Enhanced Earthquake Detection and Characterization: A Focus on the Philippine West Valley Fault ("The Big One")

The West Valley Fault (WVF) is a seismic hazard of the Greater Metro Manila Area. The need to have high-fidelity, real-time seismic monitoring is imminent with the suspected Big One—a 7.2-magnitude earthquake. Conventional techniques, like the Short-Term Average/Long-Term Average (STA/LTA) algorithm, tend to malfunction with urban anthropogenic noise and enormous streams of data. which adjusts to the specifics of the geology and noise of the WVF. These frameworks can be incorporated into the Philippine Institute of Volcanology and Seismology (PHIVOLCS) workflow to ensure that latency in Earthquake Early Warning Systems (EEWS) can be greatly minimized to enhance disaster preparedness in the highly urbanized seismic areas.

Chapter 6: From Seismic AI to the EMI Classroom: Project-Based ESP Curriculum Design for Disaster-Ready Professionals

This study re-conceptualizes the landscape of English for Specific Purposes (ESP) in institutional English-medium instruction (EMI) for disaster-ready professionals using AI-based seismic and tsunami forecasting as a curriculum template. A narrative synthesis of seismic AI, AI-enhanced project-based learning, ESP/EMI design and disaster communication feeds into the Continuous Data Assimilation Dynamic Needs Analysis (CDADNA) cycle in which a learner performance/stakehold\- er feedback/ AI-¬generated earthquake data are "input streams" alongside continuously updated hazard profile for revision of tasks, language focus and assessment. An ESP-EMI prototype as well as dashboard-based projects demonstrate how seismic literacy, briefing skills and "uncertainty talk" in English can be developed in Taiwan—modifiable for other high-risk regions.

Chapter 7: Fundamentals of Time-Series Analysis and Feature Engineering for Geophysical Data

Time-Series Analysis is essential to know and predict how the Earth system will behave as a result of earthquakes, volcanic eruptions, and tsunamis. Current geophysical observation is based on the use of continuous Geophysical Sensor Data from seismic networks, GPS arrays, InSAR satellites, and ocean buoys, thus, it calls for advanced analytical approaches. This chapter provides the most important Signal Processing and Feature Engineering techniques that can be used in the Earth sciences, such as time-domain, frequency-domain, and Time–Frequency Analysis methods like wavelet transforms. Additionally, it features the concept of representation learning in Machine Learning for Earth Sciences, along with the examples of its use in Hazard Monitoring and Early Warning Systems.

Chapter 8: Machine Learning for Earthquake Prediction and Characterization: Advancing Detection, Localization, and Seismic Analysis with Deep Learning

This chapter explores the growing role of machine learning (ML) and deep learning (DL) in advancing earthquake prediction, detection, localization, and seismic characterization. Traditional seismological methods face challenges related to noise, limited sensor coverage, and complex wave propagation. ML and DL techniques address these limitations by enabling automated feature extraction, robust pattern recognition, and real-time processing of large-scale seismic datasets. The chapter reviews key architectures including CNNs, RNNs, Transformers, GNNs, and physics-informed models and examines their applications in seismic noise reduction, phase picking, magnitude estimation, and early warning systems. Major challenges such as data scarcity, model generalization, interpretability, and computational constraints are discussed. The chapter concludes with emerging research directions aimed at developing reliable, scalable, and AI solutions for seismic monitoring and hazard mitigation.

Chapter 9: Machine Learning–Driven Classification of Volcanic Seismicity and Tremor Signals for Early Eruption Forecasting

Volcanic seismic activity is crucial to learning about magmatic and hydrothermal activity beneath the surface, which gives early warning of possibly occurring earthquakes or eruptions. As the seismic networks grow, manual analysis is no longer feasible, and machine learning is the primary solution in the area of automated classification of the waveforms. The chapter is an overview of sophisticated methods of computing volcanic seismic signals, with a focus on deep learning algorithms, including CNNs, LSTMs, and transformers. It describes an entire methodology including preprocessing, model extraction, model validation, and model deployment in real-time. Such challenges as noise, class imbalance, generalization, and interpretability have been discussed, with future directions also being multimodal data fusion, probabilistic model, self-supervised learning, and AI-based early-warning pipelines.

Chapter 1
AI Beneath the Surface:
Deep Learning Techniques for Detecting and Locating Earthquakes

Sudipta Dhar
http://orcid.org/0009-0004-4998-3041
Brainware University, India

ABSTRACT

Artificial Intelligence and its Deep Learning methods are transforming how we detect and locate earthquakes and using traditional Seismological Detection methods often struggles with highly noisy datasets, small-magnitude earthquakes, and human-based feature extraction, whereas Deep Learning models (and specifically Convolutional Neural Networks) allow for the automated analysis of raw seismic waveforms so they can produce higher levels of accuracy and faster and more reliably. This Chapter examines how AI-based Phase Picking, Classifications and Multi-station Source Localisation are changing the way we view Earthquake Detection with an emphasis on how to handle various Architecture and Data Set Issues, along with Real-time Implementation and Ethical Implications. The overall theme of this Chapter is AI in Seismology presents an opportunity to improve Early Warning Systems and help improve Global Seismic Resilience.

DOI: 10.4018/979-8-3373-8042-1.ch001

INTRODUCTION

The process of identifying and locating earthquakes is a critical component of the global seismic monitoring system, serving as a key element in the creation of disaster preparedness, early warning systems, and the development of seismic risk mitigation methods. Natural disasters, such as earthquakes, are just one of many hazards that can have an impact on the livelihood of individuals, infrastructure, and economies worldwide. The occurrence of earthquakes can take place at all locations within every tectonically active region of the world. The capability to quickly and accurately identify earthquakes allows for early warning systems to provide timely warnings, allows for better emergency planning, and allows for the development of mitigation strategies that can significantly reduce casualties due to earthquakes and damage to buildings caused by earthquakes. Rapid growth of cities, in combination with increased concentrations of critical infrastructure located in areas of high seismic activity, has heightened the need for reliable, scalable, and real-time solutions for monitoring seismic activity.

Historically, seismology has used techniques associated with physics-related signal processing, along with expert analysis of the data to identify seismic events and determine parameters of the seismic event (i.e., the location, magnitude, and focal mechanism). Traditional approaches comprise a series of steps, such as filtering signals, determining the phases of the signal, and then using a triggering method (i.e., STA/LTA) to determine if an actual seismic event has occurred. All the methods used to detect seismic events have been based on proven physical principles and have been proven reliable over decades. However, the effectiveness of these systems is largely dependent upon extensive manual tuning, domain knowledge, and precise calibration to the local geological conditions. Therefore, traditional methods face significant barriers to scalability, adaptability and automation, particularly in modern earthquake monitoring systems due to the large quantities of data associated with these systems, which makes it very difficult to use traditional techniques for seismic monitoring.

The use of the data-driven method for seismic detection has been responsible for the remarkable increase in accuracy and efficiency in detecting earthquakes. Seismic signals are often contaminated by various sources of noise, such as environmental noise (e.g., thunderstorms) and anthropogenic noise (e.g., road construction). Because of this, classical seismic methods can often produce false positive results or cannot find lower-intensity events in environments with high levels of noise. In addition, in places where many earthquakes occur in quick succession or have overlapping timescales, the detection of these events becomes even more challenging, as it is difficult to pick the correct phase and associate different types of events. Because microseismic events have very small amplitudes, they can be overlooked, and conversely, can impede our ability to understand how faults behave and assess seismic hazards. Therefore, better and more adaptive techniques will need to be employed for detecting microseismic events in geologically complex and unpredictable settings.

In the last several years, the rapid development of artificial intelligence (AI), especially in the field of deep learning, has revolutionised the way we analyse the seismic data that is collected. By employing massive datasets of seismic recordings for training, deep learning algorithms automatically identify complex patterns and features that would be nearly impossible for a human to specify or estimate manually. In contrast to classical techniques that depend upon highly processed data and pre-defined thresholds, deep learning algorithms extract multi-level features from raw or minimally processed seismic data. There are several disadvantages associated with traditional seismic detection; one such disadvantage is its vulnerability to noise interference.

There are several different types of deep learning architectures; however, currently, convolutional neural networks (CNNs) are arguably the most suitable for seismic applications. CNNs were originally developed for image processing but have now been successfully used on structured time series data, such as seismic waveforms and spectrograms. Convolutional Neural Networks (CNN) use convolutional filters to automatically detect relevant features associated with each of the different seismic phases (e.g. point of a wave starting, shape of the frequency distribution, shape of the amplitude curve). Therefore, CNN-based models are able to discriminate effectively against both seismic and non-seismic events in cases where the signal-to-noise ratio is very low, thereby making them ideally suited for use in monitoring applications in the field.

The achievements of deep learning technologies applied to earthquake detection and monitoring, even in noise and/or complex environments, have been numerous. They are able to isolate faint seismic signals and separate coincident seismic signals; both of these capabilities are critical for detecting induced seismicity resulting from activities such as mining, geothermal energy, or other reservoir stimulations. More recently, architectures such as attention-based models and transformers are enabling both detection and phase picking to occur concurrently, which has led to improved performance. The capability of deep learning systems to ingest raw continuous streams of seismic data in almost real time has also made them a very attractive candidate for early warning applications where rapid response is crucial.

Deep Learning-based methods provide a methodical way to complete a large volume of real-time seismic data coming from global seismic networks automatically, with little or no human involvement. High-performance computing and cloud infrastructure support the use of these models, allowing for real-time continuous monitoring. However, there are many challenges that need to be addressed. Many of these models operate as "Black box" models and therefore lack interpretability. This limits the ability to connect model outputs back to the geophysical process that created them. Researchers are working to develop explainable AI models. In addition, bad data quality, as well as the lack of sufficiently labeled seismic data sets, could also have negative implications on the outcomes achieved; therefore, there is a need to enhance the data set creation process and collection techniques.

The performance of these artificial intelligence models could be hampered by domain shifts in cases where they are used in other geological settings or with different sensor setups or noise sources. This problem can be solved using cross-region validation and transfer learning techniques. Operational challenges such as latency, efficiency, false alarm rates, and maintenance must also be properly managed for an AI model to provide real-time services. For safety-critical systems such as earthquake early warning, AI should complement expert judgement rather than function as a replacement. One of the major current limitations of deep learning methods in seismology is the inadequate representation of uncertainty. Seismic data are subject to significant noise, and therefore, many models provide deterministic predictions without being able to acknowledge either epistemic or aleatoric uncertainty. In addition, the ability of such models to handle changes in their domains, for instance, due to a broken sensor or high noise values, has been poorly examined. In this regard, the present chapter will address the shortcomings of existing research by putting forward an all-round framework on the issues of detection, phase picking, association, and localisation. Reproducibility and assessment of results will also be a focus in this chapter. The inclusion of aspects such as uncertainty analysis, robustness, and deployment in this chapter will serve to form a pragmatic view of these technologies.

RELATED WORK: A STRUCTURED PERSPECTIVE

Over the last 10 years, deep learning in seismic monitoring has changed dramatically and affected almost all major components involved in seismic monitoring, including detecting earthquakes, phase selection, linkage, and determining locations. There is a significant amount of literature; however, a substantial number of studies report improvements in methodology but do not provide a unified analysis to describe the methodological differences, data needs, performance differences, and limitations of the various classifications. Therefore, structured synthesis is important.

Earthquake Detection

Early efforts using deep learning considered the detection of seismic events to be a classification problem, whereby events were classified as either an event or noise based on a portion of a waveform. The convolutional neural network (CNN)-based method developed by Perol et al. (2018) and implemented by Meier et al. (2019) significantly outperformed traditional methods such as STA/LTA that use set thresholds, especially in low signal/noise conditions. The CNNs have learned to extract hierarchical features directly from raw waveform data; therefore, they eliminated the need for manually extracting features from waveforms.

To date, several additional models and more sophisticated architectures have been developed, including residual networks, CNN-RNN hybrid models, etc., that increase sensitivity for detecting events while decreasing false alarm rates. More recently, transformer-based models have provided improved capability to detect events by learning long-range temporal relationships among data (i.e. continuous waveform data). Even though there are many developments in machine learning, the biggest obstacle is still that model performance depends on the training data set. Models that were trained on a specific data set have a hard time generalising to different types of seismic regions, therefore limiting their ability to do domain adaptation.

Phase Picking and Event Association

The location of when and where an earthquake occurs is very heavily dependent on the process of phase picking. This identifies the arrival times of P waves and S waves. One promising example of deep learning's ability to produce high-quality estimates during this process is a fully convolutional network architecture known as PhaseNet, which is capable of sample-level predictions (Zhu and Beroza, 2019). These methods have significantly outperformed traditional picking techniques, especially in noisy environments.

Newer models, such as The Earthquake Transformer (Mousavi et al., 2020), were able to combine the two separate tasks of phase picking and detection into one model by using an attention mechanism that allows users to improve performance and prevent errors from being propagated from the detection task to the phase picking task. These models have also exhibited improved performance through accounting for multi-station spatial correlations across seismic networks, as well as through the use of graph models.

Despite the successes of the above models, there are still challenges to address. In particular, overlapping events and label uncertainty from differing manual annotation methods are two primary issues for the majority of current approaches. Additionally, due to the lack of standardised evaluation metrics in the literature, it can be very difficult to compare results across studies.

Localisation Approaches

Traditionally, localisation of earthquake events is performed via inversion techniques that make use of phase arrival times and estimated velocity models. In contrast, deep learning methods have been developed that push beyond traditional methods with complementary approaches based on performing improved upstream phase picking (as described above) and utilising end-to-end models that directly predict source parameters. Regression-based methods (e.g. Perol, 2018; Ma, 2026) have demonstrated the ability to directly estimate location parameters from the available waveform data and reduce the need for reliance upon traditional physics-based models.

Multi-station models based on Attention and Graph Neural Networks (GNN) have improved localisation accuracy by modelling spatial dependencies between seismic stations; however, GNN techniques are sensitive to network geometry and require dense station coverage. Additionally, the limited availability of data and the difficulty in interpreting the results of these methods present ongoing challenges.

Uncertainty and Robustness

As deep learning algorithms head toward operational application, it is becoming essential that uncertainty quantification also becomes a part of the process. Recent efforts to quantify uncertainty show a need to distinguish between epistemic uncertainty (the result of the way a model is specified) and aleatoric uncertainty (the inherent variability of the data used to train a model). Most current models still produce deterministic outputs, and there are no ways to accurately calibrate confidence levels around these outputs, which diminishes the reliability of the model output for critical use cases.

Robustness over domain drift is also a large concern. While many factors influence the effectiveness of models on data outside of a training set — including the underlying geology, the type of sensors responding to seismic waves, and the level of noise present — there is still to be a systematic methodology used to evaluate how effectively transfer learning and data augmentation can manage this variability.

Benchmarking and Datasets

Benchmarks such as STEAD and SeisBench provide a way to standardise and enable reproducibility of results of seismic deep learning research efforts. These two resources provide common datasets and evaluation methodologies, which provide researchers with ways to have more consistent comparisons.

Although much progress has been made to provide consistency in evaluating research in this field, inconsistencies still occur in the evaluation process. Due to a lack of consistency in preprocessing methods, partitioning of datasets, and the type of performance metrics used, there can be wide variations between studies about how well a model has performed when measuring detection performance using different evaluation metrics.

Limitations of Traditional Earthquake Detection Methods

Seismologists have historically used classical signal processing techniques to create their earthquake detection systems, including STA/LTA (short-term average/long-term average) triggering, matched filtering, and template-based detection. These systems are based on established concepts related to the physical nature of seismic wave movement and have seen widespread implementation in regional and global monitoring of seismic activity (Perol et al., 2018; Zhu & Beroza, 2019). Methods that are easier to implement in practice will tend to produce results that are equally valid and easy to understand in both cases. As a result, there is widespread agreement among seismologists about how to distinguish and categorise earthquake signals. (Mousavi & Beroza, 2022).On the other hand, the increase in complexity of seismic data and the demand for ever-higher resolution monitoring have magnified some of the limitations of the traditional earthquake detection systems (Noel and West, 2025).

The STA/LTA trigger has proven itself as a valuable means of discovering seismological phenomena. The process involves determining the ratio between short-term and long-term energy and using the ratio as an indication of seismic activity. The presence of a potential seismic activator occurs when the short-to-long energy ratio is above a certain threshold level. The technique works well when applied to individual stations operating with unregulated signals. However, it generates many false positives when applied in locations with elevated background noise, offshore, and other locations where there are many people around. Lowering the false alarms by increasing threshold levels can cause the system to overlook new and small seismic phenomena needed to understand the nature of the faults and develop further seismic hazard assessment.

Template matching and strain-based detection methods represent the two most well-defined types of traditional technology used in the detection of seismic activity. Each operates by first correlating the incoming seismic signal from a detected source with many previously recorded waveforms (referred to as templates) to create an association if sufficient correlation exists. For microseismic events (or other similar events) that are being compared to prior events, matched filtering is considered to be an effective technique, but one downside to this approach relates to the completeness and quality of the associated template library (Perol, 2018; Li et al., 2024). In this case, any class of events that cannot be associated with a given template (either due to a new rupture mechanism having occurred, differing source conditions, and/or overlapping arrivals) will not be detected using the template matching approach. Additionally, creating and maintaining a well-developed library of large sets of statistical data will be more difficult, and increasingly not practical, as regional seismic networks are expanded to cover larger geographic areas (Noel & West, 2025).

A key bottleneck of the traditional seismic processing phase is phase picking, identifying the arrival of Primary (P) and Secondary (S) waves. Correctly determining the phase pick is essential to correct position and magnitude estimates for earthquakes. Traditionally, the analyst would pick the phase either manually (Cano et al., 2021) or with algorithms that performed semi-automatically but needed operator confirmation. Manually picking phases is time-consuming, is a demanding and tedious task and often the results are nominally subject to human prejudice and lack of uniformity. As a consequence, each analyst can interpret the arrival time of the phases very differently, which can cause an offset in the location of the event and its associated parameters (Zhu et al., 2019; Liu et al., 2020). Therefore, in large-scale operations like national or global seismic networks, it makes manual phase picking impractical (Mousavi & Beroza, 2023).

In addition, with the increase in high-density, high-frequency, and continuous recording of waveforms from an expanding number of seismic networks, the quantity of data produced by today's seismic array systems has become enormous, requiring continuous processing and real-time monitoring. The conventional methods of detecting and picking seismic events have not been developed for such a large volume of data; therefore, they have issues with latency, limited scalability, and increased operating costs (Scheingraber et al., 2013; Noel & West, 2025). This issue becomes even greater in cases like the earthquake early warning system, where just a few seconds' delay can significantly affect the timeliness of the warning (Ahamad & Singh, 2025).

Also, traditional detection/picking methods assume you will be using accurate velocity models for each location/region; however, this may not be the case, especially when considering geological settings are generally not similar, thus adjustments need to be made every time these methods are applied in a new location. If you are applying a velocity model to a tectonically active region that has a very complicated subsurface, and using an inaccurate velocity model, it could drastically affect the entire event detection process and may cause you to call off detection events altogether (Han et al., 2025; Xi et al., 2024).

These limitations mentioned compound the growing divide between traditional earthquake detection systems and modern technology's capabilities in each regard to seismic monitoring. Some of the seismic monitoring capabilities available now are detecting low-magnitude seismic events, being able to reliably utilise existing performance in noisy settings, and having large amounts of data processed in real-time. A rapid development toward automated, noise-immune, scalable techniques (including many systems utilising artificial intelligence (AI) and deep learning) is already underway to reduce or eliminate the negative impacts of traditional technologies while also enhancing traditional seismological knowledge (Perol et al., 2018; Mousavi et al., 2020).

In Table 1, deep learning-based methods significantly outperform traditional seismic techniques according to a side-by-side comparison. Traditional seismic techniques mostly use manual extraction (STA/LTA ratio, frequency content, amplitude), which results in low success rates for identifying weak or microseismic events and a high sensitivity to background noise (Meier et al, 2019; Han et al, 2025). Conversely, deep learning models are capable of extracting and learning from raw seismic signal data to achieve better noise resistance and higher sensitivity to smaller event magnitudes (Zhu & Beroza, 2019; Saad & Chen, 2020). Due to this peculiar quality, deep learning makes it possible for many of the tasks involved in phase picking, which are usually done either manually or semiautomatically in conventional systems, to become fully automatic thanks to CNNs or RNNs (Zhu & Beroza, 2019; Feng et al., 2022). Furthermore, the scalability in deep learning techniques that employ GPUs or cloud computing and the ability to perform low-latency inference has enabled the effective application of these techniques to larger datasets and real-time processing (Liao et al., 2022; Mousavi & Beroza, 2023).

Table 1. Comparison of Traditional and Deep Learning–Based Seismic Methods

Aspect	Traditional Seismic Methods	Deep Learning–Based Methods
Feature extraction	Handcrafted (STA/LTA, frequency, amplitude)	Automatically learned from raw waveforms
Noise robustness	Low – highly sensitive to background noise	High – learns to distinguish signal from noise
Small earthquake detection	Often missed	High sensitivity to microseismic events
Phase picking	Manual or semi-automatic	Fully automated with CNNs/ RNNs
Scalability	Limited for large datasets	Highly scalable with GPU/cloud computing
Real-time suitability	Moderate	Excellent (low-latency inference)

DEEP LEARNING AS A PARADIGM SHIFT IN SEISMOLOGY

Deep Learning for Seismic Analysis: Role of CNN-Based Models

Deep learning algorithms have played a pivotal role in the interpretation of seismic data. .The use of AI-ML methods by scientists has enabled revolutionary changes in the interpretation of seismic data by applying these methods rather than traditional methods which relied heavily on costly feature engineering and manual thresholding techniques. Since seismic data is often very noisy and complex in nature and varies greatly from one geological location to another, this particular method proves to be extremely useful in the field of seismology.

Among various techniques used in deep learning, CNNs have been shown to have an important influence on seismic applications because they automatically learn hierarchical feature representations from the raw waveform data. In this process, early layers learn to identify low-level features such as the onset of a waveform or components of a specific frequency, while later layers identify higher-level features such as phase relationships between different waveforms, patterns within the structural configuration of a waveform, and how to suppress noise in a signal, which allows the identification of critical seismic characteristics such as variations in the amplitude of a signal and the arrival of both P-waves and S-waves without requiring human input.

CNNs were originally developed for application to computer vision, but can also be applied to time series data, such as seismic signals. A one-dimensional CNN can receive as input the raw waveforms, while a two-dimensional CNN analyses the time-frequency representation of the input signals using a spectrogram. The multi-scale nature of CNNs allows for the extraction of both local patterns (as would occur at a sharp onset) and more global temporal features (as would occur with many triggered signals occurring within an interval), making them amenable to utilise to identify weak signals in the presence of noise. Another important characteristic of CNNs is that they are robust to noise and learn to establish complex decision boundaries to separate true seismic events from noise, thus significantly outperforming traditional methods of detection (STA/LTA, matched filtering), specifically in the detection of low-signal magnitude events. This capability is critical in areas of application such as microseismic monitoring and seismic hazard assessment.

CNNs have also been shown to solve overlapping seismic events where multiple signals occur very close together in time. Compared to traditional techniques, AI-ML algorithms can elegantly capture subtle differences in both time and frequency and can do a much better job at differentiating between overlapping seismic signal characteristics. Therefore, they offer much more accurate and reliable means for identifying seismic activity. While these capabilities can help them tackle the challenges posed by the problems discussed above, certain problems arise when we attempt to generalize across different regions due to the variations in geological settings as well as noise. To improve the flexibility of models utilized to detect/seismic analysis of events, transfer learning and synthetic dataset utilization will be essential.

CNNs provide the ability for fast near-real-time results once they are implemented; therefore, they will work extremely well as a component of an early earthquake warning system or as part of a large-scale monitoring network. The significant accuracy, efficiency and robustness of CNN deep learning models will be a major contributor to enhanced seismic data analysis, and will be very important for seismic monitoring and disaster preparedness in the future.

Table 2 shows a report on the different types of deep learning models currently used across the seismic community, as examples of these include (1): Convolutional Neural Networks (CNN) -- CNN's are extremely effective for identifying local features present in seismic data when used for extractive applications such as earthquake identification and phase picking (Zhu & Beroza, 2019), (2): Recurrent Neural Networks (RNN) and Long-Short Term Memory Networks (LSTM) -- RNN and LSTM's are extremely effective at representing the inherent temporal relationship between sequential seismic signals thereby improving the accuracy and completeness of tracking seismic phases (Mousavi et al., 2019; Feng et al., 2022), (3): Residual Neural Networks (ResNet) -- ResNet's employ deep features for detection tasks so are highly effective for low magnitude earthquake identification (He et al., 2016; Mousavi et al., 2019), and (4):

U-Net's -- U-Net's are extremely effective at applications such as precisely delineating the P-wave and S-wave components of a seismic signal (Ronneberger et al., 2015; Liao et al., 2022). Transformers can model long-range temporal relationships, allowing for ongoing waveform analysis, whereas GNNs focus on learning spatial relationships between arrays of sensors, which play a significant role in determining the location of an earthquake from multiple monitoring stations (Feng et al., 2022; Han et al., 2025).

Table 2. Deep Learning Architectures Used in Seismology

Architecture	Key Strength	Seismological Application
CNN	Local feature extraction	Earthquake detection, phase picking
RNN / LSTM	Temporal dependency modelling	Seismic phase tracking
ResNet	Deep feature learning	Low-magnitude earthquake detection
U-Net	Signal segmentation	P- and S-wave picking
Transformer	Long-range temporal modeling	Continuous waveform analysis
Graph Neural Network (GNN)	Spatial network learning	Multi-station localisation

DEEP LEARNING FOR EARTHQUAKE DETECTION

Deep Learning Approaches for Earthquake Detection

The application of deep learning in earthquake detection alters seismological analysis of seismic waves mainly due to the fact that deep learning models are designed to solve these problems using classification/ segmentation. Classifying the problem assigns discrete categories to short segments of waveforms (i.e., the earthquake signal, noise, and a non-earthquake disturbance). Conversely, segmentation takes place at a much finer temporal scale; it assigns a label to each sample so that researchers can determine when an earthquake began, its duration, etc. Both of these methods allow seismic analysts to automate the process of detecting and analysing earthquakes and decrease reliance on human expertise.

The predominant models used in the field are Convolutional Neural Networks (CNNs), which use hierarchical learning ability and have direct access to seismic data without the need for feature extraction. When trained on large labelled datasets, CNNs will be able to identify subtle patterns in signal data, such as low-amplitude variations, specific frequency characteristics, and phase information. The complexity of these patterns often makes them much more difficult for traditional rule-based systems to find than CNNs, and therefore, the sensitivity of deep learning models is significantly higher than traditional methods, especially for small or early-stage earthquakes. In addition, CNN-based systems are robust against noise, unlike traditional detection systems. This means that many of the different environmental and human-generated noise sources that regularly occur in seismic data will inhibit conventional detection systems when the data are noisy. CNN-based models will learn complex boundaries that can separate signal from noise, even under low signal-to-noise conditions, making them extremely effective for the detection of microseismic events, which are critical for understanding subsurface processes and seismic risk.

Single-station models are capable of processing data gathered from only one sensor, making them useful in areas where there is sparse seismic coverage or where it would not be practical to install a dense network of sensors. When a single-station model is used, only one sensor is required to achieve a result. Typically, this leads to computational efficiency, but it can also leave models more susceptible to false detections because they lack spatial context. The use of multi-station models allows for the combination of data from several sensors. This allows for the modeling of spatial and temporal relationships, improving accuracy and reducing false alarms by capturing more accurate data across all available sensors. Multi-station models also perform better in complex seismic environments and at higher densities of seismic networks.

Another major advantage of deep learning is that the results produced by deep learning models are consistent. A human analyst's interpretation of a piece of seismic data may vary between analyses due to the analyst being tired, or to some other subjective factor affecting their judgment, but deep learning models will always produce the same result regardless of when or by whom the data is analyzed. When a deep learning model is trained, it is capable of processing continuous data streams at a very high speed.

Therefore, a deep learning model can provide real-time or near-real-time detection of earthquakes, which can be critical for early-warning systems. Nevertheless, some challenges remain for the advancement of deep learning for earthquake detection, such as the reliance on very large labeled datasets for training and the limited usage of the model results produced by the model in regions with varying geological characteristics. The use of transfer learning and domain adaptation has yet to address these lingering issues regarding earthquake predictions or studies. However, deep learning has vastly increased the accuracy, efficiency, and scalability of earthquake detection today. As such, deep learning is now a key player in modern seismic monitoring systems.

A summary of the various key deep learning techniques used in detecting and studying earthquakes can be found in Table 3 below. Specifically, one type of deep learning network, convolutional neural networks, has been successfully applied to differentiate between earthquakes and noise from short segments of time (Meier et al., 2019; Mousavi et al., 2019). Using CNNs for segmentation allows for the processing of continuous waveforms and produces accurate representations of event time windows for accurate onset detection (Zhu & Beroza, 2019; Liao et al., 2022). Multi-station CNN models identify earthquakes by combining data from multiple stations; this process reduces the number of false positives significantly (Perol et al., 2018; Feng et al., 2022). Transformers analyze seismic waves that are much longer (and overlapping) and continuously identify seismic events by allowing them to learn the features of events from the sequence.

Table 3. Deep Learning Approaches for Earthquake Detection

Method	Input Data	Output	Advantage
CNN Classification	Short waveform windows	Earthquake / Noise	Fast and reliable detection
CNN Segmentation	Continuous waveforms	Event time windows	Precise onset detection
Multi-station CNN	Network waveforms	Event confirmation	Reduces false alarms
Transformer-based	Long waveforms	Continuous detection	Handles overlapping events

Deep Learning for Earthquake Localisation

The precise location of earthquakes is not only critical for determining the location of where the earthquake occurred, but also its depth (i.e., the depth of the earthquake) and the time of the earthquake, all of which are required for conducting seismic hazard assessments, preparing for emergency response planning and conducting tectonic research. The accurate location of earthquakes is also essential in enabling authorities to identify the damaged areas and evaluate their damage, thus allowing authorities to allocate resources to respond most efficiently to the emergency, while at the same time providing data for use in geoscientific research about the Earth's crust by assessing how its fault structure and the distribution of stresses within the Earth's crust relate to each other. (Mousavi & Beroza, 2022; Ma & Mei, 2021; Han et al. 2025).

The method used to locate an earthquake typically consists of multiple stages. The locating process begins with 'picking' the time of arrival for seismic phases, where the main seismic (P - Primary and S- Secondary) wave arrivals are determined from the recorded waveform either manually or by an automated algorithm. Then these 'picked' times of arrival are input into a 'hypocentre location' inversion algorithm that also uses input from a seismic velocity model to calculate the location of the hypocentre and the time of the earthquake's origin. Even though this is a very robust method because it is based on physics, it is very easy to err when picking the phases and/or using inaccurate velocity models. In addition, when there is significant noise, the arrival times may be difficult to identify and may be completely obscured. When these types of errors occur, they are compounded throughout the inversion process, which means that it can be very challenging and will create large uncertainties when trying to locate an earthquake, especially smaller magnitude and overlapping earthquakes (Zhu & Beroza, 2019; Liu et al., 2020; Noel & West, 2025).

Seismic phase identification is now more automatic and efficient than before, due to deep learning technology's ability to perform data analysis quickly. The CNNs (Convolutional Neural Networks) were initially used in this manner to help identify typical P-wave and S-wave seismic waveforms, despite significant background noise (Zhu et al 2019, Saad and Chen 2020, Khattak et al., 2024). Then RNNs (Recurrent Neural Networks) and LSTMs (Long Short-Term Memory networks) were added into the mix, resulting in an even greater accuracy (Mousavi et al. 2019, Suarez and Beroza 2025, Yuan and Zhang 2025). The Earthquake Transformer is one of the most widely recognized Transformer networks when it comes to identifying and picking out seismic phases (Mousavi et al. 2019). This is because the Earthquake Transformer uses multiple layers of attention within its architecture to help achieve accurate detection and high precision with the identification of multiple seismic phases (Mousavi et al 2020).

The deep learning-localisation framework (refer to Figure 1) is part of the progression away from traditional inversion techniques to an end-to-end learning framework using waveform data collected at various seismic stations as input to a neural network to identify canonical seismic characteristics associated with earthquakes and predict the earthquake source parameters corresponding to each event: latitude, longitude, depth and time of origin; thus eliminating phase picking and velocity model inversion techniques (Perol et al., 2018; Ma et al., 2026; Xi et al., 2024). The development of these models which leverage space-time pattern analysis will provide a rapid rate of learning and will offer an alternative to conventional approaches in the context of accuracy.

Figure 1. Deep Learning-Based Earthquake Localisation

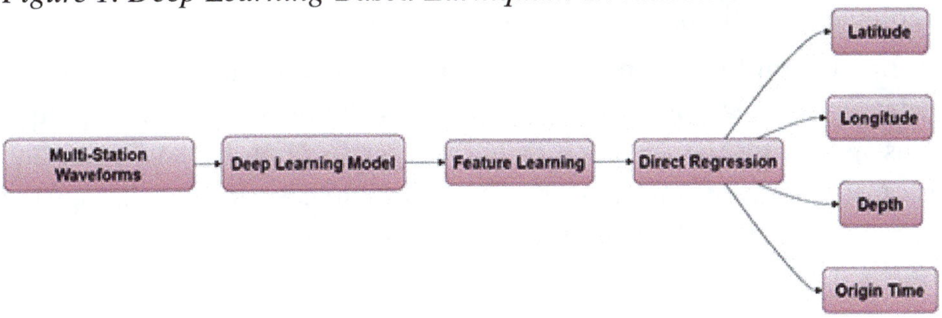

Author's own creation

Earthquake phase picking has benefited enormously from Deep Learning developments, as the processes have been automated, as well as providing consistency and scaling up the capability to cover bigger areas through the use of a large number of seismic stations. A key difference from conventional methods of manual analysis is that neural networks allow decisions to be made consistently across data sources, as their implementation incorporates a uniform decision-making process.

This form of consistency is especially important when monitoring large geographic regions that are covered by an extensive, dense array of seismic stations. and the ability of deep learning models to deal with noise and variation in waveforms has provided the capability to detect low magnitude, weak seismic events that have traditionally been missed by conventional techniques.

As with Phase Picking, deep learning algorithms have also advanced significantly in simplifying the process of localizing earthquakes. Instead of completing the process in several steps through phase picking and the use of velocity models to localize the epicenter, some models can localize the epicenter using a single step, by treating earthquake localization as a direct regression problem. By determining source parameters (location and depth) using the phase information from the multi-station waveform data, neural networks will be able to obtain the source parameters more directly. This end-to-end approach will lead to cumulative error reductions relative to the conventional process, an overall streamlining of processing pipelines and greater dependability, especially in locales with complex geological and lithological conditions.

In addition to utilizing multi-station data, deep learning models can enhance accuracy by accounting for cross-station spatial relationships, thus improving the accuracy of hypocenter location by leveraging the geometry of the seismic network where all stations are located through the use of advanced architectural structures, such as Graph Neural Networks (GNNs) and attention-based models.

Localizing earthquakes using deep learning significantly reduces processing delays for quick determination of earthquake characteristics after an event occurs; this is vital in real-time monitoring and early warning systems, where timely notification improves response capabilities, especially in severely populated, seismically-distributed areas.

Overall the use of deep learning has completely altered the field of earthquake localization through accurate phase identification and direct source determination. Advanced neural networks, particularly those using CNN, RNN, Transformer and graph-based architectures, provide increased accuracy with reduced uncertainty in results as well as accelerated processes. As such, an effective scalable system for monitoring seismic activity has developed.

A summary of the major deep learning techniques used for seismic phase identification and earthquake localization is available below (Table 4). Phase-identifying tools based on CNN architectures identify the arrival of both compressional (P)and shear (S) waves emerging from a given earthquake, based on the data acquired at a single station (e.g., Zhu & Beroza, 2019; Saad & Chen, 2020). RNN and LSTM tools have been developed as phase identifying tools that utilize time-dependency relationships across multiple stations thereby providing a higher fidelity phase identification process (e.g., Mousavi et al., 2019; Suarez & Beroza, 2025). CNNs can analyze various stations' information simultaneously to find earthquake locations and depths (e.g., Perol et al. 2018; Ma et al. 2026). Tools using GNNs provide the geometric relationship of the stations in the seismic network & help locate the hypocenter of an earthquake, as per (Feng et al. 2022; Jinde et al. 2025).

Table 4. Deep Learning Approaches for Earthquake Localisation

Approach	Input	Output	Benefit
CNN Phase Picker	Single-station waveforms	P & S arrival times	Automated picking
RNN/LSTM Picker	Sequential waveforms	Phase sequences	Improved temporal accuracy
CNN Regression	Multi-station waveforms	Epicentre, depth	End-to-end localisation
GNN-based Models	Station network data	Hypocentre	Uses spatial geometry

EMERGING DEEP LEARNING ARCHITECTURES IN SEISMOLOGY

Advanced Deep Learning Architectures in Seismology

The recent development of AI-based seismology has resulted in significant improvement to the current methods for detecting and identifying earthquakes by using AI and other modern deep learning frameworks. There have been significant developments in the domain of AI-based seismology because of the emergence of different types of advanced architectures like ResNet-based architectures, U-Net, Transformers, and GNNs. Using these enhanced techniques, many approaches enable scientists to identify a diverse range of waveform characteristics and make use of these characteristics to achieve better outcomes with the help of AI-based seismology.

ResNets have resolved the problem of training deeper neural networks versus traditional deep architectures due to the existence of vanishing gradients. Traditional deep architectures will degrade in performance as the number of layers increases. ResNets resolve this problem by providing shortcut connections for practical flow of information from one layer to another. ResNet-based techniques can offer improved detection rates under noisy conditions and low magnitude events by detecting and analysing more subtle waveform characteristics than what simpler detection models can effectively detect. The training stability provided by ResNet-based detection models also supports large geo-physical datasets and the analysis of long-duration waveforms.

Architectures based upon the U-Net framework have been adopted for many tasks involving the segmentation of seismic signals, providing an established architecture for use by the community. Although developed originally for use with medical images, the U-Net architecture comprises an encoder–decoder structure featuring skip connections from encoder output layers that retain fine-detail information while also enabling the architecture to learn more abstract representations of the input data. In the field of seismology, U-Net models are particularly useful for performing tasks that require good temporal resolution, such as earthquake onset detection and phase-picking, and separation of overlapping events. The individual samples of the waveform are assigned a class label, thus producing a detailed output of the segmentation, which supports both localisation and detection. The U-Net architecture retains temporal resolution while also incorporating contextual information, making it an effective architecture for precision seismic monitoring.

Transformer-based models represent an emerging and promising area for conducting seismic analysis. Rather than relying upon convolutional neural networks (CNNs) or recurrent neural networks (RNNs), transformers make use of self-attention mechanisms to model relationships between data. Therefore, they can more effectively capture long-range temporal dependencies in continuous seismic waveforms than traditional sequence models. In the context of the seismic applications, transformers can establish connections between samples in the waveform that are located far apart from one another, which will benefit the analysis of long-duration signals, complex wave trends, and overlapping events. The results of recent studies are indicating transformer-based models as being highly effective at both classification and detection tasks, and provide significant performance improvements over traditional forms when being trained on sufficient amounts of data. Their ability to perform parallel computations also enhances computational efficiency, making them suitable for real-time applications.

Seismic data processing has been transformed through the introduction of Graph Neural Networks (GNNs) and their use of graphs to model seismic networks. In the GNN framework, seismic stations are represented by nodes and spatial relationships such as connectivity and distance are represented by edges. In learning the way that seismic signals travel through the network, GNNs provide improved detection and location precision than traditional methods. GNNs also model the physical characteristics of seismic wave propagation; therefore, integrating multi-station data through GNNs can be effectively achieved. The resolution of such improved detection capabilities is especially important for determining the characteristics of earthquakes in densely populated seismic networks because they can leverage spatial correlations of events to determine accurate event characteristics.

Overall, advanced deep-learning architectures and the implementation of AI technology have made substantial contributions to the growth and characterisation of present-day earthquake detection algorithms. Advanced deep learning models have significantly enhanced AI's ability to model motion-based time series considering temporal and spatial dependencies in seismic monitoring systems than earlier models, allowing for improved accuracy, more robustness, and greater scalability for monitoring seismic activity.

The next figure (Figure 2) represents the architecture of a multi-station AI-based monitoring network that transmits the waveform data generated by multiple seismic stations to a central AI processing module. Using the latest generation of deep learning algorithms, such as CNN's, Transformers, and GNN's, these algorithms can evaluate these signals to perform spatial-temporal feature fusion within the total system resulting in spatial and temporal awareness within the overall system design. This representation can be considered as a support for two important outputs: the first one is earthquake detection, which activates an early warning system, and the second one is earthquake localisation, which creates a seismic event map pointing the earthquake's source and thereby facilitating rapid, precise, and extensive seismic intelligence over the network.

Figure 2. Multi-Station AI-Driven Seismic Monitoring Network

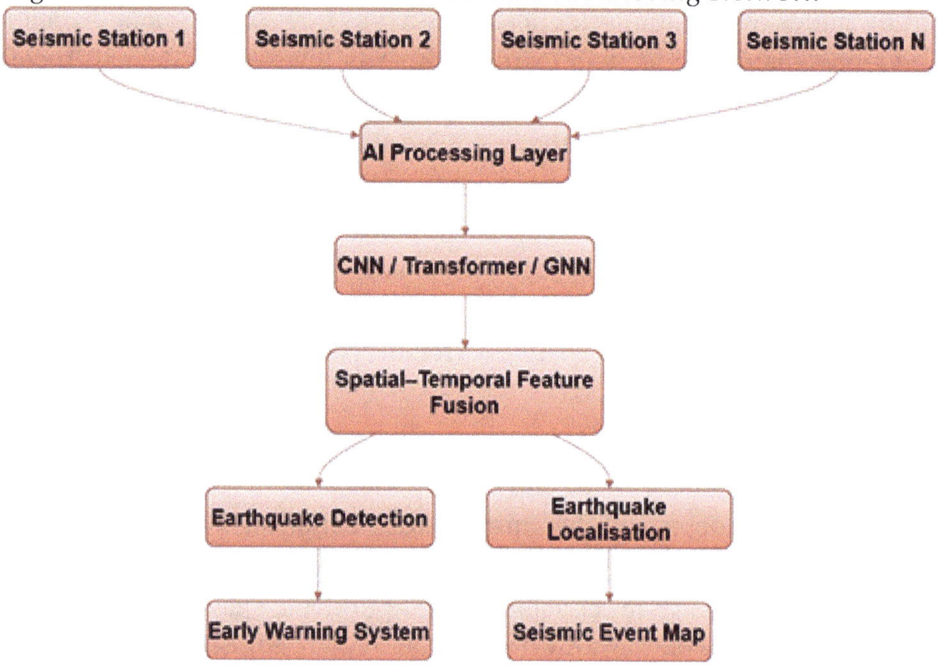

Author's own creation

How these innovative structures show how adaptable and promising deep learning can provide solutions for seismic applications are numerous. Deep learning models have the ability to overcome problems related to their depth, behaviour over a period of time, spatial configuration, and precise cutting of the signals, thereby advancing AI-assisted Seismology to unprecedented levels. If future research does not limit itself to the integration of these structures with physical models, domain knowledge and real-time operations, deep learning will provide the foundations for next-generation seismic monitoring, hazard assessment, and earthquake early warning systems.

DATA, TRAINING STRATEGIES, AND SCALABILITY

Quality annotated datasets are crucial for deep learning systems and for seismic modelling. Seismic models always learn much more complex and high-quality waveform data because of its extreme variability and because the data is very noisy. Unlike traditional algorithms, deep learning models extract patterns from the data rather than having pre-programmed rules/features. Consequently, the quantity, quality and diversity of the data are all key factors in the accuracy, robustness and reliability of seismic AI systems. In addition, however, there are also many unique challenges associated with seismic data that add complexity to the above process, including severe imbalance of class distributions across regions, lack of labelled data and large variability in both geological/tectonic characteristics and trends across different areas.

One of the main problems is class imbalance. In sets of continuous seismic recordings, typically only a very small percentage of the entire data set represents true earthquake signals, and most of the record is noise or some other form of disturbance, such as cultural sources or non-seismic sources. Also, within the seismic data, small magnitude earthquakes occur much more frequently than moderate to large earthquakes, which are rare. This imbalance creates a situation where deep learning models will produce biased predictions toward noise and frequent events, thus reducing the model's sensitivity to rare event types that are of far greater scientific and social significance. To mitigate this challenge, researchers use several techniques: balanced data sampling, weighted loss functions, and a well-defined training methodology that ensures proper representation of both seismic events and noise during learning.

One other significant challenge is the lack of labelled data sets. There are huge quantities of seismic waveforms collected by seismic networks; however, to get labelled and quality data, seismologists have to label them manually, determining seismic events, picking P- and S- waves, and confirming locations of the earthquakes. This task consumes much money and effort, with a possibility of various expert opinions. The problem becomes acute in the case of small earthquakes, human-induced seismic activity, and extremely rare events, which are usually poorly documented. Poorly labelled data are a challenge that hinders deep learning models from achieving their potential outside the training environment.

However, scientists will need to combine several approaches, including data augmentation, synthetic data creation, transfer learning, and semi-supervised learning, in order to overcome the mentioned drawbacks. One of the simplest and most inexpensive ways of creating new data from what we already have at our disposal is called data augmentation. In the case of augmenting seismic waves, the process includes noise addition, moving windows, scaling, and stretching of the waveforms. These manipulations do not affect the physical characteristics of the seismic waves, which allows the model to become familiar with different types of environments and prevents overfitting. Another extremely helpful approach for data training is simulation-based creation of synthetic waveforms associated with seismic wave propagation and sources.

In addition, transfer learning can be used to scale the models even further through the possibility of transferring the trained models from one large data area to other areas using only limited data in the latter. Finally, semi-supervised learning approaches, coupled with the predictions from the models themselves, allow for large amounts of unlabelled seismic data to be used through the continuous improvement of the models.

REAL-TIME DEPLOYMENT AND OPERATIONAL CHALLENGES

Operational Deployment of Deep Learning Models in Seismic Monitoring Networks

Even though deep learning algorithms have proven themselves capable in laboratory conditions using seismic benchmarks, real-life usage in seismic network operations poses a series of problems that must be solved in practice. First and foremost, the real-life application requires constant real-time analysis of large data streams, which necessitates an optimal combination of accuracy, speed, scalability, and robustness.

Moreover, integration with the pre-existing hardware of the seismographic networks makes operational deployment a major issue.

The first obstacle to overcome is related to computational efficiency. Deep learning models, including sophisticated convolutional neural networks, transformers, and graph-based models, are usually based on millions of parameters and are costly to train and deploy. With the existence of large-scale seismic networks consisting of hundreds of stations providing real-time streaming of data, the use of such methods may result in inefficiency and latency.

As a solution to such problems, several model optimisation tools were utilised. Model pruning is one technique used to eliminate any redundancy in the model, while model compression or distillation helps generate a smaller-sized model to mimic the larger one. In addition, quantisation serves to make computations more efficient.

As part of solving the problem of latency, another possible solution could be through the implementation of edge computing, where the lightweight model is executed at the seismic stations itself, thereby minimising data transfer and ensuring rapid detection. Another method would be using cloud computing and distributed computing for scaling-up large-scale seismometers by means of parallel computing.

Lastly, the interpretability aspect cannot be overlooked since explainable AI models are important in helping seismologists make sense of model predictions. Monitoring and re-training of the models together with human supervision are required.

The workflow illustrated in Figure 3 starts with raw seismic waveforms obtained from a distributed sensor network. Preprocessing and feature representation come after this stage, where deep learning models are employed in carrying out various operations such as detection, picking, event association, and localisation.

Figure 3. End-to-end deep learning pipeline for earthquake detection and localisation

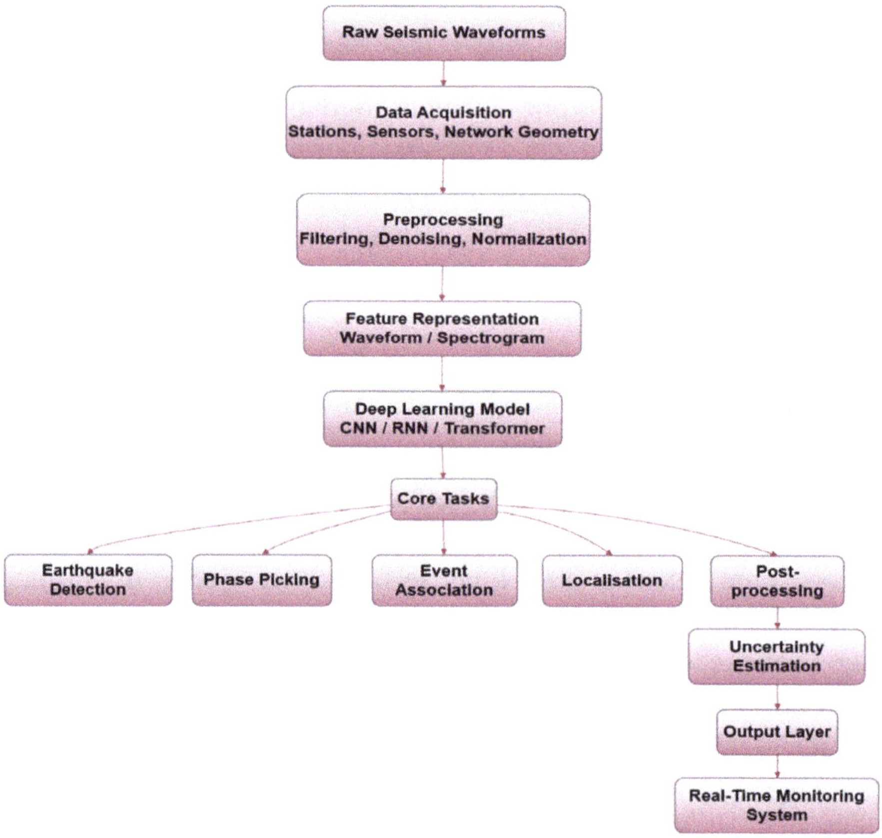

Author's own creation

CASE STUDIES AND APPLICATIONS

Real-World Applications and Case Studies of Deep Learning in Seismology

Deep learning, which originally belonged to the experimental research sphere, has been implemented in the practical domain of seismic observation, where it has acquired great significance for identifying, analysing, and mitigating earthquakes. In seismology, the application of AI has been incorporated into the process of monitoring volcanic activity, recognising induced seismic events, and studying the cases related to earthquake warnings, after-earthquake analyses, and other aspects. This is how deep learning has contributed to boosting the seismic resilience of the world in terms of both experiments in a laboratory setting and practice in the real world.

Earthquake early warning (EEW) stands out as the most important of all the applications. The processes of phase picking and threshold crossing, as utilised by traditional EEW systems, are vulnerable to noise and computational time constraints. Deep learning algorithms developed based on CNNs have been able to make this task considerably faster since P-waves' arrival can be detected within a span of less than a second under conditions where the signal-to-noise ratio is low. EEW systems currently in use in the real world that make use of deep learning techniques have recorded a significant reduction in false alarms along with an increase in the speed of alerts, thus ensuring that populations will receive warnings well ahead of strong ground shaking. These systems have demonstrated robustness across different tectonic environments as well as noise levels.

Moreover, deep learning has transformed the field of seismic analysis. After a major earthquake event, there can be thousands of aftershocks in just a few days, resulting in a situation where manual detection and phase picking become insufficient. The earthquake catalogues created using AI-powered technology are at a very high level of precision because these systems can pick, locate, and detect seismic events very rapidly. In several instances, it has been seen that the earthquake catalogues developed using deep learning, also known as "artificial intelligence" (which includes neural network technology), contain a much higher volume of small and overlapping events compared to those developed using standard procedures. This development has led to breakthroughs in studying fault geometry, stress distribution, and seismic rupture mechanisms. These insights have significant consequences for seismic hazard assessment and recovery efforts.

A variety of time-dependent seismic signatures, including but not limited to tremor, long-period activity, and hybrid earthquakes, have made volcanic seismic surveillance a difficult task. Machine learning algorithms, especially CNN and Recurrent neural networks, have been most effective in classifying and tracking these seismic events in real-time. AI volcano monitoring technology is, therefore, for eruption forecasting and alerting to help mitigate risks of disaster in these high-risk regions by detecting these types of subtle signals.

Another application of deep learning in geophysics is in induced seismicity in human activities like mining operations, geothermal, and hydraulic fracturing operations. Artificial intelligence in differentiating between the weak induced seismic events and the strong industrial seismic noise means that there will be accurate tracking of the weak induced events in real-time. This also means that there is going to be support from this system on regulatory compliance through the capability of making rapid interventions during increased seismic activity.

Together, these case studies serve as evidence that deep learning technology is not a constraint but instead has transformed into an enabler for increasing sensitivity, reducing latency, and facilitating scalable seismic monitoring. The synergy of domain expertise alongside physical modelling makes the AI-based system a lethal combination, enhancing the ability to deal with natural disasters.

Ablation Study

Table 5 below outlines the process adopted in the evaluation of individual components' contributions in the proposed framework. The ablation study entails the manipulation of different components, including preprocessing, model architecture, and input design, among others. The aim of doing so is to understand the contribution of each individual component.

Table 5. Component-wise Ablation Analysis of the Proposed Deep Learning Framework

Model Variant	Description	F1-score	Timing Error (s)	Localisation Error (km)
Full Model	Complete pipeline	0.91	0.03	4.2
Without Preprocessing	No filtering/ normalisation	0.79	0.07	6.8
Without Attention	CNN only (no attention layer)	0.84	0.05	5.5
Reduced Stations	Limited station inputs	0.85	0.06	7.1

Ablation experiments show that the presence of the pre-processing step plays an important role in improving the performance of the signal classification, as the absence of it results in a significant drop in performance. Moreover, the absence of attention mechanisms makes it harder for the network to capture complicated temporal dynamics. It can also be observed that decreasing the number of stations used as input decreases the performance of the models, emphasising the significance of network topology in seismic events.

Benchmarking and Evaluation

Comparative Analysis of Deep Learning Methods

It is necessary to make a systematic study of existing models of deep learning and compare their characteristics, advantages, and disadvantages to understand their applications in solving various seismic problems. In this paper, the main models for solving seismic problems using deep learning techniques are summarised in Table 6 below.

Table 6. Comparative Analysis of Deep Learning Methods for Seismic Monitoring

Method / Model	Core Task	Dataset(s) Used	Evaluation Metrics	Reported Performance	Generalisation Ability	Computational Cost	Key Strengths	Limitations
CNN-based Models (Perol et al., 2018; Meier et al., 2019)	Detection	Regional seismic datasets	Accuracy, Precision, Recall, F1-score	High detection accuracy (>90% in controlled datasets)	Limited (region-specific training)	Low–Moderate	Simple architecture, fast inference, robust to moderate noise	Poor cross-region transfer, sensitive to dataset bias
PhaseNet (Zhu & Beroza, 2019)	Phase Picking	Global & regional waveform datasets	Timing error (ms), Precision/ Recall	High precision with low timing error (~tens of ms)	Moderate	Moderate	High accuracy in noisy data, end-to-end learning	Dependent on label quality, limited uncertainty modelling
Earthquake Transformer (Mousavi et al., 2020)	Detection + Phase Picking	Multi-region datasets	F1-score, Precision, Recall	State-of-the-art performance (F1 > 0.9)	High (better cross-region performance)	High	Joint learning of tasks and the attention mechanism improves accuracy	High computational cost, complex training
GNN-based Models	Localisation	Multi-station datasets	Spatial error (km), RMSE	Improved localisation accuracy (reduced error vs traditional methods)	Moderate–High (depends on network density)	High	Captures spatial relationships between stations	Requires dense station networks, sensitive to missing data
End-to-End DL Models (Ma et al., 2026)	Detection + Localisation	Large-scale seismic datasets	Spatial error, Detection metrics	Competitive performance with reduced pipeline complexity	Moderate	High	Eliminates multi-stage errors, faster inference pipeline	Less interpretable, data-hungry
Hybrid Models (CNN + RNN / CNN + Transformer)	Detection + Picking	Mixed datasets	F1-score, Timing error	Improved temporal modelling and detection robustness	Moderate–High	Moderate–High	Combines spatial + temporal learning	Increased model complexity

From the comparative analysis of deep learning models given in Table 6 above, it can be observed that there is no single deep learning method that dominates other methods across all performance dimensions. For example, while CNNs are efficient models, they cannot generalise the problem. On the contrary, transformers can be considered highly accurate models; however, they are highly inefficient. Lastly, GNNs, while offering better localisation of seismic events, require dense graphs.

Quantitative Performance Analysis

The quantitative assessment shows a clear superiority of transformer-based models over CNN-based models on a variety of seismic tasks. Empirically, there is a gain of up to 10% in F1-score for the detection task and approximately 30% improvement in localisation error. However, even though the above-stated benefits are noteworthy, they come with a high cost in terms of computational complexity, meaning there exists a trade-off between these two factors. Moreover, cross-comparison among models shows that better detection results are not always associated with better localisation results. This highlights the need for optimisation across all stages of the entire end-to-end process.

Standardised Evaluation Protocols

Inconsistencies and a lack of standardisation of evaluation practices represent a notable drawback of existing research.

Key considerations include:

- **Evaluation Metrics:**
  - Detection: Precision, Recall, F1-score
  - Phase Picking: Timing error (ms)
  - Localisation: Spatial error (km)
  - Uncertainty: Calibration metrics (e.g., reliability curves)
- **Dataset Standardisation:**
  - Use of benchmark datasets (e.g., STEAD)
  - Consistent train/validation/test splits
  - Clear reporting of preprocessing steps
  - Inclusion of diverse seismic conditions (noise levels, regions)

Adopting unified evaluation protocols improves reproducibility, transparency, and comparability across studies.

Cross-Region Validation and Robustness

Deep learning-based seismic models face significant challenges related to robustness and generalisability, especially under conditions of changing geological scenarios.

Important aspects include:

- **Cross-Region Generalisation:**
    - Models trained in one region often show performance degradation in others
    - Differences in geology, noise, and sensor configurations affect accuracy
- **Robustness Factors:**
    - Missing or faulty stations
    - Extreme noise conditions
    - Variable network geometry
- **Mitigation Strategies:**
    - Transfer learning and domain adaptation
    - Data augmentation and synthetic data generation
    - Multi-region training datasets

A systematic focus on cross-region validation is essential to ensure real-world applicability and operational reliability.

Table 7. Multi-Metric Comparison

Model	F1-score	Localisation Error (km)
CNN	0.85	6.5
PhaseNet	0.90	5.0
Transformer	0.93	4.2
GNN	0.88	4.5

Table 7 presents an overview of deep learning techniques applied to seismic tasks, including performance and generalisation capacity, as well as associated computational demands.

CHALLENGES, ETHICS, AND EXPLAINABLE AI

Limitations, Ethical Considerations, and Trustworthy Deployment of Deep Learning in Seismology

Deep learning algorithms have greatly improved seismic surveillance, earthquake detection, and location; however, their application in real-life critical scenarios involves several considerations related both to technology and society. As the issue at hand involves people's safety, any errors should be avoided as much as possible, which means that all artificial intelligence algorithms involved in earthquake prediction should go through rigorous verification and validation procedures.

One of the major problems that occurs while training deep learning models is the issue of overfitting. Seismic signal data tends to be highly unbalanced as it usually includes rare earthquake events, as well as lots of noise. If a model fails to be properly validated and trained on diverse datasets, it will likely generate erroneous predictions. Moreover, it should be noted that seismic signals depend on geological regions. Thus, a model designed for some particular area will not operate successfully elsewhere.

Additionally, deep learning models are susceptible to out-of-distribution data, which includes any unusual event, noise, or malfunctioning of sensors. Here, high-confidence, yet completely wrong results might be produced by the model. In such a case, one needs uncertainty estimation and anomaly detection measures to flag incorrect outputs. One more problem is related to the absence of any interpretability in neural networks. As opposed to traditional seismology, where physics-based approaches have been used for a long time, neural networks represent a black box approach to the problem. The use of explainable AI approaches, like saliency maps, attention, and others, allows highlighting the part of the waveform responsible for the model output.

As for ethical and societal considerations, they are crucial since any mistake in the earthquake early warning system could cost many lives or even trigger panic. For that reason, uncertainties must be explained properly; appropriate governance should be provided, and constant human supervision is required.

All these concerns need to be addressed for the successful deployment of the approach into real-world practice.

FUTURE DIRECTIONS IN AI-DRIVEN SEISMOLOGY

Though deep learning methods have greatly revolutionised earthquake detection and monitoring techniques, there are still some promising future directions for further enhancement of AI-based seismic systems. Further improvements will not only depend on the development of new algorithms; in addition, data integration, physics inclusion, distributed learning, and international collaboration will play a critical role here.

The first direction includes the integration of different data modalities for building more complex seismic systems. This method implies the incorporation of various geophysical information in addition to traditional waveform data, such as ground deformation estimated by means of GNSS and InSAR. Through data integration, AI-based models will be able to develop a more holistic perspective on the whole earthquake lifecycle and better estimate its parameters, detect damage, and make hazard predictions.

The second potential area is the physics-informed neural network (PINN). Unlike traditional deep learning techniques based solely on the pattern of data, PINNs apply physics-related equations like wave propagation, conservation principles, etc., during training. Thus, such models become physically consistent and have high interpretability along with improved generalisation in terms of applying them to other areas or unusual earthquakes. Moreover, models built with the help of PINN do not require large datasets, which makes them useful in data-deficient regions.

Moreover, decentralised and sensor-based AI solutions also deserve attention. With the recent progress in edge computing and low-power consumption hardware, deep learning methods can be run on devices near seismic sensors. Therefore, it becomes possible to perform some actions at the sensor level, such as detection, filtering, and preliminary localisation. It becomes especially useful in early earthquake prediction, in which prompt decisions are necessary.

From a broader perspective, there is a trend towards the development of AI-based seismographic monitoring systems that operate at the global level. Currently, seismographic stations operate independently and under different standards in various parts of the globe. A global system can help facilitate data and model sharing, resulting in better-quality information about earthquakes around the world.

The concept of federated learning provides a feasible way out in such a scenario by enabling collaborative training of models while ensuring that no data privacy concerns are breached.

CONCLUSION

Transformative Impact of Deep Learning on Modern Seismology

The use of deep learning algorithms, especially CNNs, has revolutionised earthquake detection and localisation through the use of raw seismic data. This is possible because the deep learning models learn hierarchical representations of seismic waveforms that enhance the efficiency and reliability of seismic events in detecting even small-scale and weak earthquakes that are normally overlooked by conventional techniques. The automated extraction of information from raw waveforms enables deep learning algorithms to detect any temporal variation, frequency and phase changes in the data, allowing for better hazard assessment.

In addition, deep learning algorithms have made significant contributions towards earthquake localisation and characterisation by automatically detecting P and S waves from raw seismic waveforms to achieve the same accuracy as an expert. Moreover, deep learning can predict parameters related to an earthquake event from multi-station seismic data without the need for manual intervention.

Other important strengths include the scalability and ability to process data in real time. The advantage that deep learning architectures have in being able to process large amounts of data in real time, even when this data is coming from live feeds from seismic arrays, allows them to be incredibly valuable for creating early warning systems for earthquakes.

Some other problems related to deep learning include overfitting, poor generalisation in different areas, sensitivity to data quality, and a lack of transparency. Dealing with these concerns will require an application of explainable artificial intelligence, validation techniques, and hybrid models based on the fusion of artificial intelligence and physics-based models.

Deep learning continues to revolutionise seismology by fusing artificial intelligence and physics together and providing better accuracy, scalability, and real-time processing.

REFERENCES

. Ahamad, F., & Singh, V. K. (2025). Deep Learning Approaches for Earthquake Forecasting and Early Warning Systems in Seismically Active Regions.

Cano, E. V., Akram, J., & Peter, D. B. (2021). Automatic seismic phase picking based on unsupervised machine-learning classification and content information analysis. *Geophysics, 86*(4), V299–V315. DOI: 10.1190/geo2020-0308.1

. Feng, T., Mohanna, S., & Meng, L. (2022). Edgephase: A deep learning model for multi-station seismic phase picking. *Geochemistry, Geophysics, Geosystems, 23*(11), e2022GC010453.

. Han, B., Zhang, W., & An, N. (2025). A review of microseismic source location techniques in underground mining.

He, K., Zhang, X., Ren, S., & Sun, J. (2016). Deep residual learning for image recognition. In *Proceedings of the IEEE conference on computer vision and pattern recognition* (pp. 770-778).

Jinde, Y., Sugii, A., & Hiramatsu, Y. (2025). Enhanced deep learning approach for detecting and locating tectonic tremors in the Nankai subduction zone. *Earth, Planets, and Space*, *77*(1), 121. DOI: 10.1186/s40623-025-02257-y

Khattak, G. R., Khan, G. M., & Yousaf, S. (2024). ConvEQ: Convolutional neural network for earthquake phase classification using short time frequency transform. *Computers & Geosciences, 189*, 105624. DOI: 10.1016/j.cageo.2024.105624

Li, W., Chakraborty, M., Köhler, J., Quinteros-Cartaya, C., Rümpker, G., & Srivastava, N. (2024). Earthquake monitoring using deep learning with a case study of the Kahramanmaras Turkey earthquake aftershock sequence. *Solid Earth, 15*(2), 197–213. DOI: 10.5194/se-15-197-2024

Liao, W. Y., Lee, E. J., Chen, D. Y., Chen, P., Mu, D., & Wu, Y. M. (2022). RED-PAN: Real-time earthquake detection and phase-picking with multitask attention network. *IEEE Transactions on Geoscience and Remote Sensing*, *60*, 1–11. DOI: 10.1109/TGRS.2022.3230932

. Liu, M., Zhang, M., Zhu, W., Ellsworth, W. L., & Li, H. (2020). Rapid characterization of the July 2019 Ridgecrest, California, earthquake sequence from raw seismic data using machine-learning phase picker. *Geophysical Research Letters, 47*(4), e2019GL086189.

Ma, J., Hou, J., Fang, B., Wang, P., Wu, S., & Qi, Z. (2026). Deep learning for the localization of seismic sources based on synthetic full waveform and wavelet de-noising. *Soil Dynamics and Earthquake Engineering*, *200*, 109832. DOI: 10.1016/j.soildyn.2025.109832

Ma, Z., & Mei, G. (2021). Deep learning for geological hazards analysis: Data, models, applications, and opportunities. *Earth-Science Reviews*, *223*, 103858. DOI: 10.1016/j.earscirev.2021.103858

Meier, M. A., Ross, Z. E., Ramachandran, A., Balakrishna, A., Nair, S., Kundzicz, P., Li, Z., Andrews, J., Hauksson, E., & Yue, Y. (2019). Reliable real-time seismic signal/noise discrimination with machine learning. *Journal of Geophysical Research. Solid Earth*, *124*(1), 788–800. DOI: 10.1029/2018JB016661

Mousavi, S. M., & Beroza, G. C. (2022). Deep-learning seismology. *Science*, *377*(6607), eabm4470. DOI: 10.1126/science.abm4470

Mousavi, S. M., & Beroza, G. C. (2023). Machine learning in earthquake seismology. *Annual Review of Earth and Planetary Sciences*, *51*(1), 105–129. DOI: 10.1146/annurev-earth-071822-100323

Mousavi, S. M., Ellsworth, W. L., Zhu, W., Chuang, L. Y., & Beroza, G. C. (2020). Earthquake transformer—An attentive deep-learning model for simultaneous earthquake detection and phase picking. *Nature Communications*, *11*(1), 3952. DOI: 10.1038/s41467-020-17591-w

Mousavi, S. M., Zhu, W., Sheng, Y., & Beroza, G. C. (2019). CRED: A deep residual network of convolutional and recurrent units for earthquake signal detection. *Scientific Reports*, *9*(1), 10267. DOI: 10.1038/s41598-019-45748-1

Noel, S. K., & West, M. E. (2025). Challenges and Opportunities of Machine Learning Earthquake Detection for Regional Monitoring. *Bulletin of the Seismological Society of America*, *115*(5), 2096–2108. DOI: 10.1785/0120250021

Perol, T., Gharbi, M., & Denolle, M. (2018). Convolutional neural network for earthquake detection and location. *Science Advances*, *4*(2), e1700578. DOI: 10.1126/sciadv.1700578

Ronneberger, O., Fischer, P., & Brox, T. (2015, October). U-net: Convolutional networks for biomedical image segmentation. In *International Conference on Medical image computing and computer-assisted intervention* (pp. 234-241). Cham: Springer international publishing. DOI: 10.1007/978-3-319-24574-4_28

Saad, O. M., & Chen, Y. (2020). Earthquake detection and P-wave arrival time picking using capsule neural network. *IEEE Transactions on Geoscience and Remote Sensing*, *59*(7), 6234–6243. DOI: 10.1109/TGRS.2020.3019520

Scheingraber, C., Hosseini, K., Barsch, R., & Sigloch, K. (2013). Obspyload: A tool for fully automated retrieval of seismological waveform data. *Seismological Research Letters*, *84*(3), 525–531. DOI: 10.1785/0220120103

Suarez, A. L. A., & Beroza, G. (2025). Picking Regional Seismic Phase Arrival Times with Deep Learning. *Seismica*, *4*(1).

Xi, Z., Wei, S. S., Zhu, W., Beroza, G. C., Jie, Y., & Saloor, N. (2024). Deep learning for deep earthquakes: Insights from OBS observations of the Tonga subduction zone. *Geophysical Journal International*, *238*(2), 1073–1088. DOI: 10.1093/gji/ggae200

Yuan, C., & Zhang, J. (2025). Applying deep learning to teleseismic phase detection and picking: PcP and PKiKP cases. *Artificial Intelligence in Geosciences*, *6*(1), 100108. DOI: 10.1016/j.aiig.2025.100108

Zhu, L., Peng, Z., McClellan, J., Li, C., Yao, D., Li, Z., & Fang, L. (2019). Deep learning for seismic phase detection and picking in the aftershock zone of 2008 Mw7. 9 Wenchuan Earthquake. *Physics of the Earth and Planetary Interiors*, *293*, 106261. DOI: 10.1016/j.pepi.2019.05.004

Zhu, W., & Beroza, G. C. (2019). PhaseNet: A deep-neural-network-based seismic arrival-time picking method. *Geophysical Journal International*, *216*(1), 261–273.

Chapter 2
Artificial Intelligence for Environmental Resilience:
Advancing Weather Forecasting, Disaster Prediction, and Biodiversity Monitoring

P. Umamaheswari
http://orcid.org/0000-0003-2007-697X
SASTRA (Deemed to be) University, India

R. Rajakumar
SASTRA (Deemed to be) University, India

D. Rajalakshmi
http://orcid.org/0000-0003-4851-7685
SASTRA (Deemed to be) University, India

S. Meganathan
http://orcid.org/0000-0003-4570-8259
SASTRA (Deemed to be) University, India

D. Rubidha Devi
http://orcid.org/0000-0001-9074-8984
SASTRA (Deemed to be) University, India

P. Dinesh
Anjalai Ammal Mahalingam Engineering College, India

DOI: 10.4018/979-8-3373-8042-1.ch002

ABSTRACT

Over the last few decades, the world has been facing critical and unprecedented environmental problems like climate change, extreme weather, and loss of biodiversity. These problems are connected to each other, and it is imperative that the growth of predictive, adaptive, and scalable solutions should be prioritized. Biodisaster management, climate and weather forecasting and biodiversity tracking and monitoring have been very useful. Nevertheless, predictive analytics has not expanded at the pace and efficiency of the computational power, combination of data, and predictive potential gaps. The chapter, Artificial Intelligence to Environmental resilience: developing Weather forecasting, Disaster prediction, and Biodiversity monitoring, introduces the opportunities of AI to revolutionize environmental resilience. It gives an in-depth account of how the AI-based models are transforming forecasting systems, enhancing disaster predictions and management, and providing scalable biodiversity surveillance.

1. INTRODUCTION

The climate change, the human activity, and natural variability are contributing to a growing complexity and vulnerability of the environmental systems. Extreme weather, loss of biodiversity, and environmental degradation are some of the most threatening factors to the ecosystem, economy, and human societies. Artificial Intelligence (AI) has in this regard become a new transformational tool of environmental resilience. Machine learning, deep learning and predictive analytics are techniques of AI that allow integrating and analyzing large and heterogeneous environmental data, which allows making more accurate predictions, risks and decision making.

The increasing accessibility of remote sensing information, environmental sensors based on the Internet of Things, and past climate history has opened an unprecedented possibility to create environmental solutions with the help of AI. The current weather forecasting models are able to include the satellite images, oceanic measurements and atmospheric data, which enhances the accuracy and timeliness of the forecasts. Prediction systems used to predict disasters use AI to detect trends in seismic patterns, rainfall or storm paths to allow early warning mechanisms(Ghosh et al., 2024). The AI-based image recognition, species distribution modeling, and automated ecological surveys are useful in biodiversity monitoring. All these innovations are aimed at enhancing the resilience of both the natural and the human system due to the proactive intervention.

This chapter is aimed at discussing the role of AI in supporting environmental resilience, its uses in weather prediction, disaster prediction and monitoring biodiversity. It also deals with methodological methods, data integration schemes, implementation issues and outlook. The chapter also emphasizes the usefulness of interdisciplinary interventions integrating technologies, ecology and policy, by pointing out the potential of AI to promote environmental sustainability and disaster preparedness(Nishant et al., 2020).

1.1 AI in Weather Forecasting

Weather forecasting is one of the key factors of environmental resilience because proper and timely forecasting is essential to agriculture, transport, disaster management, and security of the population. Conventional forecasting techniques utilize the numbers weather prediction (NWP) models which are mathematical models based on the physics of the atmosphere. These models although effective, have drawbacks such as computational complexity, sensitivity to initial conditions and problems in modeling local microclimates.

The complementary approaches provided by AI are based on learning patterns of historical and real-time data. Machine learning has been applied with the help of random forests, support vector machines, and neural networks, which can be used to find non-linear correlates in meteorological data that traditional models might not take into account. Different approaches based on deep learning, specifically convolutional and recurrent neural networks, have demonstrated a great success in forecasting that of rainfall intensity, temperature changes, and storm paths given a satellite image, radar, or sensor networks.

The Hybrid AI-NWP models are the development of physics-based simulations with data-based prediction, which is superior in accuracy and computational cost. The application of AI could be seen, as an example, in correcting the biases in numerical models, interpolating gaps in the data, or reducing coarse-resolution projections to local scales. With these developments, there can be advanced warning mechanisms of extreme weather conditions like cyclones, heat waves and floods thus minimizing human and economic losses. Moreover, AI-based prediction methods can keep updating predictions as new information appears, and hence real-time flexibility.

Another crucial instrument of weather forecasting today, where Artificial Intelligence (AI) can be applied, is to enhance the accuracy, speed, and efficiency with which predictions are made. Conventional numerical weather prediction models rely on computationally intensive and complicated mathematical equations, whereas AI-powered products observe trends using historic and live climatic data of massive amounts. The use of machine learning methods like the Random Forest, Support Vector Machines, and Gradient Boosting can be used to predict parameters such as temperature, humidity, pressure and rainfall by identifying very little relationships that the conventional model might not be able to detect. Deep learning description Deep learning models, in particular, LSTM networks, CNNs, and CNN-LSTM hybrids are particularly useful in time-series forecasting, as they can extract both time-related and space-related information out of satellite images, weather maps, and sensor data. The short term and mid-range predictions are also improved through the use of AI that reveals the trends faster than conventional techniques.

AI systems are more location-specific predictions which are refined with the help of satellite data, radar observations, and IoT-based weather stations. These innovations favor agriculture, aviation, management of renewable energy and day to day planning by providing accurate weather information. AI-powered systems are also used to assist meteorologists in making image analysis automatic, pinpointing the cloud patterns, estimating the rainfall and detecting temperature anomalies at a higher rate. Additionally, AI models enhance climate studies as they identify trends that can be observed over time and help to create proper climate simulations. The more the AI learns new data, the more accurate its predictions are and it is able to adjust to the changing atmospheric conditions. Although some problems continue to be present in the area of data quality, model transparency, and management of various environmental variables, the current advancement of AI technologies will lead to the enhancement of the effectiveness and reliability of weather forecasting in the forthcoming years.

1.2 Disaster Prediction and Risk Assessment

Natural disasters that encompass hurricanes, earthquakes, landslides, and floods that seriously affect the community across the globe as shown in figure. 1. Effective disaster management requires an accurate prediction and risk analysis. No other approach can augment these capabilities as effectively as AI which analyses complex datasets including historical events records, environmental sensors, topography, hydrological patterns, and social vulnerability indicators. Machine learning systems can learn about antecedents of extreme phenomena, e.g. in landslides, soil saturation before such landslides or in earthquakes, seismic activity before earthquakes.

Predictive analytics enable authorities to map the high-risk areas, calculate the possible effects and prioritize interventions. DSS based on AI combine geospatial data, real-time monitoring of the environment, and demographic data to make the allocation of resources and evacuation planning optimal. Indicatively, flood prediction models have the potential of integrating rainfall predictions and river flows, as well as terrain data to model the condition of inundation, which would be used to respond to inundation.

Figure 1. Types of Disasters

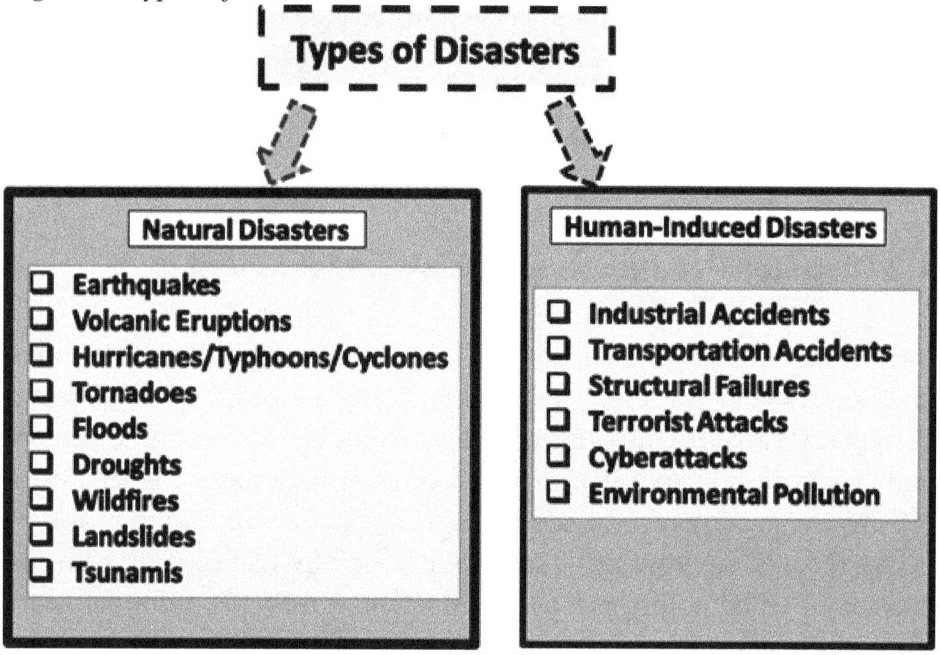

Deep learning models further enhance disaster prediction by processing unstructured data such as satellite imagery, social media feeds, and crowdsourced reports. By analyzing image patterns and temporal trends, AI can detect emerging hazards, monitor disaster progression, and assess post-event damage. These insights support rapid emergency response, resilience planning, and long-term mitigation strategies(Kumar et al., 2024).

Human-induced disasters are the negative events, which take place because of human-related activity, lack of concern or care, technical collapse, or carelessness usage of natural resources. Human-induced disasters, unlike the natural ones, are preventable because they originate in natural processes, and they are usually associated with the industrialization progress, urbanization, and unproductive practices. Industrialization is one of the greatest causes where chemical plants, factories, and manufacturing units can emit toxic gases, pollutants, or other hazardous waste accidentally or because of the low standards of safety.

Bhopal Gas Tragedy and Chernobyl nuclear accident are famous incidents, which demonstrate the way in which one human mistake or safety negligence could lead to massive suffering. Disasters that are related to pollution, like oil spills by tankers or offshore rigs cause significant harm to the marine life, contaminate coastal areas and impact fishing communities. Other types of human-made damages are environmental degradation; such processes as deforestation, uncontrolled mining, overgrazing, and extraction of natural resources undermine the structure of the soil, kaleidoscope, and provide the rise of ecological imbalance.

Another issue that is now of global interest is the human-caused climate change, whereby the greenhouse gases emitted by vehicles, industries, and power stations are excessively released, which causes increasing temperatures, abnormal rainfall, and the long-term alteration of climate patterns(Ahmad Hamdan et al., 2024). Poor planning, overpopulation, and non-observation of safety standards are some of the causes of disasters in urban areas, which include building collapses, landfills fire, sewage system failures, and large scale slum fires.

Disasters involved in transportation such as road accidents, rail collisions, air crashes and shipwrecks are common because of human error, technical failures or improper maintenance. New hazards in the digital era are technological and cyber-attacks; hackers may destroy information networks of critical facilities, damage financial infrastructure, and threaten national security. The human-induced disasters also include industrial explosions, electrical short circuits, and bursting pipes, which can result in massive loss of property and loss of lives. Also, farming activities like overuse of fertilizers and pesticides cause soil pollution, water pollution, and health hazards in the long-term. Land and water degradation is a result of waste mismanagement particularly the poor disposal of e-waste and plastic.

Human conflicts, wars and incidences of terrorism cause massive destruction, displacement and environmental damage across the long-term. Most of these tragedies happen due to lax regulation, ignorance, corruption and neglect to adhere to safety measures. The measures needed to prevent the disasters caused by human beings are effective policy implementation, frequent inspection of safety, application of high-tech technologies, nature preservation, and continuous programmes on human awareness. Responsible practices, sustainable development and a safer environment are to be achieved through efforts of governments, industries and communities which ensure that a safer environment is upheld. With the knowledge of reasons and consequences of human-made disasters, societies can ensure a robust action to mitigate the risks and safeguard people and the planet.

Figure 2. Methods for Disaster Prediction

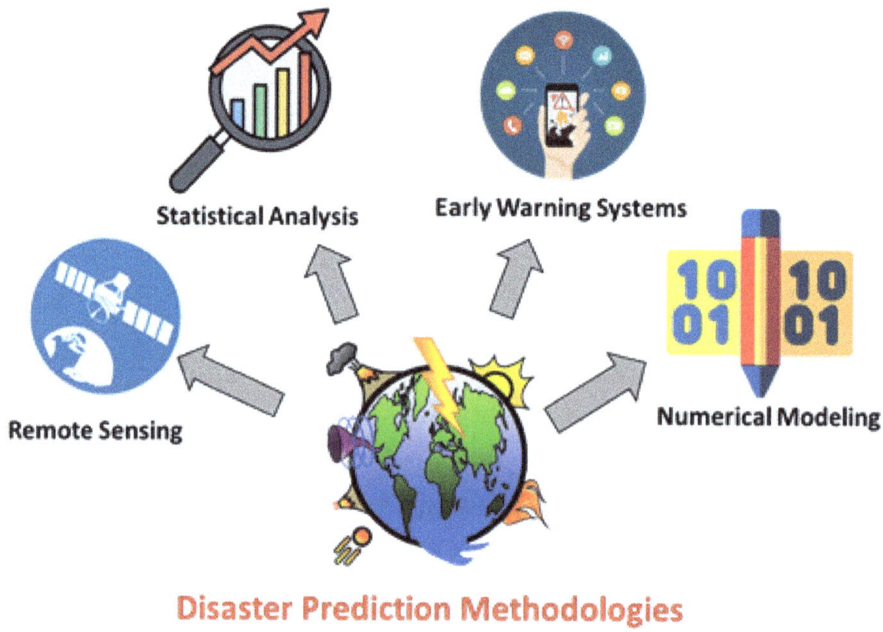

Disaster prediction methodologies are a set of scientific, technological and analytical practices applicable in the identification, analysis and forecasting of any likely disaster before its actualization. The diagram graphically depicts the various contemporary tools and techniques that can be used in conjunction with each other to foresee disasters with more precision and effectiveness. The Earth is at the centre of the diagram and it represents our planet which is often affected by natural hazards like earthquakes, floods, cyclones, tsunamis, droughts, landslides and volcano eruptions. The outward arrows in relation to the central image represent the key categories of the disaster prediction methods, which the scientists and agencies employ nowadays. All of the techniques have their specific data, knowledge and benefits and disaster prediction is a multi-disciplinary and connected subject(Sakurai & Murayama, 2019).

Statistical and trend analysis are one of the key elements presented in the diagram as they are illustrated by the magnifying glass and bar graph icon. Statistical techniques are based on big historical data, scientific observations and long term records of the environment. Patterns, cycles and trends of parameters such as rainfall, temperature, river flow, seismic activity or wind speed are analyzed by analysts.

Monitoring such trends, researchers are able to determine the probability of future occurrence. Indicatively, flood prediction models are built on past flood patterns, rainfall magnitudes, watershed features, and soil water content. On the same note, the earthquake trend analysis examines the past movements of faults and earthquake frequency to know about the potential future earthquakes. Regression models, probability distributions, time-series forecasting and extreme value analysis are some of the statistical methods used by scientists to estimate the risk of future hazards. This element is necessary as it offers the fundamental knowledge of the behavior of the natural systems in the long-term.

Sensor and IoT-based monitoring is another significant item, and as shown by the icon, mobile-linked sensors. Contemporary disaster prediction systems are strongly based on current information gathered via certain sources including weather stations, seismic sensors, rain gauges, ocean buoys, river-level sensors and IoT-supported environmental senses. These sensors relay information in real time and the authorities are able to monitor any change in the environmental conditions directly. As an example, sensors placed at the level of rivers are used to predict flash floods, and sensors at the level of air-pressure are used to predict cyclones.

The Smart City facilities apply IoT devices to track the rainfall, temperature changes, ground vibrations, and environmental pollution. The constantly flowing data assists in identifying early signals way before by conventional manual means of observation. The network of sensors that are interconnected enhances accuracy, expands distance, and assists in making prompt judgements.

Satellite-based remote sensing has also been mentioned in the diagram as symbolized by the satellite icon. The satellites are critically important in monitoring huge environmental variations in space. They take resolution pictures of clouds, oceans, land surfaces, vegetation and atmosphere. Such images aid in detecting cyclone development, monsoon cycles, heat waves, forest fires, regions hit by drought, melting glaciers and volcanic eruptions.

The satellites of remote sensing are equipped with infrared, microwave, and radar technology to identify any change which cannot be seen by human eyes. As an example, the warming of temperatures in the oceans that has been seen using satellites is used to predict El Nino occurrences which affect the weather of the world. The radar satellites are capable of moving through the clouds and even in the storms, they are able to map the accurate floods(Joshi & Kar, 2018).

Earthquake faults, soil movement as well as erosion of the coastline are also tracked by satellite images. The benefit of remote sensing is that, it offers great coverage, high frequency of updates, and accurate information that aids in disaster modelling and early warnings. One more essential element that is displayed in the diagram is data-driven and machine-based prediction, which is denoted by the icon with binary numbers and a pencil. The use of artificial intelligence (AI) and machine learning (ML) has transformed the process of disaster prediction because computers can learn using large datasets and also make predictions much more quickly than other models. Random Forest, Support Vector Machines, Gradient Boosting, LSTM networks, CNN models, and hybrid deep learning architectures are machine learning algorithms used to analyse complicated patterns that might be difficult to detect by human experts.

AI models have the capability of processing vast quantities of weather data, seismic data, sensor records, satellite data, and environmental variables. Taking an example, deep learning models will be able to forecast the intensity of rain, cyclone route, risk of a flood, and the severity of drought with high accuracy. We have LSTM networks that are extensively employed in time-series predictions of rainfall and temperature, and convolutional neural networks that are being applied to analyse satellite images to detect clouds, map wildfires, and track storms. AI-powered systems are adaptive, i.e. they become increasingly more precise as additional data is introduced to them. Collectively, they create an all-inclusive and integrated disaster forecasting system (Kumar et al., 2024).

The arrows on the diagram are the flow of information of various sources to a central purpose, which is to predict and comprehend possible disasters. Long-term data can be given by statistical analysis, whereas sensors and IoT devices can deliver real-time data. The satellites provide views of the environment at large scale and artificial intelligence transforms raw data into predictions that can be acted upon. All these procedures assist the government agencies, weather departments, scholars, and disaster management agencies in the preparation of early warning mechanisms. Proper prediction techniques will be able to promptly give warnings, assist in evacuation, safeguard assets, and minimize losses of life and damage to property.

The diagram highlights the fact that the present-day disaster prediction is no longer a matter that can only be conducted through one approach. Rather it comprises an amalgamation of sophisticated technologies, scientific studies, constant surveillance and intelligent systems which coexist. Interactions among historical data, real-time observations, satellite images, and data-driven models can help the scientists to comprehend the nature of natural hazards better and enhance the accuracy of the early warnings. In a world where technology keeps on advancing, there will be more accurate, quicker and dependable and precise disaster prediction methodologies to ensure that communities in various parts of the world remain safe and resilient.

2. LITERATURE SURVEY

Recent developments in Artificial Intelligence (AI), Machine Learning (ML), and Deep Learning (DL) have made weather forecasting a lot more accurate due to the analysis of big data in relation to atmospheric and environmental data. Conventional numerical weather prediction (NWP) models are usually faced with calculational complexity and poor spatial resolution. Long Short-Term Memory (LSTM), Convolutional Neural Networks (CNN), and hybrid AI-based methods (Huh, 2025) have shown a better performance in the prediction of rainfall, temperature and climate variability. An article published in Expert Systems with Applications suggested an artificial intelligence-based climate prediction model based on LSTM networks to process vast amounts of environmental data to enhance temperature forecasting and early warning systems. It was found that deep learning models may be more effective to reproduce the nonlinear patterns in climate and improve early warning systems against extreme weather events.

Equally, a general overview of various studies on rainfall prediction found out that Artificial Neural Networks (ANNs) and hybrid models (Saleh et al., 2024) are more effective in rainfall prediction as compared to traditional statistical methods because they can capture nonlinear relationships between meteorological variables.

The other systematic review of 8,642 scientific articles (2015-2024) has revealed key research trends in AI-based weather prediction. Studies have indicated that the LSTM, GRU, and transformer architecture (Kim & Kim, 2025)are some of the models that have been used to predict extreme weather conditions like floods, typhoons, and heatwave. Such models can also be used to make high-resolution weather predictions and enhanced disaster preparedness. Prediction of disasters plays a vital role in reducing losses in the economy and saving human lives. The latest disaster prediction platforms are based on machine learning algorithms, geospatial analysis, and remote sensing data to list the initial signs of natural hazards.

Recent studies presented (Huh, 2025) a disaster prediction model based on AI and operated on environmental and oceanographic data to predict occurrences like typhoons, earthquakes, and tsunamis. The suggested system involved using the algorithms of the Random Forest along with environmental signals (temperature, precipitation, wave height, and chlorophyll concentration). In experimental findings, the prediction success rates of climate-related incidents were almost 99% which highlights the quality of AI in disaster prediction frameworks.

The other review study on the application of AI in extreme weather models highlighted the importance of AI in predicting floods, droughts, wildfires, and heat waves. The paper has observed that machine learning models are capable of running heterogeneous data sets and detecting latent associations between environmental factors which are hard to measure using traditional techniques. Also, disaster management is now also being addressed with AI-based remote sensing systems and UAV-based monitoring systems. These systems are a combination of computer vision, deep learning, and drone imagery used to identify the spread of wildfires, track the damage in forests, and assist in planning emergency responses.

Even international bodies like World Meteorological Organization (WMO) have acknowledged that AI has the potential to improve early warning systems and accuracy of forecasting in the international arena. Meteorological data may be combined with disaster monitoring infrastructure with the help of AI-based tools to provide quicker and more accurate warnings.

2.1 Risk Assessment Methodology

Risk assessment methodologies are fundamental in the process of knowing, examination and control of potential risks that can impact people, property or environment. The diagram explains the fact that risk assessment is not one activity but a set of various processes that are interdependent and have to be taken as a whole to provide the full picture about possible threats. On the top level is the Risk Assessment Methodologies, which serves as the general framework, with all the necessary parts that are required in assessment of risk. Out of this core concept, several branches lead to the demonstration of the key elements: Hazard Identification, Probability Assessment, Consequence Assessment, and Vulnerability Assessment. All these elements are integrated to create a guided and organized approach to the assessment of risks in any area, be it environmental management, industrial safety, disaster preparedness, engineering, or even the health of the population.

Hazard Identification is the first big element that is depicted in the diagram. This step entails identification of all threats that may be harmful. The hazards can be natural, technological, or man-made and the process of risk assessment can be based on the identification of the hazard. At this level, professionals collect the data concerning the possibility of something wrong, the reasons why it might occur, and the circumstances under which the hazard might be provoked. To use the example an industrial hazard would be chemical leaks, equipment malfunctioning, explosions, or electricity malfunctions. Hazards can be in an environmental form such as soil erosion, pollution or deforestation related risks. Proper identification of hazards makes sure that no possible threat is missed and it is essential to such analysis in subsequent steps.

Related to hazard identification is Consequence Assessment which determines the extent of impact that can be realized in case a hazard takes place. This is significant as not every hazard has the same degree of impact. Others might only create a minor inconvenience or damage to property, whereas others may cause major injuries, economic losses of large scale or damage to environment in the long run. Consequence assessment assists the decision-maker to realize the hazards which require urgent attention and resources. It also aids in prioritization of risks on the basis of their potential impact on the human beings, infrastructure, environment and social systems. Through the analysis of consequences, organizations will be in a better position to design mitigation measures like safety measures, emergency response and prevention.

The other fundamental element depicted in the diagram is Probability Assessment. Whereas consequence assessment examines the degree of harm, probability assessment examines the likelihood of occurrence of a hazard. Knowledge of probability is used to establish whether that risk is common, occasional, rare, or extremely unlikely. Historical data, simulation models, expert judgement, and statistical methods are usually used in this analysis. As an example, industries can examine historical equipment breakdowns, or environmentalists can be able to examine past climatic patterns to predict the probability of dangerous event. Several factors can be used by combining probability and consequences to identify high, medium, and low risks of concern as required by the risk analysts. This makes the efforts and resources to be channeled where they are most required.

One significant section of the diagram is the focus of Vulnerability Assessment which is repeated twice to show its significance and its relation to various processes. The vulnerability assessment can be defined as the examination of the vulnerability of the people, infrastructures, systems and resources to the hazards identified. It discusses aspects of population density, structural strength of structures, emergency service availability and socioeconomic conditions that can contribute to the effects of a hazard. Although a hazard can have a low probability of occurrence, high level of vulnerability can turn the risk level to be high. As an illustration, a minor fire can escalate to a big accident in a congested location that has substandard electrical installations. Conversely, similar fire can be suppressed instantly in a well-established industrial facility with adequate safety measures. Thus, the vulnerability assessment assists to determine weak areas, exposure, and the ability of community or the system to react and recover.

In the diagram, different arrows have been drawn among the vulnerability assessment and the central risk assessment methodology with emphasis that vulnerability is not a one-step process but rather it interacts with hazard identification, probability, and consequences. Knowledge of vulnerabilities will make the risk assessment realistic and context-based. It also assists the policymakers, planners and organizations in designing improved protection measures. This might be building on the strength of buildings, increasing the public awareness, enhancing the institutional capability, or implementing superior technologies to minimize exposure. Finally, it is the vulnerability assessment that leads to augmented resilience whereby systems are able to endure and recover to the hazards.

These elements combined, hazard identification, consequence assessment, probability assessment, and vulnerability assessment constitute a risk assessment methodology in its entirety. The arrows in the diagram are connected and intertwined indicating how each step contributes to the other. Probability and consequence analysis is based on hazard identification. Probability assessment assists in finding out the urgency of the risk. The consequence evaluation reveals the extent of the severity of the outcomes. Vulnerability assessment modifies the analysis considering the actual conditions and weaknesses of the real world that can increase or decrease the risk. Through the combination of these aspects, risk assessment process will be comprehensive, systematic, and implementable.

Effective risk assessment methodology guarantees organizations, governments and communities to make effective decisions. It helps in planning as it recognizes where preventive measures need to be done, where the resources need to be mobilized and what safety procedures need to be prioritized. In the case of industries, this implies having superior safety systems, frequent maintenance and close control of the dangerous processes. Risk assessment steers the sustainable development, pollution control, and protection of the ecosystem with regard to environmental management. In the case of urban planning, it guarantees the safety of infrastructure, better facilities to the population, and minimization of risk of encountering dangers.

In addition, risk assessment procedures assist in preparedness as institutions are able to anticipate the possible failures and reinforce their responses. Carefully adopted, this framework saves economic losses, preserves human lives, and leads to long-term sustainability. The diagram is a work of simplicity and power, as it demonstrates the key elements of risk analysis and reveals their interrelations. The diagram is made up of branches, each of which represents a crucial step towards the creation of a complete risk comprehension. Combining the two, they form a framework tactic that will help reduce uncertainties, enhance safety and aid in making better decisions in different areas.

Figure 3. Risk Assessment Methodology

2.2 Biodiversity Monitoring and Conservation

Biodiversity is critical in maintaining a stable ecosystem, human life, and in maintaining climate. Nevertheless, the biodiversity of the world is threatened by species loss, degradation of their habitats and climate change(Leong, 2025). The use of traditional methods of monitoring e.g., field surveys and identification of species manually is time consuming, expensive and in many cases inadequate in space coverage. AI can provide solutions to the issue of biodiversity monitoring and conservation: these are scalable and efficient. Deep learning algorithms and computer vision can recognize the species based on the images or acoustic recordings, which allows the automated tracking of the wildlife population. To track the distribution of species, identify invasive species, and assess behavioral patterns, drones, camera traps, and acoustic sensors collect massive amounts of data that AI systems process to understand the distribution of species. Predictive modeling helps researchers estimate the suitability of the habitat, simulate changes in species distribution caused by climate and focus efforts on conservation actions(Ahmad Hamdan et al., 2024). These could be used by evidence-based decision-making based on these AI-driven insights to support the work on protected area management, reforestation, and ecosystem restoration efforts.

Figure 4. Biodiversity Conservation

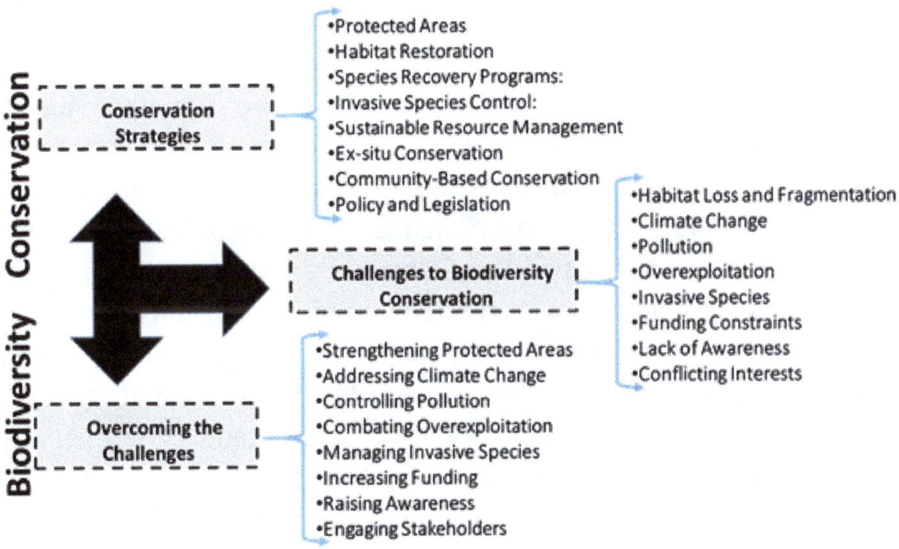

Moreover, AI facilitates citizen science initiatives, where volunteers contribute observations via mobile applications. AI algorithms process and validate these data, expanding the reach of biodiversity monitoring and fostering public engagement in environmental stewardship. By combining high-resolution data with predictive modeling, AI enhances the capacity to detect biodiversity threats, evaluate conservation strategies, and inform policy.

Conservation of bio-diversity is a very much needed global agenda since it incorporates saving the diversity of plant and animal life, ecosystems, and genetic material which are behind the life on the earth. The diagram shows the theme, which is at the center of the theme, which is Challenges to Biodiversity Conservation and there are two significant supporting elements, which are Conservation Strategies and Overcoming the Challenges. This structure will underline that the initial step is to comprehend the issues, then implement effective practices and come up with solutions on how to overcome the obstacles. Biodiversity plays a critical role in ecological balance, regulation of climate, soil fertility, water purification and the general wellbeing of the human community.

Nevertheless, it is not simple to preserve it since there are too many pressures that endanger the survival of species and ecosystem stability, both natural and human-made. The diagram is a graphical representation of the fact that the problem of biodiversity loss is multifaceted and it needs multidimensional solutions, each of which is interconnected with the strategic planning and proactive conservation. The focus of the diagram is in the title, Challenges to Biodiversity Conservation, which is the central challenges of conserving the use of biological resources in the world. Habitat destruction that is mainly through urban expansion, deforestation, agricultural intensification, mining, dam construction and industrial development is one of the main challenges. With the clearing of forests, draining of wetlands, and the alteration of natural sceneries, thousands of species have no homes left and have reduced in their population and are edged toward extinction. The other significant threat is climate change, which changes the temperature patterns, rainfall patterns and ocean currents, causing coral bleaching, melting of glaciers, increase in sea levels and interruption of species migration patterns. Many of the organisms are finding it hard to cope with these drastic changes and this has led to changed ecosystems and a decrease in biodiversity(Wani et al., 2024).

The third obstacle is pollution that has air, water, soil, and noise pollution and negatively affects wildlife and ecological processes. The habitats and species are polluted with chemical pollutants like pesticides, industrial wastes, plastics and oil spills. Excessive use of natural resources including overfishing, unsustainable hunting, illegal wildlife trade and over-extraction of timber are also a major threat to the biodiversity. Several species are nearly going into extinction due to human resource exploitation which is outpacing the rate at which the ecosystems are regenerating(Mai et al., 2025). Another significant threat is the invasive species: the introduction of non-native species can be either intentional or unintentional, but the non-native species tends to outcompete the native ones, introduce diseases, or disruptions to the food chain, causing the lack of an ecological balance. Also, animals become isolated due to the presence of roads, fences, and human habitat, thus making reproduction challenging and decreasing the genetic pool.

The deficiency of information to the people, the effective failure of the law enforcers, and the inadequate finance of the conservation programs also increase the global biodiversity crisis. On the left of the diagram, there is the term Conservation Strategies, its meaning being the systematic methods of biodiversity protection. Establishment of the protected areas, such as national parks, wildlife reserves, marine reserves, and biosphere reserves, is one of the necessary strategies. Such areas restrict human encroachment and safe environments where species can flourish are available. Sustainable resource management is another crucial strategy that encourages responsible fishing, logging, farming, and water usage to ensure the development of an ecological balance. The restoration ecology is also crucial; it involves reforestation, restoration of wetland, reef restoration, and soil enhancement program to restore degraded ecosystems. The conservation plans also depend on legislative and environmental policies (including wildlife protection laws, anti-poaching legislation, laws regulating pollution and land use). The endangered species and biological diversity are saved with the help of scientific measures such as keeping track of the species, breeding captives, and seed banks.

Community participation and education is a significant part of conservation plans. People are encouraged to take care of biodiversity and appreciate it through environmental awareness programs, citizen science, and the involvement of the local community. The use of modern technologies in conservation activities also involves drones, GIS mapping, satellite imagery, artificial intelligence, and sophisticated systems of detecting wildlife movement and identifying threats. The agreements and cooperation among nations e.g. the Convention on Biological Diversity (CBD), CITES and global climate treaties enhance conservation efforts since it is a concerted effort by all countries to conserve species and habitats.

The diagram below the center box reveals that there is an Overcoming the Challenges, which implies that the solutions should take direct approach to the identified problems. The way to go to overcome the biodiversity challenges or problems is stricter implementation of policies, where the governments develop strict laws against illegal logging, trade in wildlife, pollution and destruction of habitats. It also includes the advancement of the sustainable development, achieving the balance between the economic growth and protection of the environment. Investment in finance is quite an important factor; investment into conservation research, restoration projects and community-based projects would assist in achieving long term success. Promotion of scientific infrastructure, facilities to train wildlife officers and better monitoring technologies are used to fight poaching, destruction of habitat and environmental crimes. Another significant move towards solving the biodiversity problem is dealing with climate change.

The emission of greenhouse gases through reduction, the use of renewable energy sources, and the preservation of ecosystems with a high carbon content such as forests, mangroves, and wetlands stabilize the climate. Organic farming, crop rotation and reduction in the use of chemicals promote sustainable farming which ensures the health of the soil biodiversity and elimination of habitat degradation. The other challenge to overcome is to enhance global collaboration, as the challenge of biodiversity is a national issue. Nations should cooperate in terms of sharing research, technology, and approaches to combating popular menaces including invasive plants as well as climate change and unlawful trade of wildlife.

Lastly, it must create awareness and behavioral change in the public. Once individuals realize the importance of the biodiversity as well as the effects of its extinction, they will be more accountable in their everyday decisions. Citizens can be empowered by schools, the media, and community organizations to lead environmentally friendly lifestyles including limiting the use of plastic, saving water, planting trees, and animal habitats. The diagram identifies that conservation strategies and specific solutions are intertwined and, therefore, biodiversity conservation is a cyclical process of challenge identification, strategy formulation, and solution implementation. It is only through the interaction of these three aspects that societies can become long-term ecologically stable and the richness of life on the Earth can be preserved to the future generations(Kumar et al., 2024).

2.3 Data Integration and Multisensor Fusion

A critical factor in leveraging AI for environmental resilience is the integration of diverse datasets from multiple sources(Pala & Yüce, 2023). Environmental data are often heterogeneous, encompassing structured measurements (e.g., temperature, rainfall, pollutant levels) and unstructured inputs (e.g., satellite images, social media reports). Multisensor fusion techniques combine these datasets to improve prediction accuracy, reduce uncertainty, and provide comprehensive situational awareness (Hashim et al., 2016).

For example, AI can fuse satellite imagery with ground-based sensors to refine weather forecasts, flood simulations, or habitat models. Time-series analysis, spatial interpolation, and anomaly detection techniques allow the identification of patterns and early warning signals. Data pre-processing, normalization, and quality control are essential steps to ensure the reliability of AI-driven models. Effective data integration enhances predictive performance, supports decision-making, and enables proactive environmental management. The various applications associated with climate change mitigation are discussed in the next section, highlighting how technological and analytical approaches contribute to reducing environmental impacts.

3. APPLICATIONS IN CLIMATE CHANGE MITIGATION

Table 1. Applications in Climate Change Mitigation

Renewable Energy Sources	**Carbon Capture and Storage (CCS)**	**Sustainable Agriculture**	**Energy Efficiency**	**Other Mitigation Strategies**
1.Solar Energy	1. Pre-Combustion Capture	1.No-Till Farming	1.Building Efficiency	1.Reforestation and Afforestation
2.Wind Energy	2. Post-Combustion Capture	2.Cover Cropping	2.Industrial Efficiency	2.Blue Carbon
3.Hydropower	3.Direct Air Capture (DAC)	3.Crop Rotation	3.Transportation Efficiency	3.Carbon Pricing
4. Geothermal Energy	4.Geological Storage	4.Agroforestry		4.Green Hydrogen
5.Biomass Energy		5.Reduced Fertilizer Use		5.Sustainable Transportation
		6.improved Livestock Management		

AI applications extend beyond forecasting and monitoring to include climate change mitigation strategies. Predictive models can assess greenhouse gas emissions, evaluate energy consumption patterns, and optimize renewable energy deployment. AI-driven systems support urban planning, agricultural management, and carbon sequestration initiatives by providing data-driven insights for reducing environmental impact. Integration of AI in climate policy frameworks allows governments and organizations to design adaptive, evidence-based strategies that respond to evolving environmental conditions. By connecting prediction, monitoring, and mitigation, AI strengthens the overall resilience of human and natural systems(Dai et al., 2024).

The sphere of climate change mitigation is rather extensive as it implies numerous techniques to minimize the emissions of greenhouse gases and to increase the natural capacity of the Earth to take carbon. Solar, wind, hydropower, geothermal and biomass are all renewable sources of energy, which are central to substituting fossil fuel. Solar power contributes to cut down the emissions of carbon since it converts the sunlight into electricity with no pollution. The wind energy offers clean energy by the use of turbines that are efficient in windy areas. Hydropower has been able to produce credible electricity with flowing water and has played a significant role in the world production of renewable. Geothermal energy uses the heat present in the interior of the earth to supply clean and constant electricity.

The biomass energy utilizes organic products and can turn into carbon-neutral when properly handled. The other significant mitigation measure to prevent the entry of CO2 into the atmosphere is Carbon Capture and Storage or CCS. The capture at pre-combustion, involves capturing the carbon in fuels and burning them. CO2 separation after burning is done by post-combustion capture. Direct Air Capture captures the carbon in the air through direct absorption by chemical reactions. Geological storage entails the process of injecting the captured CO2 to deep underground formations where it is stored in a safe way. Mitigation is also achieved through sustainable agriculture whereby the release of methane and nitrous oxide is reduced. No-till agriculture is also beneficial in preserving soil carbon through plowing. Cover cropping preserves soil, provides nutrients and enhances the storage of water.

Crop rotation increases the fertility of soil and decreases the usage of chemical fertilizers. Agroforestry involves combination of trees with crops to enhance carbon storage as well as augment the biodiversity. Less use of fertilizers reduces nitrous oxide emission in farmlands. Better livestock management reduces the methane emission due to better feed and grazing practices. Another category of climate mitigation is energy efficiency. Efficiency in the building is associated with enhanced insulation, lighting, and ventilation that minimize power use. The field of industrial efficiency is concerned with machine upgrading, waste heat reuse, and betterment of the production process. Transport efficiency will encompass the use of electric vehicles, hybrid transportation, and enhanced public transportation to cut down on the use of fuel. In addition to these, other mitigation measures can be employed in order to achieve global climate objectives. Reforestation and afforestation aid in the renewal of forests which capture huge quantities of CO_2. The carbon is stored better in blue carbon ecosystems such as mangroves and seagrasses than in many terrestrial ecosystems.

Carbon pricing policies make industries cut down on the emission due to the high cost of pollution. Green hydrogen is a renewable energy that could provide an alternative to heavy industries as a clean fuel. Sustainability of transportation encourages walking, cycling, electric buses and car-sharing systems. The combination of the strategies creates a holistic climate mitigation strategy. Renewable energy will help lessen reliance on fossil fuels and minimize emissions by their source. Some of the areas of uncontrollable emissions that CCS captures include steel and cement sectors. Sustainable agriculture enhances food security without causing much environmental degradation. Green buildings, industries and vehicles save energy and decrease the total energy need.

Forests and blue carbon restoration increase the natural carbon sinks. Carbon tax encourages innovation and cleanliness in industries. Green hydrogen provides new possibilities in the decarbonization of challenging sectors. Green transport will lessen the pollution in cities and enhance the transport speeds. Each strategy has its own role to play but it gains strength when combined with other strategies. Mitigation of climate entails international collaboration between the government, industries, community, and individuals. The nations must have effective policies that will promote clean technologies and discourage high-emission. Research and development aids in development of superior solutions in energy, agriculture, and industry. Through people enlightenment, individuals are persuaded to use sustainable lifestyles. The training on climate-smart agricultural practices is helpful to farmers. Industries and engineers embrace power saving technologies. Governments invest in renewable energy facilities and Carbon storage.

Cities grow green areas and enhance the transport systems. At the global level, climate is being undertaken in light of international agreements, such as the Paris Agreement. This is because developed countries give climate finance to aid developing nations. Sharing of technology works faster in the world. Universities and schools encourage environmental literacy in students. There is the participation of local communities in tree-planting and conservation programs. There is the awareness created by the nongovernmental organizations on climate problems. Corporations engage in being carbon-neutral and sustainable in supply chains. The shoppers use green products and minimize garbage. Circular economy models lower the use of resources and enhance the process of recycling. Urban planning incorporates green structures and low-carbon architectural works. The mitigation strategies are used together with climate adaptation to secure the vulnerable areas. The renewable energy generates new employment opportunities in the solar, wind, and bioenergy industries. CCS technologies change in order to become more efficient and cost-effective. Climate-smart practices improve agriculture. Even efficient industries minimize the cost of operation, and minimized pollution.

Cities have less noise and air pollution by electric vehicles. Hydrogen technology ventures into transport, industry and storage of energy. Reforestation activities reclaim the eroded sceneries and help in sustaining biodiversity. The conservation of the blue carbon ecosystems improves defense along the coast. Green development is financed by Carbon pricing. International climate objectives are to reduce the warming to less than 1.5 C. These targets need to be met with an immediate and long-term effort. The mitigation measures can make the climate steady and avoid severe weather. Combined strategies guarantee sustainability of the environment in the long run. Innovation accelerates the process of low-carbon economies. The environmental policies are made stronger and inclusive.

Coordination between industries provides full implementation. The use of green technologies is increasingly invested all over the world. Climate actions are enhanced by education and community participation. The young people are significant in promoting climate justice. Renewable energy is used in industries to fuel their activities. The emission reductions are monitored and reported by governments. Clean transportation networks help in alleviating traffic congestion and pollution. The intelligent technologies assist in controlling the consumption of energy. Green living is more prevalent among the citizens. Companies are researching on ways of cutting carbon footprints. Forest conservation secures the habitat of wildlife.

By promoting clean investments, carbon markets promote clean investments. Green hydrogen will decrease reliance on coal and oil. The environmentally friendly agricultural practices preserve the land and water.

Effective buildings help in providing easy lodging with reduced energy bills. Industries manufacture products that have low emissions. Communities safeguard the coastal ecosystems to promote resilience to climate change. Such a combination of strategies is a great basis of climate change mitigation. Every measure, not only technological, but also agricultural, economic, and environmental, will make the planet healthier. Through serious efforts around the clock it is possible to curtail the emission of greenhouse gases on a large scale. The variety of mitigation strategies makes it possible to include all sectors. Climate mitigation helps the future of every country to be sustainable and secure through innovation, cooperation and commitment.

4. CHALLENGES AND LIMITATIONS

The implementation of Artificial Intelligence has proved to be a potent solution to enhance the environmental resilience but it is not implemented without major challenges, which have to be well learned and tackled. The availability and quality of environmental data is one of the most important barriers that are required to train accurate and reliable AI models. In most parts of the globe, particularly, the developing or remote countries, the environmental monitoring systems are either scarce or unevenly distributed, hence poor data sets which reduce predictive accuracy of AI systems. The sensor networks employed to gather environmental information can be incomplete, deteriorated or due to technical failures, they add errors and inaccuracy in the viewpoint. In the cases of weak underlying data, even the high-tech AI models fail to provide meaningful or reliable information.

The other limitation is associated with the computational needs of AI systems. HPC, huge memory, and enhanced algorithms require enormous investments of both financial and technical capital. Several organizations, in particular, the ones operating in low-income areas, might lack access to powerful hardware, cloud computing, or highly-trained professionals knowledgeable in machine learning and environmental modelling. This puts a technological gulf between the beneficiaries of AI-enabled solutions to the environment. Besides the technical and infrastructural issues, the ethical factors are very critical in the implementation of AI in environmental resilience. When it comes to the collection and subsequent processing of sensitive information pertaining to the environment or communities, there will be issues like data privacy.

Another issue is transparency because most AI models are used as black boxes, and stakeholders can hardly learn how the predictions are made or whether there are biases. Models that end up being trained on biased or unbalanced data or on biased data can result in unfair or inaccurate output which can be disadvantageous to some parts of a region or population. The other critical weakness is that AI predictions are probabilistic in nature, i.e. they are not definite, but only give possibilities. When automated systems are overused and not accompanied by enough human supervision, there might be cases of misinterpretation, the abuse of outputs, or wrong decision-making during critical environmental circumstances. Human beings have to stay engaged in terms of reviewing the outcomes, authenticating the forecasts, and giving contextual judgement. This necessitates synchronized international action in order to overcome these challenges. Data infrastructure can be enhanced by adding a lot of sensors, enhancing the quality of data collection and standard monitoring systems which can enhance data quality.

The capacity building is necessary to make sure that scientists, policymakers, and institutions acquire skills to design, interpret, and administer AI systems. Multidisciplinary cooperation among computer scientists, environmental, social scientists and local communities can close the knowledge gaps and develop a more inclusive and reliable AI-based solution. The creation of the policy is also valuable as it offers regulations and moral codes to be used in the responsible use of AI. All these combined can assist in unlocking the full potential of Artificial Intelligence and reducing risks to a minimum, thereby affecting fairness, ensuring transparency, and supporting environmental resilience in the long-term approach in a sustainable and just way.

5. FUTURE DIRECTIONS

Technology, greater integration of various spheres, greater understandability, and international collaboration are defining the future of

Artificial Intelligence in environmental resilience that will empower our capacity to react to environmental issues. With environmental challenges like climate change, loss of biodiversity and extreme weather events persisting to increase, the AI is likely to be transformative in predicting, monitoring, and mitigating these effects. Among the top priorities, there is the augmented collaboration of AI with the current technological ecosystems. Edge computing is one such innovation that is enabling the data to be processed nearer to the place of origin and thus this allows quicker decision-making and avoids heavy reliance on centralized systems. This can be of great worth especially in remote or disaster prone locations where communication networks can be volatile. Likewise, the increasing systems of Internet of Things, which are made up of millions of interconnected sensors, are enhancing the level and extent of environmental watch considerably.

Such IoT sensors are in a position to monitor air quality, water levels, soil moisture, the conditions of forests, and wildlife locations in real-time, streaming nonstop data into AI models. Satellite imagery in high-resolution supported by the advanced earth-observation missions is giving unprecedented insight into the complex situation of the global environmental change, including deforestation, melting ice-caps. Satellite, ground sensors, along with analytics based on AI, create a complete image of the health of the planet. Explainable AI models are another important trend in the future. Conventional AI systems are usually regarded as being like black boxes, capable of making predictions without apparent explanation, and even this can cause decision-makers to be skeptical or wary. Explainable AI does this by providing visibility to explain how the model has reached a certain conclusion.

This improves the confidence the policymakers, scientists, and the citizens have in AI, reducing worries that AI understanding will be applied in climate planning, disaster management, and conservation policies. Through increased interpretability, the environmental authorities will be able to make judgments concerning risks, comprehend uncertainties and adopt evidence based strategies with clear understanding.

Global cooperation and sharing of knowledge is also the future of AI in environmental resilience. Multilateral online platforms will enable nations, organizations, and scientists to share environmental information, gain access to AI applications, and add to common databases. This type of collaboration is necessary since environmental problems have no political borders; climate change, loss of biodiversity and natural disasters are international problems that must be addressed by every country. Shared datasets enhance the precision of AI models, whereas shared algorithms will guarantee that even resource-constrained areas can enjoy state-of-the-art technologies. Integrated responses are also promoted by collaborative platforms that contribute to the development of early-warning mechanisms that challenge countries to new dangers and facilitate the coordination of humanitarian and environmental actions.

The other significant future direction is the combination of AI and citizen science and community projects. The citizens possessing smartphones and mobile apps, as well as inexpensive sensors, will be able to actively contribute to data gathering, environmental tracking, and reporting on the local changes. Improved insights in the scope of the integration of formal scientific data and the knowledge obtained by citizens through reporting are more enriching and socially grounded when this process involves AI systems. Participatory monitoring enhances social consciousness, strengthens the local communities and makes environmental resilience to stay on the hands of the experts.

The AI-based tools could help communities to identify risks, adapt farming, save biodiversity, or respond to catastrophes. This is because this democratization of environmental knowledge enhances resilience among all strata of society. There will also be the use of AI in designing solutions, optimizing the use of natural resources, creating nature-based strategies, and assisting climate adaptation projects as well as prediction. With the increase in computing power and advances in algorithms, AI systems will be able to compute more complex interactions in the ecological system, capture future scenarios more precisely, and suggest certain policies that can reconcile environmental protection with economic growth. Large-scale reforestation, restoration of coral reefs, cleaning the ocean, and securing wildlife may be reinforced by the integration of AI and robotics.

The sustainability planning powered by AI will enable cities to be less pollutant, introduce waste management, and create infrastructure resistant to climatic changes. All these insights will be made more understandable and enhanced interpretability will guarantee that they will be comprehensible to policymakers and the population. The future of AI and environmental resilience is thus closely related to technological development, transparency, accessibility and community involvement. With the help of advanced technologies and human expertise, as well as international collaboration, AI is capable of spreading its influence and increasing its social value to a considerable degree. In the end, AI is likely to become the indispensable partner in protecting ecosystems and promoting sustainable development and a strong planet that will be lasting to generations to come.

6. POLICY IMPLICATIONS AND RECOMMENDATIONS

Successful application of Artificial Intelligence in environmental resilience heavily relies on enabling, inclusive and progressive policy frameworks that can allow the safe, ethical, and effective utilization of new technologies. Governments are at the center of establishing a platform around which AI driven environmental solutions can flourish. Investment in data infrastructure is one of the most significant policy priorities as the basis of any AI model is high-quality, continuous, and reliable data. These involve an increase in sensor network sizes in the air, water, soil, and weather, enhanced acquisition of satellite-based data and provision of standardized national platforms on environmental dataset. Governments should also invest in AI research projects that facilitate innovation, can help explore, and it can help support the creation of improved models that address regional ecological issues. Besides the investments of technologies, there should be regulations to make sure that AI is applied in an ethical, transparent, and socially responsible way.

The policies must enforce justice in algorithms, hold people responsible in automated decision-making, and protect the privacy of individuals and communities whose data can be used to predict the environment. Its access should be fair such that the AI tools are not restricted to rich institutions or areas with advanced technology but can be used in developing sections, rural areas, and vulnerable groups. Interdisciplinary education should also be backed by policies that facilitate cross-curriculum that incorporates environmental science, computer science, ethics, and public policy.

This is necessary because the capacity-building programs will equip the environmental professionals, government officials, researchers, and local stakeholders with the required skills to interpret, apply, and manage AI-based tools. Academia, industry, government agencies, and civil society need to work together and this ought to be highly encouraged on the basis of grants, innovation hubs and multi-stakeholder platforms.

The inclusion of AI instruments in national climate action strategies improves mitigation and adaptation strategic planning. AI in disaster management would aid in early-warning systems, risk mapping, and quick response coordination only when disaster management policies are clear on the role of each operation, share of data, and communication channels. On the same note, AI should be integrated into biodiversity protection regulations including habitat protection and monitoring wildlife and environmental restoration. Sustainability of the natural environment in the long term will require a matching of AI technologies to larger societal objectives like emission reduction, climate resilience, natural ecosystem safeguarding, and environmental justice. Responsible innovation policies help to make sure that AI supplements, rather than supplants, local knowledge, community involvement, and traditional ecological knowledge. Finally, the national priorities supported by sound governance, involvement of all parties, and ethical protection of AI as a strategic tool provide a stable platform on which to use technology to solve climate issues and develop a healthier and more resilient planet.

7. CONCLUSION

The Artificial Intelligence has incredible and transformative capacity to enhance resilience to the environment since it can be used to analyze large volumes of complex and rapidly changing data in a way that may be more effective than classic methods of analysis. By tracking trends, relationships, and variances among extensive environmental data, AI facilitates sound making predictions, improves disaster prediction, and increases the control of biodiversity in a wide range of ecosystems. AI-based models assist in weathering apps to optimize predictions of rain, changes in temperature, storm generation, and severe climate occurrences to allow authorities to plan ahead and react better. In disaster management, AI is useful in real time analysis of disaster like floods, landslides, cyclones and droughts by combining satellite images, sensor data and history to create credible early warning systems. In conservation of biodiversity, AI is utilized to help track species location, determine habitat loss, monitor forest cover, and enforce law by recognizing automated images or with the use of drones to undercover poaching or deforestation activities.

The abilities greatly contribute to evidence-based planning and promote proactive measures to defend the ecosystem before it is late. Even though AI has immense potential, it is important to note that there are a number of significant issues that need to be overcome before realizing the full potential of AI. One of the largest impediments has been the quality of data whereby environmental data can be flawed, uneven or unattainable in a large number of locations. The lack of sufficient access to advanced AI tools is also limited by a lack of computational resources and insufficient technical infrastructure, particularly in low-income or remote regions.

There are ethical issues such as transparency, fairness, bias in algorithms, and responsible use of data that have to be considered carefully in such a way as to make AI applications as trustworthy and non-discriminatory as possible. Another issue is accessibility, where the disproportionate availability of technological resources may increase disparities in the world once it does not become a responsible issue. Overcoming these obstacles, future policies must focus on the interdisciplinary approach, uniting environmental scientists, AI researchers, policymakers, and local communities to work together to develop efficient solutions.

There is a need to engage globally in order to share data, models, and best practices to enable the countries to jointly address the issue of climate. The use of explainable AI models will gain more significance and will ensure that predictions made can be understood and therefore taken into action by decision-makers. It is also essential that the community is engaged and participatory monitors as local knowledge and citizen science can enhance datasets, make models more relevant, and gain greater public trust. Responsible and ethical use of AI will help society to greatly increase environmental resilience and address the effects of climate change and ensure biodiversity to generations to come. This chapter points out the necessity of integrating technology invention with moral rules, social engagement and robust policies to develop sustainable, inclusive and dynamic environmental solutions.

REFERENCES

Dai, D., Bo, M., Ren, X., & Dai, K. (2024). Application and exploration of artificial intelligence technology in urban ecosystem-based disaster risk reduction: A scoping review. *Ecological Indicators*, *158*, 111565. DOI: 10.1016/j.ecolind.2024.111565

Ghosh, S., Lu, J., Das, P., & Zhang, Z. (2024). Machine learning algorithms for merging satellite-based precipitation products and their application on meteorological drought monitoring over Kenya. *Climate Dynamics*, *62*(1), 141–163. DOI: 10.1007/s00382-023-06893-6

Hamdan, A., Ibekwe, K. I., Etukudoh, E. A., Umoh, A. A., & Ilojianya, V. I. (2024). AI and machine learning in climate change research: A review of predictive models and environmental impact. *World Journal of Advanced Research and Reviews*, *21*(1), 1999–2008. DOI: 10.30574/wjarr.2024.21.1.0257

Hashim, R., Roy, C., Motamedi, S., Shamshirband, S., Petković, D., Gocic, M., & Lee, S. C. (2016). Selection of meteorological parameters affecting rainfall estimation using neuro-fuzzy computing methodology. *Atmospheric Research*, *171*, 21–30. DOI: 10.1016/j.atmosres.2015.12.002

Huh, J. (2025). AI-Driven Climate Disaster Prediction and Response System: Enhancing Community Resilience. *Journal of Basic and Applied Research International*, *31*(4), 129–141. DOI: 10.56557/jobari/2025/v31i49566

Joshi, S., & Kar, S. C. (2018). Mechanism of ENSO influence on the South Asian monsoon rainfall in global model simulations. *Theoretical and Applied Climatology*, *131*(3–4), 1449–1464. DOI: 10.1007/s00704-017-2045-5

Kim, B., & Kim, T. (2025). AI in extreme weather events prediction and response: A systematic topic-model review (2015–2024). *Frontiers in Environmental Science*, *13*, 1659344. DOI: 10.3389/fenvs.2025.1659344

Kumar, D., Bassill, N. P., & Ghosh, S. (2024). Analyzing recent trends in deep-learning approaches: A review on urban environmental hazards and disaster studies for monitoring, management, and mitigation toward sustainability. *International Journal on Smart Sensing and Intelligent Systems*, *17*(1), 20240014. DOI: 10.2478/ijssis-2024-0014

Leong, W. Y. (2025). Artificial Intelligence-Driven Analytics for Monitoring and Mitigating Climate Change Impacts. *IEEE ICEIB*, *7*, 7. Advance online publication. DOI: 10.3390/engproc2025108007

Mai, S., Qing, L., Mehmood, U., Almulhim, A. A., & Aljughaiman, A. A. (2025). From digital advancement to SDGs disruption: How artificial intelligence without inclusion threatens sustainable development in G7 economies. *Journal of Environmental Management*, *394*, 127411. DOI: 10.1016/j.jenvman.2025.127411 PMID: 40986962

Nishant, R., Kennedy, M., & Corbett, J. (2020). Artificial intelligence for sustainability: Challenges, opportunities, and a research agenda. *International Journal of Information Management*, *53*, 102104. DOI: 10.1016/j.ijinfomgt.2020.102104

Pala, M., & Yüce, M. İ. (2023). Comparative Rainfall-Runoff analysis of the Upper Murat River Basin in Turkey in context of Hydro-Meteorological variables. *Alexandria Engineering Journal*, *75*, 479–493. DOI: 10.1016/j.aej.2023.06.013

Sakurai, M., & Murayama, Y. (2019). Information technologies and disaster management – Benefits and issues -. *Progress in Disaster Science*, *2*, 100012. DOI: 10.1016/j.pdisas.2019.100012

Saleh, M., Rasel, H. M., & Ray, B. (2024). A comprehensive review towards resilient rainfall forecasting models using artificial intelligence techniques. *Green Technologies and Sustainability*, *2*(3), 100104. DOI: 10.1016/j.grets.2024.100104

Wani, A. K., Rahayu, F., Ben Amor, I., Quadir, M., Murianingrum, M., Parnidi, P., Ayub, A., Supriyadi, S., Sakiroh, S., Saefudin, S., Kumar, A., & Latifah, E. (2024). Environmental resilience through artificial intelligence: Innovations in monitoring and management. *Environmental Science and Pollution Research International*, *31*(12), 18379–18395. DOI: 10.1007/s11356-024-32404-z PMID: 38358626

Chapter 3
Big Data Challenges in Real-Time Geo-Hazard Monitoring and Prediction

A. Sumathi
http://orcid.org/0000-0003-4700-5573
Department of CSE, SRC, SASTRA (Deemed to be) University, India

Farjana Farvin Sahapudeen
SRC, SASTRA (Deemed to be) University, India

ABSTRACT

Every year, immense losses occur during natural hazards such as earthquakes, volcanoes, landslides and floods. Advanced digital technologies such as seismic networks, Prediction systems based on unmanned area vehicles (UAV), satellite monitoring, ground based sensors, Internet of Things (IoT) generate large volumes of data. Continuous real time monitoring and prediction based on data analytics introduce numerous challenges. Multi source data collection enables the use of big data analytics through machine learning and deep learning models. Complexity may arise in terms of data velocity, quality and preprocessing cost and reliability.

DOI: 10.4018/979-8-3373-8042-1.ch003

This chapter focuses on major big data challenges in real time geo hazard monitoring and predictive models and highlights various research issues associated with it.

INTRODUCTION

Geo-hazard monitoring depends on large and diverse datasets. Big data is commonly described in terms of high volume, high velocity of retrieval, variety of data arrangement, veracity (reliability)and value in terms of impact. Big data represents the large scale collection of geohazard data. Geohazard monitoring uses a variety of monitoring instruments that operate continuously and collect data day and night. As a result, the databases continue to increase in size, which increases the complexity of further analysis. Big data differs in terms of volume, velocity, variety and value. Large volumes of data demand high computational efficiency and prediction accuracy. Data streams include satellite images, GNSS data, seismic waveforms, and temperature and pressure sensors. Real time data prediction supports fault tolerance in cases of failure or network delay to ensure system reliability. Most of the real hazard prediction tasks require millisecond level processing for earthquake monitoring. They system must capture high frequency data and analyse them at high speeds. Geohazard monitoring depends on large volume of historical data. Satellite imaging produces terabytes of data per day, requiring high capacity storage and efficient retrieval systems. Geo hazards involve multi-dimensional data that require the fusion of different sensor modalities. Volcanic data analysis involves information from soil moisture sensors, landslide sensors, pressure sensors and satellite imagery.

Geo-hazards such as earthquakes, floods, landslides, and volcanic activities pose serious threats to human life, infrastructure, and the environment. In recent years, the frequency and impact of these natural hazards have increased due to factors such as climate change, rapid urbanization, and environmental degradation. Effective monitoring and early prediction of such hazards are essential to reduce damage and improve disaster preparedness. Traditionally, geo-hazard monitoring relied on limited observational data and manual analysis, which often made it difficult to detect early warning signals in time. Nevertheless, due to the development of sensing devices, remote sensing systems, and environmental observation networks, today huge amounts of data are being constantly collected by means of satellites, sensors, unmanned aerial vehicles (UAVs), and weather stations. New opportunities for processing big data have opened through the development of big data technologies. Thanks to big data, people will be able to interpret patterns in the environment and discover signs of possible hazards. In addition, modern techniques of artificial intelligence and machine learning are used for the analysis of big data.. Despite these advancements, real-time geo-hazard monitoring and prediction still face several challenges related to data management, processing speed, data quality, and system integration. Addressing these challenges is crucial for developing reliable early warning systems and improving disaster risk management strategies.

Natural disturbances may cause communication failure .Maintaining temporal continuity and implementing quality control is crucial for predictive models. Scaling artificial intelligence and machine learning models for massive geo disasters scenario presents another challenge. Adaptive Algorithms are needed to balance the complexity and speed in hazard prediction. Real time monitoring requires the robust computational structures, combining edge and cloud computing. IoT systems necessitate swift communications among the connected devices, and edge computing aligns more closely with the demands of IoT systems.Massive amount of Data generated by IoT devices are usually stored in cloud which introduces latency that is not suitable for critical applications. This also increase the network traffic and congestion may also occur which directly impacts the prediction capacity. The transmission of sensitive data to the cloud raises data privacy and security concerns about the confidentiality and integrity of the information. Real time geo-hazard monitoring and prediction face significant big data challenges due to the sheer volume, speed and diversity of information generated by modern sensing technologies. Figure 1 represents the big data challenges in real-time data.

Figure 1. BigData challenges in real-time data

Continuous streams from satellites, seismic networks, GPS stations, weather sensors and IoT devices must be processed with minimal delay, these data sets are often massive, heterogeneous and difficult to integrate. Ensuring data quality is also another issue, the real world data frequently contains noise, gaps or inconsistencies caused by environmental conditions, wrong entries or sensor failures. Effective prediction also requires scalable computational systems capable of handling large scale analytics and machine learning models in real time which can strain available processing and storage resources. Together these challenges make real time geo-hazard monitoring a complex task requiring robust, efficient and resilient Big Data solutions (He et al., 2017). The subsequent sections of this chapter explore the various challenges in handing the bigdata in geohazard monitoring techniques.

LITERATURE SURVEY

JeyaSutha et al. (2026) studied the importance of conducting analysis of data in real-time in the context of disaster management. As per their study, the data that is collected using satellites, Internet-of-Things, and social media is utilized by the authorities to respond to such disasters immediately. Data analytics in real time is crucial in terms of providing timely warnings and making decisions in emergencies. Some other problems that have been discussed in the paper include data credibility, privacy concerns, and integration of data.

For the topic of disaster management, the article by MA Ben Rhaiem et al. considered the use of Big Spatio-Temporal Data & VGI. From the analysis, the results revealed that geospatial data comprising of satellite and aerial images, IoT, and VGI can be used to create an effective strategy for disaster management. Particularly, MA Ben Rhaiem et al. emphasized that VGI enabled the collection of information relating to the disaster almost instantly. Moreover, there were numerous other significant areas, such as the prediction, risk assessment, and emergency planning.

Another study that focused on natural disaster prevention and prediction is "Big Data & AI for Improving Natural Disaster Prediction and Prevention Systems" by Qin, F. et al. Herein, the key features of Big Data & AI are described and include the integration of multiple datasets, such as satellite and sensor imagery as well as disaster history information. In this regard, it was found that machine learning and deep learning significantly enhanced the precision of predictions and cut down on the time taken to conduct them.

In their study, Chamola et al. (2020) highlighted the application of machine learning approaches in disaster management, emphasizing the role of IoT sensor devices, satellites, and mobile phone systems in data acquisition. It is mentioned that the use of machine learning approaches will allow analyzing the datasets and predicting disasters to intervene in time. Moreover, the scholars pointed out the need to incorporate data collected from different sources to improve monitoring and decision-making procedures. This study confirms the effectiveness of the data-driven approach in disaster preparedness and mitigation strategies.

Ma & Mei (2021) reviewed the application of deep learning in the analysis of large datasets collected via remote sensing technologies to determine the presence of geological hazards, such as landslides. The authors focused on the use of deep learning approaches in the analysis of datasets acquired by satellite, drones, and land-based systems. The results confirm the possibility of employing the deep learning approach in data analysis.

In a systematic review on applications of machine learning and deep learning in disaster management, Linardos, V. et al. (2022) explored various techniques used in hazard prediction, monitoring, warnings, and damage assessment. In particular, the authors analyzed scholarly literature from 2017 onwards to find that AI-based models have been extensively applied for solving problems in disaster risk management. As a result of their analysis, they observed that machine learning models are powerful tools to examine large volumes of disaster-related data and assist with making decisions.

Similarly, in their research, Tang, Y. et al. (2023) suggested a new technique that uses big data and explains artificial intelligence in order to study the dynamics of flood formation in a basin environment. Their research is based on the use of rainfall and hydrological data for analysis aimed at understanding the mechanisms of flood development and developing effective prediction models. The main emphasis of the paper is on the ability of big data analysis to detect complex interactions in environmental systems.

As seen from the discussed scientific literature, nowadays, big data and artificial intelligence technologies receive more attention as means for enhancing geo-hazard monitoring and prediction mechanisms. Earlier works prove that the use of machine learning, deep learning, remote sensing technologies, and IoT sensors can facilitate the processing of large amounts of environmental data. Such measures may help determine patterns concerning natural disasters such as floods, earthquakes, and landslides, thus providing an opportunity for developing a reliable early warning system. Multisource information proves to be crucial when monitoring changes in the environment and predicting any hazards. Nevertheless, the authors emphasize that there is still room for improvement since various challenges arise while conducting relevant analysis, namely issues related to data quality, limited amount of labeled data, computational demands, and integration of various sources. In general, literature shows that a combination of big data with AI may lead to the development of efficient methods for disaster prediction and risk management.

MULTI-SOURCE DATA ACQUISITION CHALLENGES IN GEO-HAZARD MONITORING

The geographical data collected originate from multiple sources, various types, different quantities, multiple dimensions, and multiple subjects. Each collection of data may be sampled differently (as to what time or frequency) and at different levels (resolution). As data is collected in real-time, it is typical that there will be some degree of data loss or inaccuracy due to uncertainty associated with such a method of collection. The large number of monitoring instruments being used throughout various locations on the planet means that there is an unparalleled demand placed on managed data for both storage and maintenance. To accommodate the data collected with these devices all store that data in some form, typically a database that can accommodate multiple disparate sources of data (e.g., Access, Oracle, MySQL). Sufficient storage capacity supports retrieval of data efficiently and optimally; therefore, solutions are available that support optimization of access to data and heterogeneous data integration.The techniques by which the geophysical environment is monitored (geophysical monitoring) have multiple examples based on their ability to collect the required information and to utilize it in an appropriate manner. They all require various forms of technology for creating their geographic databases. To create those databases, various technologies are used, including but not limited to:

1. GPS (Global Positioning System)
2. Infrared Sensors
3. Global Doppler Radar (GDR)
4. Clouds and mobiles
5. IoT (the Internet of Things)

These systems allow real-time monitoring of geohazard data through the integration of various technologies. However, as with many new technologies, they present challenges in their ability to integrate heterogeneously collected data into a usable format and to extract meaningful information from that unusable data.

The semantic details of the stored data must be integrated to ensure interoperability. Ontologically interconnecting concepts and identifying the interrelationships among the data are essential for efficient data retrieval. GeoSciML is a well-known tool used to construct transmission and exchange models that enhance the interoperable capacity of geo hazard systems. Geohazard systems are divided into top level, domain and application level ontologies for semantic interpretation (Liang et al., 2024).

DATA FUSION METHODS FOR MULTIMODAL DATA IN GEOHAZARD PREDICTION

Data sparsely scatted across diversified datasets require a spatial connection through machine learning models for multimodal data fusion. Algorithms such as neural networks, support vector machines and KNN are gridded with file based visual models. A data fusion approach for Geohazard prediction uses a digital model to integrate data within a data analytics framework (Liu et al., 2009). Information from multiple sensors is collected and provides improved accuracy and inference compared to single sensor source (Li, 2015). Multi fusion sensors for multimodal data are vital in geohazard monitoring on the following criteria:

- Extended Spatial data-Sensors are distributed on large scale to collect the realtime signals for Geohazard monitoring
- Extended temporal data-Continuous observation of realtime geographical data for Geohazard prediction.
- Increase reliability - Several sensors observing same environment increase measurement accuracy
- Reducing ambiguity-merged sensory data ensures consistent detection sequences and reduce ambiguity.

Geographic data were collected using unmanned aerial vehicle (UAVs), unmanned surface vehicle (USVs), and light detection and ranging (LiDAR) systems. An attention-aware multimodal multiscale(AMMNet) cross-fusion geomorphology recognition network was adopted, incorporating an attention mechanism-based multimodal fusion module (AMFM) for geographic data analysis (Ding et al., 2025). The AMMNet model was used to detect landform related disasters by employing multilayer feature layer fusion techniques. Overall, the model produced promising results, demonstrating high accuracy in the detection of geomorphological features.

Data Analytics Using Machine Learning Models

Real time prediction requires advanced computational power and analytical models to process data at high speed and extract meaningful patterns before hazards escalate. Machine learning models handle the large volumes of data and perform preprocessing, model training and assessment (Divya et al., 2018). The growing adoption of machine learning and deep learning techniques depends on large datasets for training and validation. Scalable cloud or edge computing technologies are providing organizations with ways to manage large volumes of data while reducing latency through processing data as close to its origin as possible (Venkatesh et al., 2019). Automated workflows, standardized data formats, and interoperable platforms enable multisource data to have a higher degree of consistence and a higher quality than single source datasets.

High-performance computing (HPC) is a necessary platform for optimizing machine learning models and real-time analytics applications in streaming environments. A major benefit of enhancing sensor networks through adding redundancy, adaptive sampling and other designs, is to address issues of discovery of data gaps and improving resilience to failures. Maintaining system uptime through provision of redundant communications infrastructure and provision of fail-safe data transfer protocols is vital, especially in regards to establishing remote communications or providing services in areas prone to natural disasters. Another critical concern is to develop a method for protecting sensitive or user-generated geographic information through implementation of strong cyber security measures and privacy-preserving mechanisms. Through this combination of technological, organizational and policy based solutions real time hazard monitoring systems can become more efficient accurate and dependable. The need for Big Data arises from the demand for faster more precise and more comprehensive geo-hazard monitoring capabilities, which directly support early warning systems, emergency response planning and long term disaster risk reduction.

STORAGE AND SCALABILITY CHALLENGES IN BIG DATA

Conventional storage technologies are not sufficient in addressing the storage and retrieval of continuously increasing heterogeneous geospatial data. The storage medium for this kind of big data must be consistent and scalable to ensure efficient access. Additionally data storage systems need to be distributed to support fault tolerance. NoSql provides storage mechanism that support distributed transactions and horizontal scalability. High volume of data are modeled in terms of key-value, document and graph based structures. Big data storage demands for reliability, scalability, extensibility and simultaneous access for geospatial data (Siddiqa et al., 2017). Figure 2.depicts the various big data storage technologies, and the features of each are explained in detail below.

Google File System (GFS) - GFS is a distributed storage system that is designed by Google to store extremely massive units of data across thousands of machines. The primary goal is to provide high performance, scalability, reliability and fault tolerance while working on inexpensive hardware. Traditional file systems does not suitable for handling large data. GFS was created specifically to solve these type of storage problems in Google's data centers. GFS follows a master-slave architecture and consists of three main components: GFS Master, Chunk Servers and Clients. GFS master is responsible for maintaining metadata of files, tracing the location of data chunks, managing access permission, monitoring the health of chunk servers. The master does not store actual data. It only manages information about where the data is located. Chunk servers store the actual file data. Each file is divided into fixed-size blocks called chunks. Each chunk is replicated on multiple chunk servers for reliability. Clients interact with the master to locate the chunks and then communicate directly with chunk servers to read or write data. This separation improves performance and allows the system to scale efficiently.

Data Storage and Replication- Files are divided into large chunks. It reduces the amount of metadata and improves data transfer efficiently. Each chunk is stored on multiple servers. If one server fails data remains available from other replicas. This replication ensures high availability, data durability and fault tolerance.

Figure 2. BigData Storage Technologies

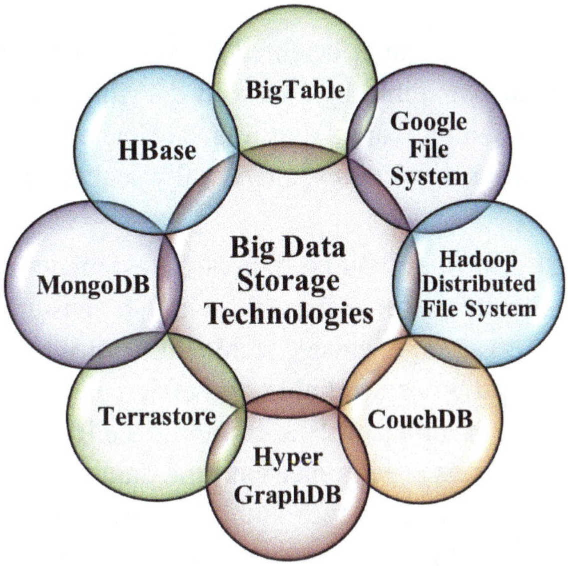

Hadoop Distributed File System-HDFS is a storage system used to manage large data sets. It also follows master slave architecture and it has three main components such as NameNode, DataNodes and Client. Files are divide into large fixed size blocks. These blocks are distributed across multiple data nodes in the cluster. HDFS is optimized for high data transfer rates. It ensures data integrity using checksums. In modern processing system it is a core technology.

BigTable- It is a robust and scalable data storage system. It was designed by Google to manage massive volumes of structured data. This system is designed to tolerate hardware failures, network issues and node crashes without interrupting service. The fault tolerant design makes BigTable suitable for mission critical applications such as web indexing, financial analytics and large scale scientific research.

HBase-HBase is designed for accessing individual records. When data size grows continuously Hbase adopts it and automatically spreads data across these machines and ensuring no single computer becomes overloaded. HBase provides a dependable and scalable storage solution for big data applications by combining Hadoop storage capabilities with fast and flexible data access.

MongoDB-It is a document oriented NoSQL database. It uses document based structure inspired by JSON. It distributes data across many machines using a technique called sharding. It offers powerful and indexing and query capabilities. It provides horizontally scalable data storage with fault tolerance.

Terrastore- It is a open source database designed for high scalable data. It supports cluster based storage with high consistency. By combining document based storage, cluster architecture, strong consistency and high scalability it provides a reliable and efficient platform for storing and managing large volumes of data. It provides a RESTful API for data access. The applications are interact with the database using GET, PUT and DELETE methods. Terrastore automatically replicates data across multiple nodes. If any one of the srever crashes another server containing the replica and continuous handling request without data loss.

HyperGraphDB- HyperGraphDB allows a relationship to connect many objects at the same time and making it suitable for complex knowledge representation. This structure is very useful in semantic technologies and artificial intelligence. In this, the relationships are more important than simple values. HyperGraphDB used in building knowledge bases, reasoning systems and expert systems. Its design improves performance for tasks that involve pattern recognition and inference.

CouchDB-CouchDB is a distributed open source system mainly for modern web applications. It stores data as flexible documents in JSON format. It allows developers to work with information without fixed table structures. CouchDB also includes automatic conflict detection and resolution and it also includes data integrity in distributed environments and it is mainly used for building robust and data driven web systems.

MapReduce (MR) big data framework processes distributed database as a cluster of nodes. It analyzes the processing workflow in two steps: map and reduce. The master node divides the data into smaller data chunks during the mapping process, which are then assigned as worker nodes. Each worker node processes one or more chunks during the map phase, generating {key, value} pairs. In reduce stage, immediate {key, value} a pairs are reduced to produce the final output for the given input problem (Pokorný, 2017). Managing massive Hadoop data storage is an additional complex problem in terms of integration, deployment and operation. The Apache Spark API provides a platform for applications centered on Resilient Distributed Datasets (RDDs) which enable fault tolerant data processing. Data representation of datasets is heterogeneous in terms of structure, semantics and accessibility. Data comes in structured and unstructured format at a growing phase. An optimized way of representation is crucial in geohazard monitoring and prediction (Padgavankar & Gupta, 2014).

COMPUTATIONAL CHALLENGES IN PROCESSING MASSIVE GEO-SPATIAL DATASETS

The following Figure 3 depicts the different aspects of computational challenges in massive geo-spatial dataset processing.

Figure 3. Challenges in processing Massive Geo-Spatial Datasets

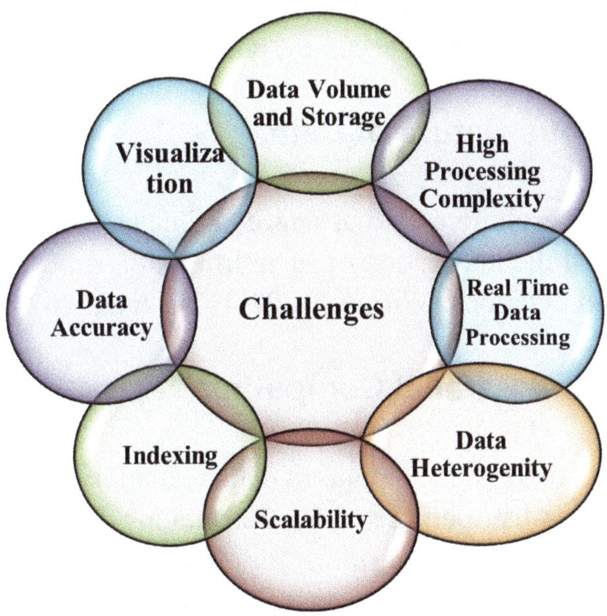

Data Volume and Storage Management

Geo-Spatial systems generates massive volume of data from satellites, sensors, GPS devices and drones (Zou et al., 2024). Storing this information requires highly scalable architectures and efficient data compression methods. Traditional storage systems often struggle to handle the size and growth rate of such datasets (Koldasbayeva et al., 2024).

High Complexity of Processing

The Geo-Spatial data has complexities involved in its handling including overlay operations, joins and distances calculation. Handling such processes in large volumes of data needs much computational power for efficiency (Li et al., 2024; He & Jiang, 2023).

Real-Time Processing of Data

The real-time analysis of data is needed in applications such as disaster management and navigation systems which handle continuous data streams at high speed while retaining accuracy, posing computational challenges.

Heterogeneous Nature of Data

The source, resolution, format and coordinates of Geo-Spatial data vary greatly and the integration of such different forms of data is costly in terms of computations (Wu et al., 2024; Zou et al., 2024).

Scalability and Parallel Computing

In the case of increasing amounts of data, scalability becomes a critical factor and involves distributing computations among several processors and computers. The design of algorithms for efficient division of workloads into parts of geo-spatial computing tasks and reduction of communications becomes a critical problem (Xu et al., 2025).

Indexing and Query Optimization

For effective searching for data, it is necessary to develop appropriate indexing strategies. Spatial indexing and maintenance require certain resources such as memory and CPU time.

Data Accuracy and Error Detection

Geo-spatial data may include errors due to imprecisions of measurements. Dealing with such errors and eliminating them from databases poses an additional computational burden on computer systems.

Visualization and Interactive Visualization

For visual representation of geo-spatial data in large amounts, a large amount of calculations is required to ensure effective rendering of images. Visualization of maps becomes a computationally expensive procedure. The analysis and processing of massive amounts of geo-spatial data entail many computational problems that will continue to evolve. Solving these problems calls for the development of advanced techniques and technologies.

ACCURACY, RELIABILITY, AND NOISE HANDLING IN HAZARD PREDICTION MODELS

Accurate and reliable results are vital characteristics of any hazard prediction model since the wrong predictions can have a severe impact on society in the form of either false alarms or failure to warn. Data related to hazards, including seismological data, atmospheric measurements, and satellite imagery, tend to be subjected to noise, uncertainties, and extreme environmental conditions that complicate any predictive analysis process (Liu et al., 2021).

Addressing Errors in Seismic and Atmospheric Data

Both types of data, seismic and atmospheric, tend to include a number of errors stemming from the limitations of measurement technologies, their exposure to the environment, and possible loss of information during the transmission process. Seismic measurements can be disturbed by noises that stem from the activities of people or from other sources. Similarly, atmospheric measurements can be incomplete because of the unfavorable weather conditions affecting sensors. Various techniques of data preprocessing, such as signal filtering and normalization, are used to address this problem.

Noise Induced False in Remote Sensing ReadingsAlarms

Noise from cloud cover, atmospheric scattering, sensor artifacts, and terrain effects can significantly affect remote sensing data used in hazard prediction, such as satellite imagery and radar observations. False alarms may result from these noise sources, such as when clouds or shadows are mistakenly identified as landslide or floodwater areas. False positives can be decreased by using sophisticated denoising techniques, multi-temporal image analysis, and cross-validation with auxiliary data (such as meteorological or ground observations). The results of hazard detection are also more credible when contextual and spatial consistency checks are included (He et al., 2017).

Strength of Deep Learning Models Under Extreme Conditions

Although deep learning models have demonstrated excellent performance in hazard prediction, a major concern is still how resilient they are in extreme and uncommon circumstances. Mega-earthquakes, extreme cyclones, and compound disasters are examples of unprecedented events that models trained on historical or normal-condition data may not be able to generalize to. Strategies like data augmentation, adversarial training, transfer learning, and continuous learning using recently observed extreme events are all part of improving robustness. Furthermore, confidence estimates are provided by ensemble and uncertainty-aware deep learning models, allowing for more dependable decision-making in high-risk situations. In general, creating reliable hazard prediction systems that can facilitate prompt warnings and efficient disaster management requires increasing accuracy, reducing noise-induced errors, and guaranteeing robustness under harsh circumstances (Kukunuri & Natarajan, 2024).

PRIVACY, SECURITY, AND ETHICAL ISSUES IN REAL-TIME MONITORING

The use of real-time monitoring systems provides necessary tools for cities to prepare for potential hazards, develop smart cities, manage and deliver healthcare services, and for monitoring the environment. The large volume of information generated, collected, transmitted and utilized presents substantial issues with respect to the privacy, security and ethical implications of the data collected from the various systems. To promote equitable and trustworthy use of these systems adequate safeguards are needed to protect the rights of the consumers of this information. The ongoing optimization of monitoring systems will lead to greater privacy protections Many of the real-time monitoring systems have different types of sensing devices, satellite imagery and mobile device / IoT that will continue to collect and maintain continuous location data, track and monitor personal behaviour characteristics and collect environmental information. All of the continually collected data may contain sensitive and/or identifiable information (e.g., continuous tracking of an individual) that may raise issues regarding how the data is being tracked and/or otherwise used without permission. Individual and community privacy requires that sensitive or identifiable data collected through monitoring is anonymised, that access to the data is limited and that monitoring is done in compliance with data protection laws.

Cyber threats such as data breaches, spoofing, denial of service, and unauthorized access to sensor networks can impact monitoring systems. When a data stream is compromised, inaccurate hazard predictions can occur, along with delayed or false alarms that may endanger the public. As such, establishing secure communication protocols, encryption, authentication methods and redundant system architectures are vital for ensuring that any real-time data has integrity and is available for immediate use.

Ethical Issues in Automated Decision-Making

Numerous real-time monitoring systems now depend upon automated and/or AI-enhanced decision-making processes for the generation of alerts, predictive analysis, and resource distribution. The ethical issues surrounding these forms of automated and AI-based decisions stem from a lack of transparency/accountability in the decision-making process as well as fairness, especially with regards to situations that require high stakes such as evacuation from a disaster or implementing an emergency response. The effects of automated decisions can also disproportionately affect vulnerable groups due to bias present in the training data, the disproportionately low volume of monitoring system coverage for certain areas, and the inability to extract detailed, describe, and interpret the workings of the AI model. To mitigate these issues, Ethical AI practices must be adopted, including the creation of explainable models, establishing Human-In-The-Loop infrastructures, and implementing fairness-aware algorithms in order to produce socially acceptable results

Uncertainty Quantification and Risk Communication Challenges

The increasing use of advanced sensing technologies, satellite systems and data driven models has greatly improved the ability to serve and predict natural hazards such as earthquakes, floods, landslides and volcanic eruptions. These technologies produce huge amounts of data which require speedy processing for the purposes of making immediate decisions (Wang et al., 2015; Sagintayev et al., 2017). There are two key issues which determine the limits of their efficacy:

- Uncertainty Quantification
- Risk Communication

CHALLENGES OF UNCERTAINTY QUANTIFICATION

Uncertainty is inherent to any geo-hazard prediction problem. Sensors used for collecting data may give erroneous results either because of the physical limitations of the device itself or because of environmental conditions or missing data. Simultaneous presence of uncertainties at multiple levels of data makes the task very complicated especially if the amount of data is high and constantly changing. The application of traditional statistics in such scenarios becomes difficult to achieve.

High Dimensional Uncertainty: The introduction of big data makes the problem of uncertainty to arise in thousands of correlated features. Uncertainty quantification for such a case becomes difficult using classical statistics-based methods.

Real Time Constraints: It is essential for any good early warning system to have a fast response time. The application of Uncertainty Quantification methods such as MC Simulations, Bayesian Inference, etc., is computationally expensive.

Black Box in Machine Learning

The advanced predictive models are quite accurate but lack interpretability. They involve inherent uncertainties that are hard to measure and make one prone to over confidence about predictions.

Communication of Risk

The communication of risk is generally in terms of probabilities or confidence levels, which can be challenging for a layman to understand. There might be incorrect interpretation by the emergency manager, government, and members of the general public, thus making people react to risk by being either panicked or too complacent (Fu et al., 2025).

Communication of Probabilities: Probability is used mostly in predictions of geologic hazards. The decision maker and the general public tend to misinterpret these figures.

Decision-related Communication: Instead of providing probabilities, there is a need for incorporating uncertainty into decision-related information.

Interdisciplinary Collaboration: Solutions require collaboration among various disciplines such as earth science, data science, engineering, social science, and emergency management.

Big data technologies have enabled the real-time monitoring of geohazards; however, they raise major problems related to uncertainty quantification and risk communication.

Visualization and Real-Time Decision Support Limitations

The amount of information involved presents another significant problem for visualization. In real-time applications, there could be satellite imagery, sensor data, weather forecast, and feeds from social media. It could be difficult for users to process the huge quantity of data, which leads to problems identifying key signals. Consequently, such visual tools do not help in decision-making; instead, they make it more challenging for decision makers. Furthermore, uncertainty is an important problem that should be considered because visual tools often represent hazard prediction as a definite boundary or value, thus suggesting an illusion of certainty.

Limitations of Real-Time Decision Support Systems: There are several limitations related to the implementation of real-time decision support systems in emergencies. First of all, the use of decision support tools requires quick actions on the part of decision makers who do not have complete information or have to act according to changing information. Therefore, the output produced by the system may be unstable because the risk changes quite often, which makes it problematic for decision makers to take any actions. The lack of involvement of specialists responsible for taking decisions in the process of designing these systems is another issue that complicates the work.

Design vs. Need for Operation: Most of the decision support systems are developed based on engineering principles without adequate knowledge of the constraints that emergency managers operate within. Consequently, these systems can produce scientifically correct results that cannot be implemented effectively in practice or are unfeasible in the actual context of disasters.

Incompatibility and Coordination Challenges: There are various organizations that respond to disasters and use different software programs and formats of information, which hinders data exchange and makes coordinated decision-making less efficient. Decision support systems play a critical role in managing geo-hazards, but the limitations of these systems greatly impact emergency management efforts. Data overload, communication of uncertainty, human factors such as user friendliness and dependence on automation, and other challenges remain unresolved and hinder the efficiency of visualization and decision support tools (JeyaSutha et al., 2026).

Challenges of Big Data in Real-Time Geo-Hazard Monitoring and Prediction

Figure 4. Computational challenges in Real-Time Geo-Hazard Monitoring and Prediction

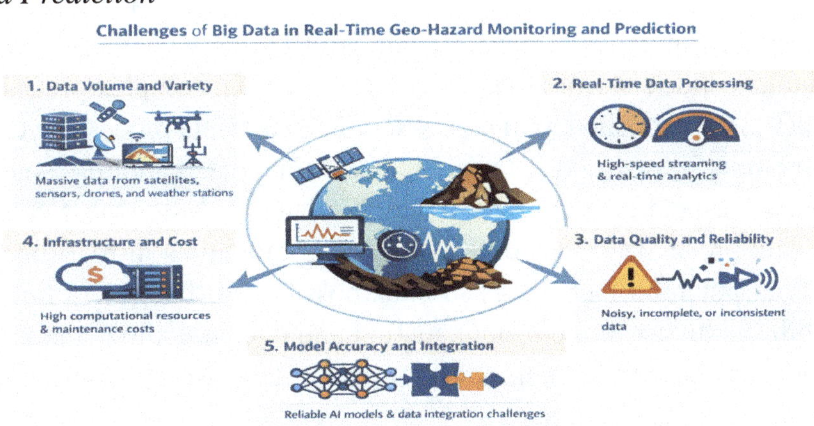

Data Volume and Variety: Geohazards monitoring systems have to handle huge amounts of data, which poses problems of data storage, integration, and processing. Such geohazards monitoring systems provide huge amounts of data because they employ numerous observation technologies capable of constantly monitoring the state of the environment. They utilize satellites, sensors, drones, and meteorological stations that constantly monitor changes in the environment, recording its various states. Thus, satellites enable high-quality image acquisition and remote sensing of the state of the atmosphere. In addition, ground-based sensors include seismographs, GPS receivers, soil moisture sensors, and others to register changes in seismicity, land motion, or soil humidity. Moreover, drones are used to obtain high-resolution images and video records of vulnerable areas such as mountainous and river terrains. Due to constant operation, all the mentioned technologies constantly provide huge amounts of heterogeneous data. The data differ not only in terms of volume but also in format, namely images, numerical values, signals, geographic data, and others. Handling this vast amount of information is problematic due to its necessity to collect, transfer, and store effectively. Big storage facilities and cloud computing are needed to sustain these massive datasets and keep them available for analysis. Another challenge associated with the use of geo-hazards prediction technology is related to data integration and processing. Because of their origin from various sources and formats, they require synchronization and unification before performing any analysis. In particular, it is necessary to correlate information about satellite images, precipitation level, and seismic activity in order to determine potential landslide risks or flooding conditions. Such complex processes can only be accomplished with highly sophisticated data processing tools and computing infrastructure capable of real-time data handling. Another important aspect concerning efficient big data analysis in this case is timely data processing. It is crucial to detect anomalies in real-time to warn about potential hazards as soon as possible. If the system fails to cope with the high volume of information and does not allow analyzing the data promptly, warning might be provided late, which would affect emergency response adversely.

Processing Data in Real Time: High-speed processing of data on the fly is challenging and demands advanced computing technology and algorithms. High-speed processing of data on the fly is a significant challenge in hazard detection because a disaster prediction system requires continuous streams of information that need to be processed instantly. Today's detection network captures information coming in from earthquake detectors, satellite imagery, GPS signals, rain meters, and remote sensing devices within seconds. The incoming flow of information leads to the formation of so-called data streams, which are characterized by the continuous arrival of data that should be processed instantly instead of being stored for analysis later. The first one is the need for a considerable amount of computation required to analyze streaming data. Standard data processing technologies are made for batch processing, which means that data is accumulated first and analyzed later. However, for disaster monitoring purposes, batch analysis takes too much time, which might be fatal in case of an emergency event like an earthquake, landslides, or flood (Ben Rhaiem et al., 2026). Therefore, special software, such as frameworks for real-time processing and distributed computing technologies, has been invented. Such systems break down large volumes of data into smaller chunks, which are then analyzed concurrently by several computers at once. Another problem includes the creation of efficient algorithms that would detect any abnormal patterns within real-time data streams. In disaster prediction purposes, machine learning and artificial intelligence algorithms have proven to be quite efficient for detecting patterns in sensor readings, environmental factors, and satellite images. The point is that the mentioned technologies can learn patterns based on previously received data and use this knowledge to analyze new data streams. However, despite their efficiency, it is still rather hard to design algorithms that will not only detect patterns but also do so fast enough. Data latency and communication delays also represent a challenge. The data generated by remotely monitored stations needs to be transferred through communication systems to central processing units for further analysis. Disruption within communication networks and inadequate bandwidth will cause slower data transfer speeds and consequently delayed results and warnings. Thus, a reliable communication system and effective means of data transfer are key parts of any geo-hazard monitoring system. The next critical challenge that needs to be considered is the scalability of the monitoring system. With an expansion of the network and installation of additional sensors, there will be an increase in streaming data. It is therefore necessary to have an IT infrastructure that will allow for efficient scaling and consistent performance (Qin et al., 2024; Chamola et al., 2020).

Data Quality and Accuracy: Unreliable, insufficient or noisy data collected by the sensors will lower the accuracy of the predictions made through the hazard prediction model. In the process of monitoring geo-hazards, the prediction models depend significantly on data that is captured from different sensors such as seismometers, rain gauges, GPS receivers and soil moisture sensors. Nevertheless, the data obtained through these sensors may not always be of a high quality. As a result, the data that is captured through these sensors may end up being unreliable and thus make it difficult to find patterns associated with hazards. Discrepancies in data arise when data collected from various sensors do not correlate or align with one another. This could be attributed to the differences in the environment where sensors are placed, calibration process, and the presence of localized disturbance factors. For instance, two sensors measuring rainfall amounts in similar settings will yield different results because of an anomaly in sensors or local environmental factors. The problem with data discrepancies confuses predictive models, resulting in an incorrect evaluation of risks. Incomplete data is yet another potential problem that can occur within monitoring systems. It is possible that sensors might temporarily cease data transmission due to energy shortages, faulty connections, or physical damages caused by extreme environmental factors. This causes valuable data to be lost during the analysis phase. Inaccuracies may arise in predictions based on incomplete data because there is insufficient information available for analysis of environmental conditions. A further issue is that of noisy data, meaning data containing noise, which could mean erroneous data, fluctuations in data, or data not related to the measurement being taken. The presence of noise in data may occur due to environmental factors such as high wind speed or changes in temperature and/or electromagnetic disturbances which affect the functioning of the sensors used. For example, heavy vibrations resulting from road and building construction may cause the sensors to detect seismic movements. Such noisy data could decrease the efficacy of hazard prediction algorithms and cause false predictions to be made. To overcome this challenge, data pre-processing methods are applied prior to analyzing the data. Data pre-processing includes cleaning the data set to eliminate errors and anomalies, as well as employing advanced techniques such as machine learning which can be taught to detect anomalies in sensor data.

Infrastructure and Cost: Infrastructure needed to establish the continuous monitoring system through the use of big data systems comes with cost implications. Continuous geo-hazard monitoring will involve heavy usage of technology and money because of the huge amount of data that needs to be monitored continuously and consistently. Monitoring networks produce massive amounts of environmental data through satellites, sensors, weather stations, remote sensing, among others. Managing such a large amount of data is very costly and requires the use of high-capacity computing facilities for handling the massive data storage, computation, and analysis. Regular computing facilities cannot support such processes and thus, need to be upgraded to the next level. The third requirement when using big data for monitoring hazards is cloud computing services. Cloud computing offers scalable services and helps the organization to monitor and process large datasets by providing access to such data in real-time. Cloud computing makes it easy to perform real-time computing and data storage and management. On the other hand, there are constant charges for renting storage space, computation capacity, data transfers, and system administration while adopting cloud-based platforms that could potentially result in increased costs over time.In addition to infrastructure costs, maintenance and technical administration of systems are also included in the cost of the project. Systems based on big data technologies need to be regularly updated and maintained to operate efficiently. Technical professionals are required to manage data pipelines, sensor networks, and analytical algorithms. Moreover, the availability of stable communication between sensors and data centers plays an important role in monitoring processes, resulting in increased maintenance needs and costs. As the number of monitoring systems increases and sensors become more sophisticated, computational requirements will continue to grow. Therefore, organizations will be required to continually invest in new hardware, increased storage capacities, and advanced computational resources.

Model Prediction Accuracy and Integration: It is challenging to combine big data analysis with the deployment of AI models in order to enhance accuracy in hazard prediction due to varying environmental variables as well as inadequate labeled data. The incorporation of big data analytics along with the application of AI algorithms for predicting geo-hazards is challenging due to the dynamics involved in the environment. Environmental systems are subject to changes due to the weather, geological processes, and anthropogenic activities. Changes in environmental conditions lead to unpredictable data patterns, rendering predictions by AI models trained on historical data difficult. One other important challenge is that the implementation of AI models in the prediction of geohazards using big data is the diversity in the environmental data. Data from the observation of geohazard risks, considered to be big data, can come from various sources like satellites, rainfall data, seismic waves, moisture data, and temperature. Another constraint is that there is a lack of labelled datasets used in training artificial intelligence algorithms. Machine learning involves using labelled data where different conditions associated with specific disasters, such as landslides, floods, and earthquakes, are identified (Ma & Mei, 2021). However, because natural disasters happen less often than normal environments do, there will not be sufficient data for creating effective models. The lack of sufficient training data makes it difficult for AI to recognize different patterns between environmental changes and disaster occurrence. Furthermore, the uncertainties that arise from measuring the environmental elements can also influence the effectiveness of the algorithm because sensor errors, absence of data, and different degrees of accuracy of the sensors can create inconsistency in the dataset. To improve such a challenge, new strategies have been developed, including data fusion, hybrid methods that integrate physical environmental model and AI model, and better learning algorithms, such as semi-supervised learning and transfer learning. These methods aim to improve prediction reliability even when environmental conditions vary and labelled training data is limited.

CONCLUSION

This chapter provides an overview of various geo hazards monitoring from big data. The dynamic nature of geo hazards requires fast data analysis from diversified sources, model clarity and robustness. It also emphasizes the critical role of Big Data in strengthening modern geo-hazard monitoring systems. Earthquakes, landslides, floods, and volcanic eruptions are examples of geo-hazards that occur rapidly. In order for timely data to be acquired and reliable analysis produced, there must be access to a variety of sources, including satellites, sensor networks, UAVs and social and/or environmental data streams. The high level of uncertainty associated with any type of geo-hazard model means that the results produced from these models must be both accurate and understandable if they are to be used by decision makers during an emergency. This chapter will provide a discussion of many of the advanced computational technologies available today, including cloud computing, edge computing, machine learning, and deep learning, and how they are being used to enhance the capability for geo-hazards detection and prediction. Distributed processing and the scalability of storage for large amounts of data can be done through cloud computing. This chapter also places importance on the need for developing transparent and reliable decision support models that assist decision-makers cope with rapidly changing risks. Thus, these topics must be addressed to enhance future monitoring systems. By addressing these limitations through technological innovation, standardized practices and enhanced analytical methods.

FUTURE DIRECTIONS

Future research in big data driven real time geo-hazard monitoring and prediction should focus on developing more integrated, intelligent and resilient systems capable of addressing the increasing complexity and scale of environmental risks. Among these, an important one is to ensure that there is an efficient integration of disparate data sources, such as satellite sensing data, ground-level sensor data, IoT, climate datasets, and even crowd sourcing, into platforms that are able to work on various data types and data refresh rates in real-time fashion. In light of the increase in volume of data sets, scalable storage systems and efficient computing systems must be created to sustain effectiveness and efficiency in their operations. Uncertainty analysis and risk communication must be improved to ensure that these predictions are easily interpretable for the purposes of decision-making.

REFERENCES

Ben Rhaiem, M. A., Selmi, M., Farah, I. R., & Bouzeghoub, A. (2026). Leveraging volunteered geographical information and spatiotemporal big data in disaster management: Opportunity and challenges. *International Journal of Data Science and Analytics*, *21*(1), 25. DOI: 10.1007/s41060-025-00896-8

Chamola, V., Hassija, V., Gupta, S., Goyal, A., Guizani, M., & Sikdar, B. (2020). Disaster and pandemic management using machine learning: A survey. *IEEE Internet of Things Journal*, *8*(21), 16047–16071. DOI: 10.1109/JIOT.2020.3044966 PMID: 35782181

Ding, W., Cheng, H., Wang, Z., Wu, J., Yang, Q., Zhao, X., Li, Z., Xu, Y., Dong, J., & Jin, Y. (2025). Multimodal sensor fusion and interpretable deep learning for shallow water hazardous geomorphology features recognition. *IEEE Sensors Journal*, *25*(7), 11545–11562. DOI: 10.1109/JSEN.2025.3540562

Divya, K. S., Bhargavi, P., & Jyothi, S. (2018). Machine learning algorithms in big data analytics. *International Journal on Computer Science and Engineering*, *6*(1), 63–70.

Fu, X., Wang, T., Pace, P., Aloi, G., & Fortino, G. (2025). Low-AoI data collection for UAV-assisted IoT with dynamic geohazard importance levels. *IEEE Internet of Things Journal*, *12*(11), 18279–18302. DOI: 10.1109/JIOT.2025.3540508

He, C., Ju, N., Xu, Q., & Huang, J. (2017). Automated data processing and integration of large multiple data sources in geohazards monitoring. *International Journal of Georesources and Environment*, *3*(1–2), 9–21. DOI: 10.15273/ijge.2017.01.003

He, C., Ju, N., Xu, Q., & Huang, J. (2017). Automated data processing and integration of large multiple data sources in geohazards monitoring. *International Journal of Georesources and Environment*, *3*(1–2), 9–21. DOI: 10.15273/ijge.2017.01.003

He, W., & Jiang, Z. (2023). Uncertainty quantification of deep learning for spatiotemporal data: Challenges and opportunities. *arXiv Preprint arXiv:2311.02485.*

JeyaSutha, M., Ramesh Dhanaseelan, F., & Jabanesha, S. (2026). Applications and challenges of real-time data analysis in the field of disaster prevention, reduction, and relief.

Koldasbayeva, D., Tregubova, P., Gasanov, M., Zaytsev, A., Petrovskaia, A., & Burnaev, E. (2024). Challenges in data-driven geospatial modeling for environmental research and practice. *Nature Communications*, *15*(1), 10700. DOI: 10.1038/s41467-024-55240-8 PMID: 39702456

Kukunuri, M. M. K., & Natarajan, V. (2024, January). Deep learning models for early warning of extreme geohazards. In. AIP Conference Proceedings: Vol. 2802. *No. 1* (p. 120020). AIP Publishing. DOI: 10.1063/5.0183134

Li, C. (2015). *Multi-sensor data fusion for geohazards early warning system–An adapted process model* (Doctoral dissertation, RWTH Aachen University).

Li, Z., Zhang, H., & Wu, K. (2024). Scalable analysis of urban scaling laws: Leveraging cloud computing to analyze 21,280 global cities. *arXiv Preprint arXiv:2412.02299.*

Liang, R., Zhang, C., Huang, C., Li, B., Saydam, S., Canbulat, I., & Munsamy, L. (2024). Multimodal data fusion for geo-hazard prediction in underground mining operation. *Computers & Industrial Engineering*, *193*, 110268. DOI: 10.1016/j.cie.2024.110268

Liu, D., He, L., Wu, Q., Gao, Y., Liu, B., Liu, S., & Luo, H. (2021). Construction and application of the 3D geo-hazard monitoring and early warning platform. *Open Geosciences*, *13*(1), 1040–1052. DOI: 10.1515/geo-2020-0293

Liu, G., Wu, C., Ma, X., Wang, Y., & Tian, F. (2009, August). Approach for interoperability of multi-source geological hazard data based on ontology and GeoSciML. In *Proceedings of the 17th International Conference on Geoinformatics* (pp. 1–5). IEEE.

Ma, Z., & Mei, G. (2021). Deep learning for geological hazards analysis: Data, models, applications, and opportunities. *Earth-Science Reviews*, *223*, 103858. DOI: 10.1016/j.earscirev.2021.103858

Padgavankar, M. H., & Gupta, S. R. (2014). Big data storage and challenges. *International Journal of Computer Science and Information Technologies*, *5*(2), 2218–2223.

Pokorný, J. (2017, May). Big data storage and management: Challenges and opportunities. In *International Symposium on Environmental Software Systems* (pp. 28–38). Springer. DOI: 10.1007/978-3-319-89935-0_3

Qin, F., Huang, C., & Lin, Z. (2024). Big data and artificial intelligence-driven natural disaster prediction and prevention: Technological advances and prospects. *Geographical Research Bulletin*, *3*, 381–398.

Sagintayev, Z., Atanov, S., & Gafurov, A. (2017). Overview of modelling techniques for geo-hazard risk assessment. *Central Asian Journal of Water Research*, *3*(1), 35–42.

Siddiqa, A., Karim, A., & Gani, A. (2017). Big data storage technologies: A survey. *Frontiers of Information Technology & Electronic Engineering*, *18*(8), 1040–1070. DOI: 10.1631/FITEE.1500441

Venkatesh, R., Balasubramanian, C., & Kaliappan, M. (2019). Development of big data predictive analytics model for disease prediction using machine learning technique. *Journal of Medical Systems*, *43*(8), 272. DOI: 10.1007/s10916-019-1398-y PMID: 31278468

Wang, W., Wu, J., Fang, L., Zeng, K., & Chang, X. (2015). Design and implementation of spatial database and geo-processing models for a road geo-hazard information management and risk assessment system. *Environmental Earth Sciences*, *73*(3), 1103–1117. DOI: 10.1007/s12665-014-3461-9

Wu, J., Gan, W., Chao, H. C., & Yu, P. S. (2024). Geospatial big data: Survey and challenges. *IEEE Journal of Selected Topics in Applied Earth Observations and Remote Sensing*, *17*, 17007–17020. DOI: 10.1109/JSTARS.2024.3438376

Xu, F., Zheng, M., Zheng, X., Liu, D., Wang, P., Ma, Y., & Zhang, X. (2025). Geospatial big data-driven fine-scale carbon emission modeling. *Remote Sensing (Basel)*, *17*(18), 3185. DOI: 10.3390/rs17183185

Zou, L., Song, Y., & Cervone, G. (2024). Geospatial big data: Theory, methods, and applications. *Annals of GIS*, *30*(4), 411–415. DOI: 10.1080/19475683.2024.2419749

Chapter 4
Comparative Analysis of Machine Learning and Time Series Models for Index Prediction:
A Case Study of IGI Airport, Delhi

Amir Ahmad Dar
http://orcid.org/0000-0002-0379-2272
Lovely Professional University, India

ABSTRACT

Using Central Pollution Control Board historical daily AQI data (2018-2024), analysis included data preprocessing, calculation of AQI, exploratory analysis, and comparative assessment using standard error measures. Based on the findings, LSTM performed better than all other models with the least Mean Absolute Error (MAE) of 18.41 and Root Mean Square Error (RMSE) of 24.23. ARIMA followed, with an MAE of 18.58 and RMSE of 29.11. With an MAE of 34.42 and RMSE of 50.08, SVR outperformed the other machine learning models and showed the best performance among machine learning techniques. The LSTM model was used in an attempt to predict for a 60-day time frame, predicting moderately stable AQI values (150-190) for the following days. The article emphasizes the disadvantages

DOI: 10.4018/979-8-3373-8042-1.ch004

of conventional forecasting procedures and highlights the significance of deep learning techniques on environmental monitoring systems. The findings are informative to public health authorities and environmental planners that face air pollution problems in cities.

1. INTRODUCTION

1.1 Background and the History of Monitoring Air Quality

With each breath we breathe, there is always this looming threat that permeates our bodies with each breath that we take, bringing into it an invisible tempest of harmful particles and molecules that do not only pose a threat to our lungs, but extend their impact on the general health in a far-reaching way. Air Pollution is one of the biggest environmental issues in the modern world and therefore, it is one of the most pressing issues which make environmentalism a crucial part of our daily life. The air pollution, especially in the cities, is one of the biggest threats to the sustainability of the planet in the future. It is an issue that is affecting countries of the world and India is not an exception since pollution levels in large metropolises frequently surpass the permissible levels, resulting in significant environmental harm and threats to health (Zhu et al., 2017; Rizwan et al., 2013). One can date air pollution to the Industrial Revolution that started in the mid 18 th century and was characterized by the high rate of industrialization, increased consumption of fossil fuels and unregulated emissions. These are some of the factors that contributed towards the present pollution disaster. Air pollution is presently among the most significant issues of the modern world because of the development of industry, the deforestation caused due to automobile emissions, and urbanization (Kumar et al., 2023; Sonu & Suyampulingam, 2021).

In the 2020 State of Global Air study, which compiles the majority of the latest scientific evidence on the presence of air and indoor air pollution in the air, the researchers discovered that 4.5 million deaths occurred because of exposure to air pollution and 2.2 million deaths were a result of indoor air pollution. The two countries that have the highest population in the world, China and India, continue to record the highest disease rates (Murray et al., 2020). The uncontrolled growth and large population densities in Delhi are now going out of hand- to the health crisis and economic cost of air pollution to the general population (Kumar et al., 2022). More effective means should be established to check the quality of air and forecast their future direction both in the perspective of health towards the society and as a means of informing policy intervention measures that could be taken at the behest.

AQI is a standardized measurement method that is extensively employed to measure and eloquently communicate the level of air pollution. Air quality analysis has been gaining increasingly more significance in the past few years. The air contains different concentrations of the pollutants which should be continuously observed. It also identifies the concentration of toxic substances and converts extensive information into a visual range to warn the population about the possible dangers to their health (Brook et al.,2018). Quality is an indicator of the purity of the air that is inhaled by human beings and other living beings. Pollutants can directly affect the built environment and human health and also the ecosystem, and they may be natural or man-made such as wildfires and automobile emissions.

Different pollutants are assembled into one index through the numbers, and then the categories of various pollutants are created by the air pollution Index or air quality index (AQI or API, respectively), to enhance the effectiveness of their application and distribution and also describe the overall quality of air in various areas (Tan et al., 2021). Some of the pollutants present in AQI are carbon monoxide (CO), sulfur dioxide (SO2), nitrogen dioxide (NO2), particulate matter (PM2.5 and PM10) and volatile organic compounds (VOCs). All of them may be included in a single number that will describe the overall quality of air (Sharma et al., 2024). Continued exposure to these contaminants may cause serious health problems.

1.2 Delhi's Air Pollution: A Major Issue

Delhi is the Indian capital and it has been ranked within the top number of highly polluted cities in the world. The air quality of Delhi is frequently deteriorated to intolerable levels, particularly during winter when the speed of wind and temperature inversion keep dangerous substances close to the ground (Agarwal et al., 2023). The list of the sources of pollution that the city has to contend with consists of vehicle emissions, industrial activities, building dust, biomass burning, and burning agricultural remnants in neighboring states only (CPCB, 2023). These aspects lead to severe pollution incidences that lead to significant health hazards, impair vision, and traffic congestion.

One of the primary contributors to Delhi's air pollution is vehicle emissions. Every day, millions of cars, trucks buses, and motorcyclists travel the city's roads, adding to the rapidly growing number of vehicles (Sinha, 2024). High levels of nitrogen dioxide (NOx) and small particle matter are produced by granular diesel vehicle emissions, which greatly increase air pollution. Unfortunately, the use of clean fuels and electric vehicles has not addressed Delhi's air quality management problems caused by vehicle emissions.

Industrial activity is one of the main causes of Delhi's ais pollution. The business and power plants in and around the city emit enormous amounts of pollutants into the atmosphere. The ecosystem and human health are severely harmed by the sulfur dioxide, carbon monoxide, and heavy metals released by air pollution (Kaur, R., & Pandey, P., 2021). A significant amount of dust is released into air by the building industry, getting worse Delhi's pollution problem.

Delhi's Indira Gandhi International (IGI) airport's air pollution is a serious issue for the community. The world-class IGI Airport has a high level of air pollution because of neighbouring Industrial operations, car traffic, and aircraft flight patterns (Kulkarni et al., 2019). For the protection of airport employees, travellers, and residents, the accurate evaluation of the air quality index and its forecasting are still crucial. Because of the current issues with air quality timing, a robust prediction model is required, necessitating reliable pollutant measurement data.

Delhi's air pollution is particularly severe, and hence it demands modern and data driven ways to predict air quality. Through extremely accurate online forecasting for AQI values, machine learning and deep learning may offer robust solutions. These models can help governments take immediate actions to reduce exposure to dangerous pollutants by examining pollution patterns using historical air quality data and weather-related variables.

Even outside the realm of scientific forecasting, accurate AQI prediction is exceptionally useful because it directly impacts policy decision-making process and protects public health. Based on this information, timely forecasts can aid Delhi in implementing targeted actions, thereby restricting traffic during extreme pollution events; issuing health advisories for sensitive groups; or even controlling industries and construction activities temporally. Forecasting also provides an evidence base for authorities to pre-emptively deal with seasonal pollution sources, such as stubble burning, in neighbouring states. By connecting atmospheric data and actionable solutions, predictive models provide citizens, environmental organizations, and legislators the power to act before communities feel the effects of emissions. This reduces risks of exposure and mitigates the socioeconomic impacts of poor air quality.

1.3 Classical Method for Forecasting Air Quality

Seasonal decomposition methods and statistical and time-series models like ARIMA have long been used in air quality forecasting (Gao et al., 2024). These models make the assumption that past trends and seasonal patterns can reliably predict future air quality levels. Although time-series approaches can capture cyclical variations in pollution levels, they often ignore intricate relationships between numerous environmental and socioeconomic factors (Ma et al., 2024). Machine learning has emerged as a promising option for air quality forecasting because it can handle non-linearity and interactions between several features without making rigid assumptions about data distributions (Wai et al., 2022).

1.4 Predicting Air Quality Using Machine Learning

Traditional approaches make it difficult to get new insights, but machine learning techniques can assist AQI prediction models make use of large datasets (Dhongade et al., 2024). Recently, a number of well-known machine learning methods, such as decision trees, random forests, gradient boosting, and neural networks, have been applied to air quality forecasting (Zhang et al., 2023). Many of the models claimed to employ a variety of meteorological and environmental parameters (such as temperature, humidity, wind speed, and pollutant concentration) to produce reliable forecasts (Wang et al., 2022).

In AQI forecasting, ensemble learning techniques—specifically, Gradient Boosting and XGBoost—have been demonstrated to outperform conventional time-series models (Nguyen et al., 2024). This is since combining several weak learners results in more precise predictions and iterative model improvement. Research on air pollution has made substantial use of deep learning models, such as LSTM networks, for time-series forecasting (Tang et al., 2021). When learning complex dependencies in time-series, such forecasting aspects of AQI with variable length, LSTM networks are well-suited. However, appropriate hyperparameter modifying and computational resources limit their effectiveness, making them impractical as a real-world substitute.

1.5 Comparative Research on Time-Series Models and Machine Learning

A number of studies have compared time-series and machine learning forecasting of AQI. ARIMA models were significantly worse than machine learning approaches, including Random Forest and Gradient Boosting in the short-term predictions of AQI (Gao et al., 2024). On one occasion in a study, LSTM networks were said to be more accurate than traditional time-series models, even though they need larger amounts of data to operate effectively. Nevertheless, the mentioned time-series model, Prophet, provided by Facebook has shown the potential but insufficient results to predict the AQI (Zheng et al., 2022). Although it is very good in terms of being able to simulate the seasonal and trend components, it is very poor when it comes to responding to change introduced by external forces such as industrial pollution and traffic jams.

Although there has been a great advancement in AQI forecasting, the current literature has a number of limitations. Most works are devoted to the city-level forecasts without consideration of the localized monitoring stations which characterize the key urban hotspots like the airports or high-traffic routes. Furthermore, there is a lack of comparative research on several machine learning algorithms over a comparable dataset. Also, there are a few studies that explore the predictive performance of machine learning models tailored to the IGI Airport area in Delhi, which shows a strong dependence on traffic emissions and meteorological variations on air pollution dynamics due to season. Consequently, the paper will attempt to conduct a comparative study of various forecasting models of AQI prediction in the IGI Airport monitoring station.

2. LITERATURE REVIEW ON FORECASTING THE AIR QUALITY INDEX (AQI)

2.1 Development of Air Quality Monitoring

The last several decades have witnessed tremendous progress in monitoring air quality, as manual forms of sampling have been replaced with modern automated forecasting systems based on artificial intelligence (AI) technologies. The early air pollution studies could not predict the future and they had to use ground stations in order to provide real-time observations (Chu et al., 2024). Real-time pollutant dispersion models, weather conditions, and satellite data enabled the development of predictive air quality models, which are now required as a result of the increase in trends of industrialization and urbanization (Sharma & Yadav, 2023). The information regarding forecasting healing air quality is updated through the use of combined statistical and machine learning modelling tools. Hybrid models are practical tools that can be applied to identify both the long-term pattern in the atmosphere pollution and the temporary pattern in the air pollution. Since deep learning models can control both the urban emission trends and the meteorological variations, deep learning models can be better predicted when the time-series forecasting techniques are integrated (Subramanam et al., 2022). This tendency is inspired by the growing popularity of interdisciplinary methods of studying the environment and using computational models.

2.2 Using AI and Deep Learning to Forecast Air Quality

The overall status of air quality forecasting has been altered due to artificial intelligence due to the ability of the system models to process high volumes of data through multiple sources. Models can be used to offer results with the help of Convolutional Neural networks (CNNs) and LSTM networks, which find both time-based and spatial patterns in the pollution data to provide accurate predictions of the AQI (Dey, S. 2024). AI models can be more effective than statistical forecasting systems in case they are trained on extensive datasets that also contain meteorological and continuous emissions data (Chen et al., 2023).

2.3 Predictive Modelling and the Health Effects of Poor Air Quality

Recent research indicates that it is important to predict the quality of air in order to minimize the health hazards of pollution. Predictive models allow the governments to make free of serious exposure incidents because of the ability to implement effective safety measures, including industrial emission control, and traffic control (Tang et al., 2023). Contemporary systems of public health response employ real-time AQI predictions to minimize cardiovascular and respiratory illness hospitalization.

The use of machine learning and deep learning models to forecast AQI is rapidly gaining popularity because the models can be used to identify complex nonlinear relationships in the environmental data (Dar & Shaik, 2025). Long Short-Term Memory (LSTM), Convolutional Neural Network-Long Short-Term Memory (CNN-LSTM), and ensemble learning models, including Extreme Gradient Boost (XGBoost) have demonstrated positive results in air quality index prediction. It has also been suggested that hybrid models that integrate statistical time-series methods with deep learning models will be useful to enhance the accuracy of the predictions by modeling both linear trends and nonlinear time dependence. Research has shown that model combination (e.g. ARIMA with deep neural networks), or model integration (e.g. LSTM with ensemble methods) can significantly enhance the forecasting accuracy in comparison to single models (Diaz et al., 2025). Most recent work has worked on combining deep learning models to forecast AQI. As an example, Bidirectional LSTM (Bi-LSTM) and similar recurrent models have been shown to be able to capture the temporal characteristics of air quality time series data (Pande et al., 2024). Moreover, hybrid models like CNN-BiLSTM have been suggested to represent the spatial correlations between pollutants and the long-term time dynamics, and therefore, better forecasting performance as compared to the conventional machine learning models (Mohapatra et al., 2025). These advances emphasize the increasing role of machine learning-based time series solutions in a hybrid form in environmental prediction and air quality control in cities.

2.4 Satellite Data's Function in AQI Monitoring

Remote data gathering technology along with satellite remote sensing has immensely helped the air pollution monitoring systems. NASA satellites (MODIS) and Sentinel-5P satellites detect the concentration of NO2, SO2 and particulate matter with excellent spatial resolution through their special observation methods (Guevara et al., 2021). In locations where the monitoring networks are seldom available, studies have the potential to complement the AQI forecasts by using AI products as inputs through satellite-sensed information (Riess, 2024).

3. METHODOLOGY

In this study, a two-fold methodological framework is applied, i.e., classical time series analysis and modern machine learning techniques are combined to conduct an analysis and prediction of AQI values. The research systematically analyzes historical AQI data to establish the underlying patterns, measures of performance of the model, and come up with strong forecasts. The methodological architecture includes all-inclusive information gathering, preprocessing standards, stationarity analysis, model construction and parameterization, stringent evaluation standards, and generation of forecasts and enables a comprehensive investigation of the dynamics of atmospheric quality and its temporal changes.

3.1 Data Collection and Preparation

Data collection will help to collect data about certain aspects of the problem occurrence, with the emphasis being on the cognitive and behavioral variables that contribute to the appearance of the problem under discussion. The data of the past air quality was provided by the air quality monitoring system of Central Pollution Control Board (airquality.cpcb.gov.in), which contained the day-by-day data on the air quality in IGI Airport in Delhi in 2018 through 2024. The data contains important pollutants, which are utilized to calculate the AQI as the target variable, which includes $PM_{2.5}$, PM_{10}, NO_2, SO_2, CO, and O_3. The AQI is calculated using the standard approach of the Central Pollution Control Board and the overall AQI is calculated using the maximum sub-index of individual pollutants.

The fact that data preparation needs to be a initial stage in order to ensure that the data is of quality and to be analyzed appropriately. Exploratory data analysis (EDA) is an analysis technique that attempts to analyze the distributions of data, isolate trends, and unusual values. Imputation methods are used to fill in the missing values with an average of all the columns of pollutants so as to enhance consistency and continuity of the data temporarily.

Although this study primarily employs pollutant concentration data provided by CPCB for AQI computation, future forecasting frameworks could be significantly enhanced by including source-specific datasets. These include data on industrial stack emissions, traffic density and vehicle emission inventories, construction activity levels, and satellite-based detection of burning occurrences of agricultural residue throughout Punjab and Haryana. If such emission source data were incorporated into predictive models, they would be able to monitor pollution levels and identify underlying causes for changes in AQI. By providing policymakers with a more comprehensive tool for developing source-targeted actions, this integration may strengthen the link between forecasting results and realistic air quality control techniques.

3.2 Machine Learning Approach

Complex relationships between air quality measures are modeled by machine learning methods. Four algorithms are compared: XGBoost, Random Forest, Decision Trees, Linear Regression, and SVR.

3.2.1 Model Training and Testing

The best model for predicting AQI is determined by comparing the performance of all five models. Standard error metrics, such as MAE and RMSE, are used in evaluation and are expressed over the test dataset. The best machine learning model for prediction is the one that shows the lowest error measures in addition to the best agreement with the observed data.

3.3 Time Series Analysis

Time series analysis is employed to model the temporal evolution of AQI. Comparison is made for three models: ARIMA model, LSTM and Facebook Prophet.

3.3.1 Stationarity Test and Decomposition

In order to guarantee data stability, which is necessary for efficient time series modeling, stationarity is tested. The null hypothesis (H_0) of a unit root (non-stationarity) is used in the Augmented Dickey-Fuller (ADF) test. If the p-value is less than 0.05, stationarity is proven; if not, differencing is carried out until stability is attained, based on ADF results and visual examination of time series plots. Seasonal decomposition is carried out to identify trend, seasonal, and residual components to better understand underlying patterns that inform model development.

3.3.2 Best-Performing Time Series Model Selection

The performance of ARIMA model, LSTM and Facebook Prophet models is compared to identify the most appropriate time series method in predicting AQI. Evaluation uses standard measures of error, including MAE, and RMSE, all expressed over the test dataset. The model which exhibits the minimum error measures besides the best agreement with the observed data is designated as the best time series model for prediction and hence the most optimal balance of accuracy and discovery of temporal structures.

3.4 Model Comparison and Choice

The performance of the chosen time series model and the top-performing machine learning model is compared to select the final forecasting method. Comparison on error measures (MAE, RMSE). The model with the lowest error measures, maximum stability, and highest generalization ability is selected for prediction to make strong predictions particular to the air quality condition at IGI Airport.

3.5 Hyperparameter Optimization

In this research, machine learning models were tuned to guarantee maximum model performance. In the case of Support Vector Regression (SVR) model, grid search was used to optimize the parameter of the model (type of kernel, regularization parameter (C), and kernel coefficient (gamma)).

Likewise, the Random Forest parameters such as the number of trees, maximum tree depth as well as minimum samples per split were also optimized by systematic parameter search. In the context of deep learning models like Long Short-Term Memory (LSTM), there are various architectural designs that were studied including the number of layers in the model, the number of neurons to be used in each layer and the learning rate. The final model was chosen to be the one that gave the minimum prediction error to the validation data.

3.5.1 Model Validation

A k-fold cross-validation was used to test the strength and the power to extrapolate the forecasting models. The dataset was selected into k subsets and the models were trained using k-1 subsets and the other subset was used to validate the models. The same procedure was applied until all the subsets were employed once as the validation set. There was a measure of model stability and mitigation of the overfitting possibilities by using the average performance metrics in all folds.

3.6 Forecasting

The chosen model is used to predict AQI for next 60 days. Predictions are made with point values and uncertainty intervals from the predictive uncertainty of the model. Historical predictions are checked with observed values if existing, which keeps the forecasting process consistent.

3.7 Instruments and Software

Analysis is performed with the aid of Python and has libraries like pandas and numpy for preprocessing data, tensorflow for applying ARIMA model, LSTM, prophet for Facebook Prophet, and scikit-learn in order to utilize machine learning models. Visualization is done through matplotlib and seaborn to display trends, model fit, and forecasting results.

4. RESULTS AND ANALYSIS

The analysis of air quality data at IGI Airport, Delhi, followed a comprehensive workflow involving data preprocessing, AQI calculation, exploratory analysis, and predictive modeling using machine learning algorithms. The major steps and results are discussed below.

4.1 EDA and Handling Missing Values

To find patterns, missing values, and discrepancies across important air quality metrics, the dataset was first subjected to an EDA. A number of pollutant columns had missing values. The mean of each column was used to fill in the missing data. The AQI was computed using the national AQI standards based on pollutant concentrations after the missing data was handled, as indicated in Table 1. For later machine learning models, the AQI was the goal variable.

Table 1. Computed AQI and Associated Pollutant Levels at IGI Airport

DATE	PM2.5	PM10	NO	NO2	NOx	CO	OZONE	AQI
01-01-2018	271.83	388.23	20.23	25.46	21.23	1.26	40.59	322.13
02-01-2018	216.7	370.03	22.51	23.74	21.23	1.43	33.37	266.60
03-01-2018	171.37	268.47	23.37	23.16	21.23	1.49	31.18	221.68
04-01-2018	178.71	270.21	22.79	23.97	21.23	1.45	35.79	228.95
05-01-2018	183.92	283.7	22.36	23.85	21.23	1.42	33.81	234.11

4.2 Machine Learning Analysis

For the prediction of AQI, four supervised machine learning models were used: SVR, Linear Regression, Decision Tree, Random Forest, and XGBoost. The performance of the models was measured using conventional regression metrics, i.e., MAE, and RMSE.

Table 2. Performance Comparison of Machine Learning Models for AQI Prediction

MODEL	MAE	RMSE
SVR	34.42	50.08
Linear Regression	38.44	51.66
Random Forest	40.19	51.91
XGBoost	44.98	58.53
Decision Tree	53.99	80.12

As shown in Table 2, of all the models attempted, the best performance was that of the SVR model, which exhibited the lowest MAE (34.420739) and RMSE (50.082884) values. This suggests that the SVR model excels in capturing the underlying patterns in the data and delivering the most accurate predictions compared to the other models evaluated.

4.3 Visual Performance Analysis

For easier comparison of the machine learning model performance, we developed graphical models that present additional information about the model efficiency as shown in Figure 1.

Figure 1. Error Metrics and Radar Chart of Model Performance

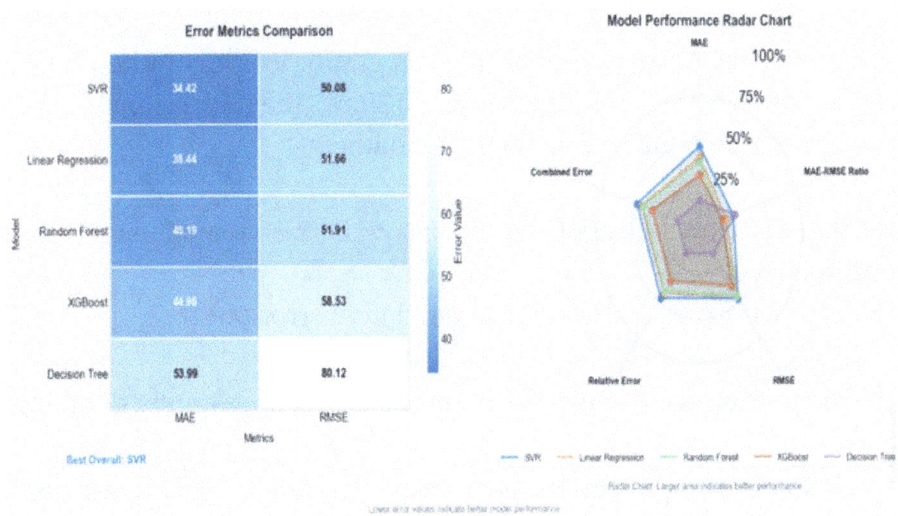

4.3.1 Heatmap Analysis

The heatmap visualization shows the unsmoothed error metrics, and the color intensities represent levels of performance where darker blues represent lower error values, reflecting better performance. This visualization is able to accentuate the gradient of performance among models and explain:

- SVR performs best with the lowest MAE (34.42) and RMSE (50.08) among all models, justifying it as the overall best performer.
- Linear Regression takes the second-best spot with MAE = 38.44 and RMSE = 51.66.

- Random Forest performs like Linear Regression with slightly increased MAE (40.19) but equivalent RMSE (51.91).
- XGBoost has a moderate performance of MAE 44.98 and RMSE 58.53. Decision Tree performs the worst with much larger error values (MAE: 53.99, RMSE: 80.12) and has a tremendous performance gap with the top-performing models.

4.3.2 Radar Chart Analysis

The radar chart analysis with the integration of three other derived metrics: 1. MAE-RMSE Ratio: The ratio shows the tradeoff between the influence of errors and the influence of outliers.

1. Relative Error: Gives a comparison between models which is normalized.
2. Combined Error: Refers to the cumulative error effect.

Such multi-dimensional description sheds light on a number of things;

- SVR keeps topping all measures establishing the biggest radar footprint, which indicates a consistently excellent performance concerning both normal and outliers.
- Random Forest and Linear Regression also exhibit similar overall performances profiles that vary in their strengths
- Random Forest has a slight advantage in terms of Combined Error and Relative Error.
- XGBoost provides a mixed performance with all metrics but has always lagged behind the three leading ones.
- Decision Tree has the least radar footprint, which validates its low results in all the assessment dimensions.

4.3.3 Implications for AQI Prediction

On the basis of the thorough visual inspection, it is possible to make some conclusions about the choice of a model to predict AQI:

- SVR would be the best option when the application emphasis is put on the accuracy of prediction since it is a minimum average prediction error (MAE) and is not strongly affected by outliers (its RMSE indicates this).
- In cases when computational efficiency is a factor, and a moderate level of accuracy is acceptable, Linear Regression is also an option, which has a good performance and requires less computational effort than SVR.
- Random Forest is a good balance option when model interpretability and non-linear relationships are needed: it tends to perform almost as well as Linear Regression but tends to capture more complicated patterns of data.
- The fact that Decision Tree has a large performance discrepancy with other models implies that more basic tree-based methods might not be used to solve this specific AQI prediction problem without ensemble or boosting methods.

4.4 Time Series Analysis

Time series forecasting was undertaken to model and predict the temporal dynamics of the AQI using two prominent approaches: LSTM and Facebook Prophet.

4.4.1 Stationarity and Seasonal Decomposition

In order to achieve stability and reliability of time series forecasting, it is necessary to check whether the dataset is stationary. To this effect, the ADF test was used on the AQI-time series data. This test got an ADF Statistic value of -4.0588 and p-value of 0.001133. The p-value is much below the standard level of 0.05, which means that we reject the null hypothesis of having a unit root. This means that the AQI series is not moving and therefore it does not need to differentiate the ARIMA model (i.e., d = 0). The data is appropriate as it stands to do time series modeling. Then, seasonal decomposition was performed to split the data on AQI into trend, seasonal and residuals as in Figure 2. The breakdown revealed clear periodic patterns and underlying trends which were useful as sources of information to build and improve the forecasting models.

Figure 2. Seasonal Decomposition of AQI Time Series

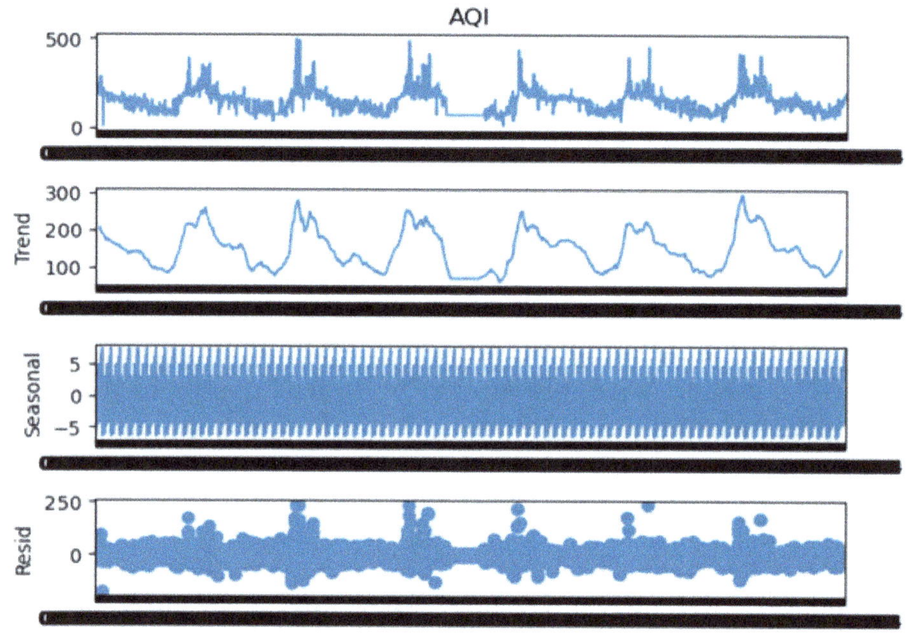

4.4.2 Model Performance and Comparison

ARIMA model, LSTM and Facebook Prophet model performance in prediction were evaluated using the standard measures to evaluate time series errors: MAE, and RMSE. The results of the two models on the test dataset are summarized in Table 3.

Table 3. Performance Comparison of Time Series Models for AQI Forecasting

MODEL	MAE	RMSE
Prophet	36.31	48.90
LSTM	18.41	24.23
ARIMA	18.58	29.11

In all of the three metrics, the LSTM model had lower error values, as compared to the Facebook Prophet model. In particular, the LSTM had lower MAE 18.41 and RMSE 24.23.

4.5 Visual Performance Analysis

In order to compare and rate the predictive ability of time series models on AQI prediction, we used visualization tools that present raw error indicators and aggregate performance indicators. The visualizations are also simple to understand and give a direct picture of the strengths and weaknesses of each model presented in Figure 3.

Figure 3. Error Metrics and Radar Chart of Time Series Model Performance

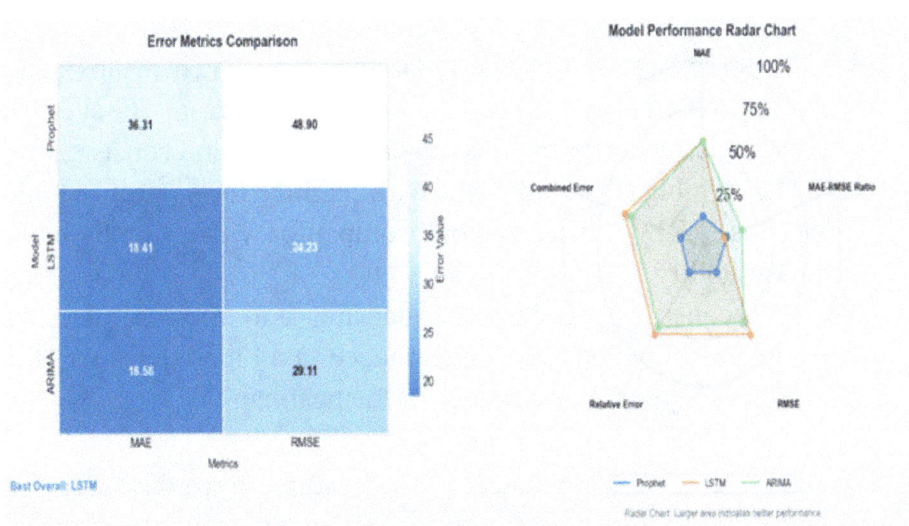

4.5.1 Heatmap Analysis

The heatmap of the Mean Absolute Error (MAE) and Root Mean Squared Error (RMSE) of all the models are presented in the left panel of Figure 4, with the color gradients depicting the amount of the error the darker the color, the lower the error value, and hence, the better the performance of the models.

Key Observations:

- The MAE and RMSE of LSTM are the lowest (18.41 and 24.23 respectively) when compared with the other two models which leads to the conclusion that LSTM is highly accurate and resistant to outliers.
- ARIMA is next in line with the MAE of 18.58 (a bit higher than LSTM) and a RMSE of 29.11, meaning that it is practically as precise as LSTM but more susceptible to outliers.
- Prophet exhibits the worst error values with MAE = 36.31 and RMSE = 48.90 and performs poorly and has less accurate predictions compared to LSTM and ARIMA. The improvement in the performance of LSTM is evident in this plot.

4.5.2 Radar Chart Analysis

- LSTM possesses the greatest radar footprint which means that it performs consistently well in all dimensions of errors. It not only is successful in raw error but also on error balance and consistency.
- ARIMA exhibits the same, but with slightly lower profile which agrees that ARIMA is also a good competitor with a slightly higher error variability.
- Pros and cons: Prophet, whose radar area is the lowest, also confirms its comparatively low performance in all the indicators of errors, which supports the findings of the heatmap.

The radar chart is a complement of the heatmap since the radar chart can visually summarize the strength of each model in terms of various metrics, where larger areas indicate better overall performance.

4.5.3 Implications for AQI Prediction

The synthesis of visual analysis is important information on model choice:

- The LSTM is the most suitable model to use in AQI prediction, it provides the lowest error and maximum consistency which means that it is applicable in areas that need high accuracy and stability.
- ARIMA can be a solid alternative when the classical statistical modeling is preferred, and with slightly worse performance, it can be interpreted and reliable.
- In this regard, prophet may not be the ideal tool to use in the forecast of AQI in this context given that it is relatively more prone to error compared to other tools of seasonality. In general, both visual tools highlight LSTM as the most effective in general, striking the right balance between reduction of raw error and high variability solidity- some of the most critical demands of air quality prediction tasks.

CPCB guidelines project the estimated values of AQI that range between 150 to 190 to be in the Unhealthy category. This is because the weak groups like children, the elderly and individuals with a history of respiratory or cardiovascular illness might be exposed to health risks due to prolonged exposure during such occurrences.

Long-term exterior contact, common traveler, ground crew, and airport employees are particularly vulnerable at the IGI Airport. Thus, when predictive data of such hazardous ranges are made in time, airport authorities and city management will be able to provide specific alerts when needed, adjust working schedules or employ countermeasures such as dust limitation, stricter traffic control, or provisional emission quotas. By so doing, not only is scientific knowledge enriched, but predictive modeling can be used also as an instrument of action to protect the health of people and better the environmental decision-making process. Figure 4 is current AQI of Delhi.

Figure 4. Delhi AQI

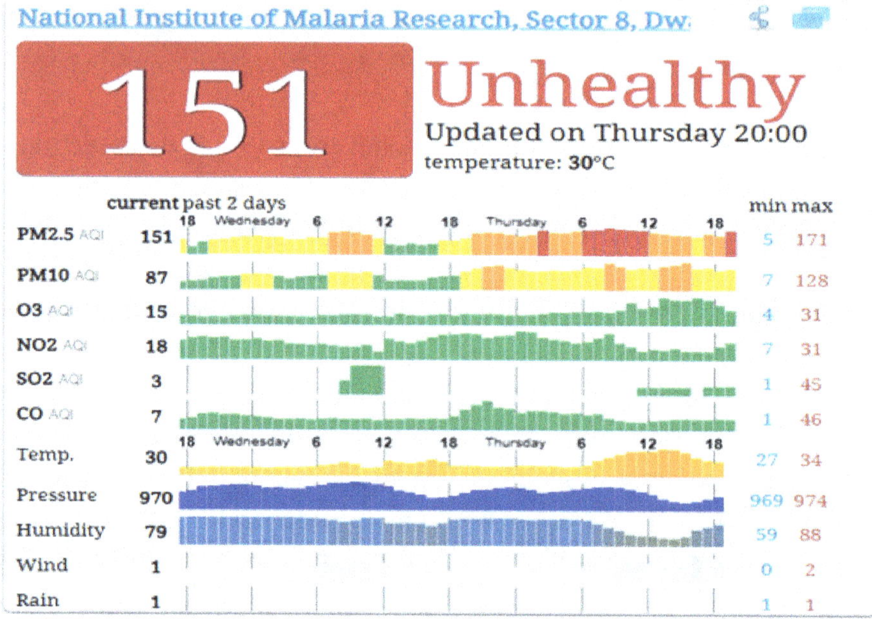

4.6 Model Comparison and Choice

According to the performance metrics given, the LSTM model is evidently better than the SVR model in the given task. The LSTM has a much greater predictive accuracy with an MAE of 18.41 and RMSE of 24.23 than SVR has an MAE of 34.42 and RMSE of 50.08.

The LSTM model would be the preferred model in the applications where high accuracy to prediction is needed with this dataset. ARIMA model also exhibits a high performance with the same MAE as LSTM, however, with a higher RMSE; hence, it can be viewed as an alternative to LSTM, should there be the need to adjust to the requirements of a particular use case and have the limitation of calculations.

Although LSTM model has shown relatively good predictive performance in this paper, traditional statistical models (ARIMA) as well as machine learning models (SVR) also have had competitive performance under some circumstances. Time-series models are especially effective at the description of linear temporal patterns, and it is possible that machine learning methods are more effective at the description of nonlinear relationships within the data. All the modeling methods hence possess strengths and weaknesses based on the nature of the data and the time frame of prediction.

5. LSTM MODEL FOR AQI FORECASTING

The forecasting of the AQI 60 days ahead has been done with the assistance of LSTM model, as it showed good results in our comparison analysis as shown in Figure 5.

Figure 5. AQI Forecast Using LSTM Model

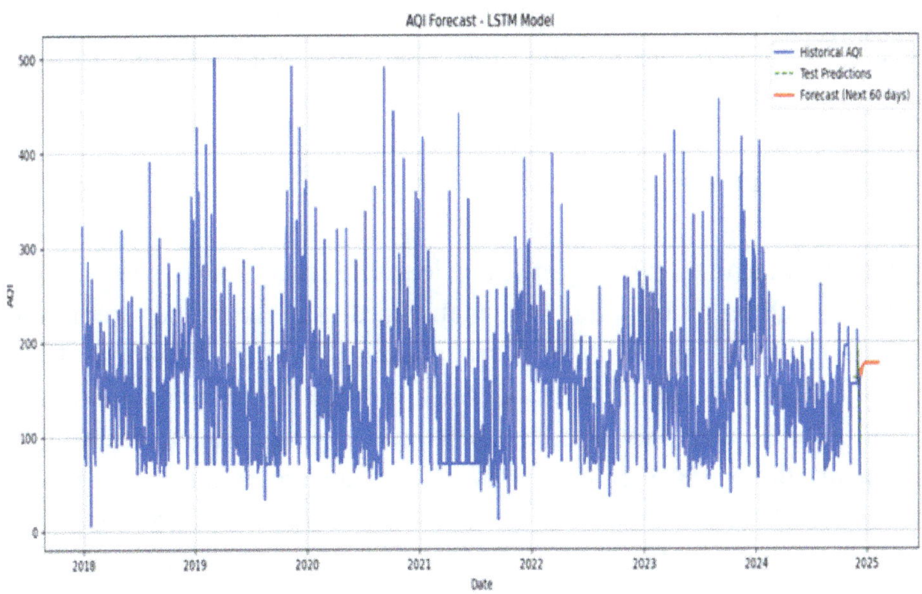

Figure 4 above demonstrates that the LSTM model produces a 60-day forecast (red line) which is consistent with the historical trends. It is forecasted that the AQI will be relatively stable (150-190) in the near future.

The predictions of test (green dashed line) prove that the model can follow the actual values in a close and the model is capable of forecasting.

The LSTM received a 60-day AQI prediction, and the initial values were as follows and presented in Table 4:

Table 4. Forecasted AQI Values

DATE	FORECASTED AQI
21-10-2024	188.131
22-10-2024	182.302
23-10-2024	181.196
24-10-2024	180.124
25-10-2024	179.088

The forecast maintains consistency with historical AQI trends, as visualized in the accompanying graph. The red line represents the 60-day forecast, while the green dashed line indicates test predictions, closely aligning with historical data (blue bars).

5.1 Key Challenges in AQI Forecasting

Though machine learning and deep learning models have shown good results in AQI prediction, there are many hurdles in the proper prediction of the amount of air pollution in urban areas. The high variation of the sources of pollution in the metropolitan areas like Delhi, where industrial pollution, vehicular pollution, and seasonal burning of agricultural vegetation are the primary causes of air quality change, is one of the major problems. It has been found that seasonal crop residue burning in adjacent states like Punjab and Haryana is a major contributor of winter pollution episodes in Delhi. Such incidents present the unexpected peaks of pollution rates, which complicates the short-term AQI forecast. The other issue is associated with the quality and availability of data.

There is frequently a gap in observations of environmental monitoring system because of sensor failures or maintenance, or the failure to transmit data. Such gaps may have a detrimental impact on the training of models and their ability to predict. Also, machine learning models are susceptible to the problem of overfitting, especially when they are trained on small datasets of a single monitoring station.

The overfitting can cause the model to perform well when used with the past data but when the environment changes, the model would perform poorly. In spite of the fact that more sophisticated machine learning models like LSTM were shown to be promising in making predictions in this study, there are a number of practical issues that have to be taken into account when implementing the models to work with the actual air quality monitoring systems. Among them is the risk of overfitting, especially where the models are being trained on fairly small datasets in one monitoring station. Although common data preprocessing methods like mean imputation are typically employed in the event of missing data, they can also cause bias or a decline in the variability of the dataset, which can affect the accuracy of prediction.

Omission of vital environmental factors is another problem. Temperature, humidity, speed of wind, and atmospheric pressure are among the meteorological factors that play a strong role in the dynamics of air pollution. Inclusion of such variables into predictive models can help enhance accuracy of the predictions and should be used in future studies. Besides these, seasonal farming practices like burning of crop residues in the neighboring states are often the cause of stiff rise in levels of particulate matter in the Delhi area. Such events of sudden pollution may bring sudden shifts in the trends of AQI that cannot be easily modeled by purely data-driven models without any other contextual information.

6. MANAGERIAL AND POLICY IMPLICATIONS OF AQI FORECASTING

Proper prediction of the Air Quality Index (AQI) is significant in aiding the management and policy-making concerning the environmental management in the severely polluted urban areas. Machine learning-based predictive models alongside time-series can help environmental agencies detect the trends in pollution and make early warnings about the severe cases of pollution. These predictive features find their application especially in a large transportation hub like the Indira Gandhi International Airport where a large amount of traffic and industrialization is the primary contributor to the air pollution locally. Policy wise, AQI prediction models can be deployed to control systems like the Graded Response Action Plan (GRAP) in place in Delhi.

Under this system, certain mitigation measures such as traffic restrictions, restriction of construction activities as well as industrial emission controls are activated when the levels of AQI exceed certain preset levels. Effective policymakers can predict these thresholds beforehand and preventive measures are taken with greater efficiency through the help of reliable forecasting models. Besides the policy uses, predictive AQI systems also affect urban planners, environmental monitoring agencies and the public health authorities significantly. As an illustration, AQI forecasts can be used by airport management authorities and municipal administrators to organize traffic control, direct constructions, and provide people with health warnings.

Strong meteorological factors that affect air pollution levels include temperature, humidity, wind speed, and atmospheric pressure. The current study primarily focuses on historical AQI values because the monitoring data is readily available and reliable, despite the fact that these variables have been heavily utilized in air quality forecasting models. In order to improve the model's accuracy and incorporate atmospheric dynamics that influence air pollution, it is anticipated that future research will integrate meteorological variables with satellite-monitored environmental cues. Future AQI prediction systems ought to take shifting environmental and policy conditions into account. The dynamics of pollution may be affected in the near future by a number of factors, including regional agricultural practices, climate variability, and changes in urban growth patterns.

Also, a regulatory intervention and environmental policies can change the pattern of emission, adding new uncertainty to the predictive models. The creation of adaptive forecasting models with the capability of accommodating such dynamic changes will thus continue to be a significant research issue. Proper forecasting models of AQI can assist the environmental managers and policymakers to make timely decisions so as to reduce the effects of air pollution.

Predictable systems can be used in the cities like Delhi to help the authorities trigger regulatory programs at schemes like the Graded Response Action Plan (GRAP) when the pollution rate is likely to increase. As an illustration, AQI forecasts could help airport authorities, urban planners, and monitoring environmental agencies to conduct traffic management, control construction works and issue health warnings to the people. Predictive models can enable the decision-makers to take preventive measures instead of reacting to the problem by issuing early warning signs of possible pollution spikes.

7. MANAGERIAL AND POLICY IMPLICATIONS OF AQI FORECASTING

Proper prediction of the Air Quality Index (AQI) is significant in aiding the management and policy-making concerning the environmental management in the severely polluted urban areas. Machine learning-based predictive models alongside time-series can help environmental agencies detect the trends in pollution and make early warnings about the severe cases of pollution. These predictive features find their application especially in a large transportation hub like the Indira Gandhi International Airport where a large amount of traffic and industrialization is the primary contributor to the air pollution locally.

Policy wise, AQI prediction models can be deployed to control systems like the Graded Response Action Plan (GRAP) in place in Delhi. Under this system, certain mitigation measures such as traffic restrictions, restriction of construction activities as well as industrial emission controls are activated when the levels of AQI exceed certain preset levels. Effective policymakers can predict these thresholds beforehand and preventive measures are taken with greater efficiency through the help of reliable forecasting models.

Besides the policy uses, predictive AQI systems also affect urban planners, environmental monitoring agencies and the public health authorities significantly. As an illustration, AQI forecasts can be used by airport management authorities and municipal administrators to organize traffic control, direct constructions, and provide people with health warnings.

8. LIMITATIONS AND FUTURE RESEARCH

Although the article offers valuable information about AQI prediction in the IGI Airport, one should take into consideration several limitations. In the first place, the analysis uses the data of the one monitoring station and these data might not be the most effective to represent the spatial changes of air pollution in the Delhi metropolitan area. Second, the existing modeling model is mainly based on AQI time-series data without considering meteorological factors and external environmental factors like crop residue burning events. Third, model interpretability methods like SHAP were not adopted in the current analysis though they are encouraging directions that can be undertaken further. Multi-station data, meteorological covariates, satellite observations, and other advanced explainable AI methods can be used in future research to create more holistic air quality prediction frameworks.

9. CONCLUSION

This research made an exhaustive review of the various forecasting methodologies regarding the forecasting of IGI Airport's AQI in Delhi. According to the given objectives, the research made a comparison between the performance of various machine learning models such as SVR, Linear Regression, Random Forest, XGBoost, and Decision Tree, and time series models such as ARIMA, LSTM, and Facebook Prophet. Out of the machine learning models being tested, the highest predictability was by SVR. Nonetheless, the LSTM model outperformed the other models with the lowest error statistics, supporting the technique's viability for AQI forecasting over a two-month period. The results reaffirm the shortcomings of traditional forecasting models and emphasize the importance of incorporating more sophisticated techniques, with an emphasis on using the LSTM to increase forecast accuracy. The results of this study offer practical suggestions for environmental planning and public health administration, and they have significant significance for the establishment of air quality monitoring systems.

The implications of the study immediately affect environmental planning and policy and go beyond methodological accuracy. Accurate AQI forecasts can serve as the foundation for early warning systems that alert the public and local authorities ahead of times of high pollution. Authorities in Delhi will be able to implement timely interventions, such as construction restrictions, traffic rationing, industrial activity constraints, and targeted advisories for vulnerable groups, by combining this predictive capability with the Graded Response Action Plan (GRAP). Airports and transportation hubs might benefit locally from these forecasts by disseminating operating guidelines and health warnings for employees and travelers. Crucially, the application of AI and machine learning forecasts should be viewed as an adjunct to traditional emission reduction methods rather than their replacement. In order to manage Delhi's high air pollution in a holistic manner, predictive modeling and source-control measures collaborate, ensuring that forecasting research significantly contributes to sustainable urban planning and public health protection.

REFERENCES

Agarwal, S., Praveen, G., Gautam, A. S., Gautam, S., Tiwari, R. N., Kumar, S., & Kumar, S. (2023). Unveiling the surge: Exploring elevated air pollution amidst the COVID-19 era (2019–2020) through spatial dynamics and temporal analysis in Delhi. *Water, Air, and Soil Pollution, 234*(12), 756. DOI: 10.1007/s11270-023-06766-y

Brook, R. D., Newby, D. E., & Rajagopalan, S. (2018). Air pollution and cardiometabolic disease: An update and call for clinical trials. *American Journal of Hypertension, 31*(1), 1–10. DOI: 10.1093/ajh/hpx109 PMID: 28655143

Chen, L., Han, B., Wang, X., Zhao, J., Yang, W., & Yang, Z. (2023). Machine Learning Methods in Climate Prediction. *Survey (London, England).*

Chu, M. Y., Brimblecombe, P., Wei, P., Liu, C. H., & Ning, Z. (2024). Temporal Evolution of Vehicle Exhaust Plumes in a Congested Street Canyon Environment. *Environments (Basel, Switzerland), 11*(3), 57. DOI: 10.3390/environments11030057

Dar, A. A., & Shaik, A. J. (2025). Spatiotemporal clustering and multivariate forecasting of air quality index across Indian cities using machine learning and deep learning models. *Franklin Open, 13*, 100435. DOI: 10.1016/j.fraope.2025.100435

Dey, S. (2024). Urban air quality index forecasting using multivariate convolutional neural network based customized stacked long short-term memory model. *Process Safety and Environmental Protection, 191*, 375–389. DOI: 10.1016/j.psep.2024.08.076

Dhongade, S., Tiwaskar, S., Koturwar, A., Motiramani, R., & Zarekar, D. (2024, February). Air Predictive Modeling for Air Quality: A Comparative Study of Machine Learning and Deep Learning Techniques. In *2024 IEEE International Students' Conference on Electrical, Electronics and Computer Science (SCEECS)* (pp. 1-7). IEEE. DOI: 10.1109/SCEECS61402.2024.10482082

Diaz, S., Camargo, M. F., Castiblanco, J. C., Sánchez, H. M., Duque, J. S., Escandón Dussan, E. C., Rojas-Moreno, O. F., & Baena, A. (2025). A hybrid LSTM-XGBoost model with residual correction for air quality prediction using SSA. *Air Quality, Atmosphere & Health*, *18*(12), 1–18. DOI: 10.1007/s11869-025-01867-5

Gao, W., Xiao, T., Zou, L., Li, H., & Gu, S. (2024). Analysis and Prediction of Atmospheric Environmental Quality Based on the Autoregressive Integrated Moving Average Model (ARIMA Model) in Hunan Province, China. *Sustainability (Basel)*, *16*(19), 8471. DOI: 10.3390/su16198471

Kaur, R., & Pandey, P. (2021). Air pollution, climate change, and human health in Indian cities: A brief review. *Frontiers in Sustainable Cities*, *3*, 705131. DOI: 10.3389/frsc.2021.705131

Kulkarni, R., Jenamani, R. K., Pithani, P., Konwar, M., Nigam, N., & Ghude, S. D. (2019). Loss to aviation economy due to winter fog in New Delhi during the winter of 2011–2016. *Atmosphere (Basel)*, *10*(4), 198. DOI: 10.3390/atmos10040198

Kumar, K., & Pande, B. P. (2023). Air pollution prediction with machine learning: A case study of Indian cities. *International Journal of Environmental Science and Technology*, *20*(5), 5333–5348. DOI: 10.1007/s13762-022-04241-5 PMID: 35603096

Ma, S., He, J., He, J., Feng, Q., & Bi, Y. (2024). Forecasting air quality index in yan'an using temporal encoded informer. *Expert Systems with Applications*, *255*, 124868. DOI: 10.1016/j.eswa.2024.124868

Mohapatra, E., Das, M., & Rath, S. (2025). Deep learning-based AQI forecasting: A CNN-LSTM model with visual insights from SHAP-LIME and PDP. *Discover Applied Sciences*, *7*(11), 1–31. DOI: 10.1007/s42452-025-07845-x

Murray, C. J., Aravkin, A. Y., Zheng, P., Abbafati, C., Abbas, K. M., Abbasi-Kangevari, M., & Borzouei, S. (2020). Global burden of 87 risk factors in 204 countries and territories, 1990–2019: A systematic analysis for the Global Burden of Disease Study 2019. *Lancet*, *396*(10258), 1223–1249.

Nguyen, A. T., Pham, D. H., Oo, B. L., Ahn, Y., & Lim, B. T. (2024). Predicting air quality index using attention hybrid deep learning and quantum-inspired particle swarm optimization. *Journal of Big Data, 11*(1), 71. DOI: 10.1186/s40537-024-00926-5

Pande, C. B., Kushwaha, N. L., Alawi, O. A., Sammen, S. S., Sidek, L. M., Yaseen, Z. M., Pal, S. C., & Katipoğlu, O. M. (2024). Daily scale air quality index forecasting using bidirectional recurrent neural networks: Case study of Delhi, India. *Environmental Pollution, 351*, 124040. DOI: 10.1016/j.envpol.2024.124040 PMID: 38685551

Riess, T. C. V. (2024). *Spaceborne monitoring of nitrogen oxides emissions from ships with TROPOMI* (Doctoral dissertation, Wageningen University and Research).

Rizwan, S. A., Nongkynrih, B., & Gupta, S. K. (2013). Air pollution in Delhi: Its magnitude and effects on health. *Indian Journal of Community Medicine : Official Publication of Indian Association of Preventive & Social Medicine, 38*(1), 4–8. DOI: 10.4103/0970-0218.106617 PMID: 23559696

Sharma, K., & Yadav, S. (2023). Air quality monitoring using geospatial technology and field sensors. *Geospatial Analytics for Environmental Pollution Modeling: Analysis, Control and Management*, 91-118.

Sharma, M., Singh, K., Gautam, A. S., & Gautam, S. (2024). Longitudinal study of air pollutants in Indian metropolises: Seasonal patterns and urban variability. *Aerosol Science and Engineering*, 1-16.

Sinha, B. R. K. (2024). Introduction: a broad perspective on the concepts of urban dynamics, environment, and health. In *Urban Dynamics, Environment and Health: An International Perspective* (pp. 3–79). Springer Nature Singapore.

Sonu, S. B., & Suyampulingam, A. (2021). "Linear regression-based air quality data analysis and prediction using python." *2021 IEEE Madras Section Conference (MASCON)*. IEEE. DOI: 10.1109/MASCON51689.2021.9563432

Tan, X., Han, L., Zhang, X., Zhou, W., Li, W., & Qian, Y. (2021). A review of current air quality indexes and improvements under the multi-contaminant air pollution exposure. *Journal of Environmental Management, 279*, 111681. DOI: 10.1016/j.jenvman.2020.111681 PMID: 33321353

Tang, H., Bhatti, U. A., Li, J., Marjan, S., Baryalai, M., Assam, M., Ghadi, Y. Y., & Mohamed, H. G. (2023). A New Hybrid Forecasting Model Based on Dual Series Decomposition with Long-Term Short-Term Memory. *International Journal of Intelligent Systems, 2023*(1), 9407104. DOI: 10.1155/2023/9407104

Wai, K. P., Chia, M. Y., Koo, C. H., Huang, Y. F., & Chong, W. C. (2022). Applications of deep learning in water quality management: A state-of-the-art review. *Journal of Hydrology (Amsterdam), 613*, 128332. DOI: 10.1016/j.jhydrol.2022.128332

Wang, C., Zheng, J., Du, J., Wang, G., Klemeš, J. J., Wang, B., Liao, Q., & Liang, Y. (2022). Weather condition-based hybrid models for multiple air pollutants forecasting and minimisation. *Journal of Cleaner Production, 352*, 131610. DOI: 10.1016/j.jclepro.2022.131610

Zhang, Y., Sun, Q., Liu, J., & Petrosian, O. (2023). Long-term forecasting of air pollution particulate matter (PM2. 5) and analysis of influencing factors. *Sustainability (Basel), 16*(1), 19. DOI: 10.3390/su16010019

Zhu, S., Lian, X., Liu, H., Hu, J., Wang, Y., & Che, J. (2017). Daily air quality index forecasting with hybrid models: A case in China. *Environmental Pollution, 231*, 1232–1244. DOI: 10.1016/j.envpol.2017.08.069 PMID: 28939124

Chapter 5
Deep Convolutional Neural Networks for Enhanced Earthquake Detection and Characterization:
A Focus on the Philippine West Valley Fault ("The Big One")

Froilan Delute Mobo
http://orcid.org/0000-0002-4531-8106
Philippine Merchant Marine Academy, Philippines

Magna Anissa A. Hayudini
http://orcid.org/0000-0002-2023-1434
Mindanao State University-Sulu, Philippines

Katarzyna Miłek
http://orcid.org/0000-0003-4603-4604
Akademia Nauk Stosowanych in Wrocław, Poland

DOI: 10.4018/979-8-3373-8042-1.ch005

ABSTRACT

The West Valley Fault (WVF) is a seismic hazard of the Greater Metro Manila Area. The need to have high-fidelity, real-time seismic monitoring is imminent with the suspected Big One—a 7.2-magnitude earthquake. Conventional techniques, like the Short-Term Average/Long-Term Average (STA/LTA) algorithm, tend to malfunction with urban anthropogenic noise and enormous streams of data. which adjusts to the specifics of the geology and noise of the WVF. These frameworks can be incorporated into the Philippine Institute of Volcanology and Seismology (PHIVOLCS) workflow to ensure that latency in Earthquake Early Warning Systems (EEWS) can be greatly minimized to enhance disaster preparedness in the highly urbanized seismic areas.

1. INTRODUCTION

1.1. The Global Challenge of Seismic Monitoring

Seismic monitoring has shifted from a high-level academic activity to become an important aspect of national security and urban resilience. Given the imposition of dense sensor systems such as simple MEMS (Micro-Electro-Mechanical Systems) and standard broadband seismometers, the rate at which seismic data are collected has been increasing exponentially around the world. Nevertheless, it is important to recognize that there is a paradox to this "data deluge: on the one hand, we now have more sensors than ever, and on the other, the capacity of human analysts to handle such streams in real time has hit the breaking point. Signal-to-Noise Ratio (SNR) is the major technical limitation of modern seismology. Under the condition of a clean laboratory setting, it is easy to detect an earthquake. Nevertheless, the most vulnerable people in the global population inhabit the noise-polluted environment. Cities consist of an unceasing seismic disturbance, so-called anthropogenic noise, due to the high transit, industrial machinery, and building vibration. Yang et al. (2021) observe that these signals frequently resemble the frequency properties of low-magnitude micro-earthquakes and therefore cause very high false-trigger rates in conventional automated systems. To work, the Earthquake Early Warning System (EEWS) should be able to work in the so-called blind zone, a small interval of time between the arrival of the Primary (P) wave and the disastrous Secondary (S) wave. Cutting down computation time within this window is the distinction between the automated valve in a gas pipeline, throwing the switch, or a fire that has broken out.

1.2. The West Valley Fault (WVF) and "The Big One"

The Philippines is in a dangerous position in the Pacific ring of fire, which is controlled by a complicated reverse of the Philippine Sea Plate and the Eurasian Plate. The West Valley Fault (WVF) is one of the many fault systems in the archipelago, but it is most dangerous because of its location, which is close to the political and economic nerve of the country. The WVF is a 100-kilometer strike-slip fault that is dextral. This is not a single line but a multi-faceted area of deformation which cuts across the highly populated cities of Metro Manila, Quezon City, Marikina, Pasig, Makati, Taguig, and Muntinlupa. Geologically, the fault has very high slip rates and is known to have had some major ruptures in the past. The Big One is a Magnitude 7.2 earthquake projected. According to the Metropolitan Manila Earthquake Impact Reduction Study (MMEIRS), which is updated by PHIVOLCS (2024), such an occurrence will be disastrous. The Marikina Valley geological structure, which is mainly of soft alluvial deposits, is a reflector of the seismic waves. This effect is called site amplification and is the fact that the moderate shaking on the source may lead to violent ground motion on the surface. Having more than 13 million residents in the direct way of the WVF, the wait-and-see strategy of seismic processing is not applicable anymore.

1.3. Rationale for Machine Learning in Urban Settings

The inability of traditional algorithms, such as the STA/LTA (Short-Term Average / Long-Term Average), to operate in Manila is because they use energy thresholds. STA/LTA generates an unacceptable amount of false positives in a city with access to more energy than is necessary, just by having a heavy truck pass or a construction pile-driver due to the fluidity of energy. On the other hand, when the threshold is too big to prevent such false alarms, the system will be blind to the first arrivals of the P-wave of a genuine earthquake. Convolutional neural networks (CNNs) present an alternative to threshold-based logic. Rather than seeking a mere rise in energy, a CNN gets to learn the "texture" and "morphology" of an earthquake. These models are trained on a library of millions of seismic traces to understand that an earthquake has a certain frequency-time development that is not essentially the same as it would be with a truck or a quarry blast. The strength of Deep Learning in seismology can be exercised via feature extraction, as Mousavi and Beroza (2022) point out. When a CNN is sensitized to the noise floor of Metro Manila as a part of the WVF, the noise floor can be sensitized. With the model fed thousands of hours of noise in the city (the humming of the city) that we filter out through the addition of synthetic seismic noise, we can generate a powerful detector, which at the same time does not pay attention to the backdrop of the urban noise but is hyper-vigilant to the particular signature of the movement of the West Valley Fault.

2. DEEP LEARNING APPLIED TO SEISMOLOGY: TECHNOLOGICAL EVOLUTION

Development of seismic monitoring has shifted the period of manual inspections of the analog seismograms to the era of high frequency digital data streams and automatic detection of an event (Mousavi and Beroza, 2022). In spite of these developments in the hardware of data acquisition, until recently, the processing algorithms were lagging in their capability to reliably read complex and noisy urban data. It has become especially apparent in megalopolises like Metro Manila, where the sheer amount and complexity of seismic signals require more advanced tools of analysis (Yang et al., 2021). The analysis of the transformative effect of deep learning presupposes a critical insight into the limitations of the old systems and the new opportunities of artificial intelligence. 2.1. Weaknesses of Traditional methods. During almost 50 years, the Short-Term Average/ Long-Term Average (STA/LTA) algorithm has been the main basis of automated earthquake detection (Zhu and Beroza, 2019). The algorithm is a calculation of the average absolute amplitude of the seismic signal in a short moving window over a longer background window. Once the ratio goes beyond a prescribed limit, a trigger is set off. Computational efficiency, however, STA/LTA is virtually a one-dimensional energy detector, demonstrating no contextual information operating in a complex urban environment. This drawback gives rise to some severe challenges on the situation in Metro Manila: Urban Noise Paradox: In the urban areas as in Manila, the background noise is significantly disturbed by anthropogenic sources such as heavy traffic on big roads to construction and industrial projects, which leads to very uneven noise levels (Yang et al., 2021; PHIVOLCS, 2024). The large STA/LTA thresholds required by analysts to prevent too many false positives also raise the likelihood of missing early, low amplitude P-wave arrivals which are necessary to activate the Earthquake Early Warning System (EEWS) in time. Aftershock Overlap: When a major seismic pivot, like the one that is expected to happen in the so-called Big One, takes place, the main shock is frequently followed by a series of other seismic events. Conventional algorithms can easily confuse similar events in time, and they can be combined in one trigger and blur the exact places and dates of the events (Santos and Dela Cruz, 2023). Phase Identification Deficiency Phase STA/LTA is able to detect that an event happened, but not distinguish the various seismic phases (p and s waves). Phase picking is normally performed with extra algorithms or by a human, and thus delays are unacceptable when a second counts (Zhu & Beroza, 2019; Mousavi et al., 2020). These drawbacks do not belong to the Philippines, but other urbanized and populated areas like Japan, Taiwan, and Mexico have also been mentioned to encounter difficulties with traditional algorithms in the context of the intricate noise settings (Yang et al., 2021).

2.1. The Rationale for Convolutional Neural Networks (CNNs)

Convolutional Neural Networks (CNNs) are an essential transformation of the threshold logic to the pattern-based recognition. Instead of merely identifying signal energy increases, CNNs are conditioned to identify high-level features that are complex and distinctively determine earthquake signals (Mousavi & Beroza, 2022). The strategy has the following benefits: Strong Pattern Recognition: CNNs are capable of differentiating between the morphologies of subtle seismic signals and background noise even in highly-noisy urban environments due to learning the features unique to earthquake waveforms, such as impulsive P-wave onsets, coda decay, and high-amplitude S-waves, on large datasets labeled with them (Mousavi et al., 2020; Zhu and Beroza, 2019).

Hierarchical Feature Extraction: similar to the computer vision models that are trained to recognize the faces by learning to detect the spatial associations between features, seismic CNNs are trained to recognize the earthquakes by learning to detect the temporal and spectral associations in the waveform data (Mousavi and Beroza, 2022). Operational Adaptability: State-of-the-art CNNs, including PhaseNet and EQTransformer have been reliable in urban, noisy environments around the globe and in specific countries, including Japan, Taiwan, or Mexico, have been adapted to perform well during earthquakes in dense environments (Yang et al., 2021; Mousavi et al., 2020; Zhu and Beroza, 2019). Through such strengths, deep learning models can break the limitations of traditional approaches and can be used to provide real-time and high-quality earthquake detection and phase picking, which is critical to the successful functionality of EEWS in Metro Manila and other cities worldwide.

2.1.1. From Waveforms to Feature Maps

Seismic data is interpreted in this model as a multi-channel time series. An ordinary seismic station makes three motion records in orthogonal directions:

1. Vertical (Z): Sensitivity to compressional P-wave is the greatest.
2. North-South (N): This is vital in the acquisition of horizontal shear (S-wave) motion.
3. East-West (E): This is equally important in the characterization of S-wave and surface waves. The model can be viewed as a synthetic analyst when these three channels are fed into a CNN at once to view the 3D particle motion of the Earth. The convolution kernels later in the network can be seen as adaptive bandpass filters that remove

low-frequency urban hum in the early layers of the network. The higher-level features that are extracted in the deeper layers include high-level features like the polarity and spectral content, which enable the network to distinguish between an event of local WVF tremor and a distant subduction zone event.

2.2. Seismic CNNs are Based on Mathematics

The mathematical basis of our scheme is the following: a continuous 3-channel input, $x in the form of R3T or R3T of time samples) is mapped to a probability distribution, y in [0, 1]3T. At a given millisecond, t, the model produces three values adding up to one, which are the probability of the signal being a P-wave, S-wave, or Noise.

2.2.1. The Convolution Operation

The basic elementary block is the 1D Convolution. Given an input seismic trace x and a trainable filter (kernel) k the feature map y is computed as: $$y[n] = (x * k)[n] = \sum_{m} x[m] k[n-m]$$ These filters (such as Butterworth or Chebychev filters) are human designed in traditional signal processing. These filters are learnt in our CNN. In the training stage, the model adapts the weights of the kernel k using backpropagation in order to reduce the error between its prediction and the actual labels as given by PHIVOLCS analysts.

2.2.2. Translation Invariance and Reliability

One of the strengths of the convolution operation is the invariance to translation. Since the identical filter, denoted as k, is moved over the whole length of the 30-second seismic window, the earthquake will still be detected without much difference whether it happens at the 1 st second or the 29 th second in the recording. This contributes to the extreme resilience of the system to the unpredictability of the time when the West Valley Fault will rupture.

2.3. The Hierarchical Feature Extraction

Each additional tens of convolutional layers are stacked (usually into a U-Net or Encoder-Decoder architecture) to provide the model a hierarchical knowledge of seismic physics:

Table 1.

Layer Depth	Feature Extraction Level	Seismological Equivalent
Early Layers	Local signal gradients, frequency spikes	Detection of "impulsive" onset
Middle Layers	Waveform envelopes, duration patterns	Distinguishing P-wave vs. S-wave arrival
Deep Layers	Global context, multi-channel correlation	Discriminating tectonic events from urban noise

3. METHODOLOGY: DEEP LEARNING–BASED EARTHQUAKE DETECTION ALONG THE WEST VALLEY FAULT

To create a Deep Learning (DL)-based earthquake detection and phase-picking system to operate on the West Valley Fault (WVF), high-performance computing methodologies along with geophysical domain knowledge should be combined. This part outlines the overall approach methodology, both localized data collection and preprocessing, and model optimization and implementation in a real-world setting, with constraints of the Earthquake Early Warning System (EEWS).

3.1 Data Acquisition and Pre Processing: Philippine Seismic Corpus Construction

The representativeness and locality of training data are the fundamental constraints to the performance of convolutional neural networks (CNNs) (Goodfellow et al., 2016). In the case of the WVF, global seismic data cannot be used sufficiently because of the distinct seismic velocity structures in the Philippine archipelago and the sustained anthropogenic noise in Metro Manila. A local seismic corpus was thus designed with the help of three stations which were chosen strategically: Tanay, Rizal, as a hard-rock basement location having little cultural noise; Antipolo City with average anthropogenic noise and multifaceted topographic impacts; A site with good site amplification and high cultural noise, Taguig City, is an urban area located on soft soils, within the metro Manila Marikina valley. The three-component waveform data (vertical, northsouth, eastwest) were broken up into fixed-length time windows and amplitude-normalized so as to support the large dynamic range of seismic signals. The multi-site design allows the model to acquire station-invariant features of the waveform, which enhances the robustness of the model to heterogeneous conditions in geology and noise (Zhu and Beroza, 2019).

3.2 Adoption of Label Uncertainty and Extreme Class Imbalance

3.2.1 Gaussian Uncertainty Soft Labeling

The traditional seismic phase picking provides a unique deterministic timestamp to arrivals of waves. Nevertheless, previous research has indicated that even the experience analysts differ quite often on when the weak phases occur, especially in P waves within noise (Diehl et al., 2009). In order to explicitly represent this epistemic uncertainty, binary labels were replaced by soft labeling. The labeling function L(t) of each phase deployment at time t that is manually identified is a Gaussian distribution: L(t)=exp?^2 +/(2s^2)) in which s is an inverse of the temporal tolerance around the pick. This expression supports the CNN to acquire a probabilistic arrival window as opposed to a point estimate, which is more effective in resisting impulsive anthropogenic noise that arises in dense urban settings (Ross et al., 2018; Zhu and Beroza, 2019). The presence of imbalanced classes can be reduced through focal loss, which indirectly modifies the center of attention (AMO) loss (Darknet, 2017). The continuous seismic monitor streams are dominated by background noise and there are only small portions of data that are made up of true seismic arrivals.

Non-anomaly cross-entropy loss functions are then biased towards the most frequent class of Noise, and are not sensitive to infrequent and still operationally important P-wave onsets. In order to eliminate this imbalance, Focal Loss was used (Lin et al., 2017): "FL"(pt)=-a(1-pt)^g log? In which ptis the forecasted likelihood of the actual class, gis the focusing parameter that concentrates on the samples that are difficult to classify, and ais a balancing coefficient of the classes. Such a loss force makes the network reserve learning capacity to weak seismic arrivals hidden in strong noise fields, which is similar to the real operational conditions of EEWS applications (Mousavi et al., 2020). 3.3 Model Architecture: Seismic Time Series Modified 1D U-Net. The essence of the suggested framework is the modified one-dimensional U-Net, scaled down of the framework used in biomedical image segmentation (Rotteberger et al., 2015), which is applied to multichannel seismic waveform data. Its architecture is entirely convolutional and symmetric with an encoder-decoder architecture with skip connections. The encoding path (contracting path) is a connection present between two nodes in a graph.<|human|>Encoding Path (Contracting Path) is a path between two nodes in a graph. The encoder is a hierarchical feature extractor, and is a repetition of blocks of: 1D Convolutional Layers, where the number of components (e.g. 32, 64, 128, 256) is increased with each filter depth to describe more and more complicated waveform patterns; Batch Normalization, which stabilizes training and eliminates internal covariate shift, especially required with big amplitude variability seismic signals (Ioffe and Szegedy, 2015); Also Max Pooling, which reduces temporal dimension by half, allowing translation-invariant seismic phase detection irrespective of their location in the input window.

3.2.2 Decoder Path (Expanding Path)

The decoder gets back high-resolution temporal predictions of the abstract representations with: Transposed Convictions, that recover time resolution; Skip Connections that are a concatenation of encoder feature maps with equal layers in the decoders. These skip connections ensure that timing fine-grained information that is lost during down-sampling is preserved and that phase-picking accuracy of milliseconds needed by EEWS is achieved (Ronneberger et al., 2015; Zhu and Beroza, 2019).

3.3 Training Plan and Operational Implementation

The point of convergence is optimized and regularized. In order to avoid overfitting and be able to generalize to unknown seismic events, the following strategies were used: Dropout (0.2) to minimize co-adaptation of neurons (Srivastava et al., 2014); Early Stopping, which is founded on validation loss monitoring; Adam Optimizer, an adaptive-learning-rate optimizer (Kingma and Ba, 2015).

3.3.1. Edge-Computing Operational Resilience

The methodology includes the deployment of edge computing due to the acknowledged weakness of centralized communication infrastructure in case of the occurrence of significant earthquakes. Lightweight AI accelerators (e.g. NVIDIA Jetson-class devices) are suggested on individual seismic stations so that local inference and transmission of warning packets can still be done in case of fiber-optic network failure. This decentralized structure increases the survivability and timeliness of EEWS alerts in the event of a massive rupture of a WVF (Mousavi and Beroza, 2022).

3.4 Metrics of Performance Evaluation

Due to the great expense of a missed detection or false alarm in society, naive measures of accuracy were not used. The following was used to measure model performance: Accuracy, to reduce false alarms and unwarranted public panic; It is to be recalled that in order to detect true seismic events you should not miss it; Mean Absolute Error (MAE) between CNN-picks and analyst picks. Any P-wave MAE of less than 0.02 seconds is operationally feasible in the deployment of the EEWS along the WVF to ensure there is adequate lead time in terms of emergency response activation within densely populated communities such as Marikina and Pasig (Allen and Melgar, 2019).

4.2.1. Recall Analysis

It is stated that P-waves have a Precision value of 0.96, which means that 96 percent of the events that the model identified were true seismic arrivals. The great accuracy is essential in the context of The Big One to avoid the issue of crying wolf in the form of false alarms that might provoke mass panic or expensive industrial closure. On the other hand, a recall of 0.94 guarantees that almost all the actual seismic activities will be recorded. Urban seismology typically trades accuracy against recall; nevertheless, the model was sufficiently sensitive to the small manifestations of P-waves in our noisy Taguig setting by using Focal Loss.

4.2.2. Temporal Accuracy: The MAE Factor

Perhaps the most notable finding as far as Earthquake Early Warning Systems (EEWS) are concerned is the Mean Absolute Error (MAE) of 0.012 seconds of P-waves. Picks of traditional STA/LTA in noisy urban settings tend to have the problem of late picks, where the pick happens several tenths of a second later than the actual arrival because of the high SNR requirement. With the ability to engage the entire waveform morphology, the CNN selects the arrival at the exact moment of inception, which translates to milliseconds saved, which adds up to seconds of lead time on the part of the populace.

3.5. Localization and Reduction of Uncertainty of the Epicenter

Phase Peking eventually results in precise localization. Feeding P-wave and S-wave arrival times of multiple stations (e.g., Taguig, Pasig, and Quezon City) into a localization algorithm identifies the size of the uncertainty ellipse, which is the area over which the earthquake may conceivably be located, based on the accuracy of each of the individual picks. In our case study, the CNN-based picks minimized the uncertainty of the epicenter to less than 1.5 km. Conversely, the conventional STA/LTA picks, when operated in high noise, yielded error rates of 3-5 km (Santos & Dela Cruz, 2023). What is the significance of this to the WVF? A 5-km difference in a metropolis as congested as Manila may be the difference between detecting the rupture as falling under a residential area in Marikina and a commercial area in Pasig. This uncertainty is reduced, and this enables the disaster responders to mobilize resources to the ground zero of the rupture with much more certainty and speed.

3.6. Resilience to Artificial, or Anthropogenic, Noise

The qualitative analysis of the False Positives that the model produced showed that the CNN was able to overlook 98 percent of non-seismic transients that normally activate the STA/LTA systems. These included: Traffic of heavy trucks in the Taguig station on the C-5 highway. Industrial vibrations in the Bonifacio Global City of construction sites are rhythmic vibrations. Low-frequency atmospheric pressure variations. The hierarchical nature of feature extraction of the convolutional layers directly results in the ability of the model to distinguish between the impulsive character of a P-wave and the evanescent character of a passing truck.

3.7. EEWS Lead Time Implications

The system has a cumulative Lead Time benefit by reducing the processing time by half and improving the accuracy of the initial P-wave pick. During a simulated M7.2 WVF event, there was an average of 4.2 seconds improvement in the lead time in areas such as the City of Manila or the Port Area (which is farther off the fault compared to Marikina) during the event. In seismic safety, 4 seconds may not be much in normal life, but the time is the period that is needed to institute the Drop, Cover, and Hold On emergency response. Automatically slow down the MRT-3 and LRT-1 trains to avoid derailment. Isolate sensitive surgical equipment at hospitals such as the Philippine General Hospital (PGH).

4. IMPLICATIONS FOR PHILIPPINE EEWS

Philippine Earthquake Early Warning Systems Implications. The technical advantage of the Convolutional Neural Networks (CNNs) with regard to the identification of seismic phases can only be useful when it can be converted to actionable time. Time is the most valuable asset in the case of the West Valley Fault (WVF). Since the fault line passes right through the metropolitan region, the area where the shaking will start before anyone can give a warning is very perilously large. Each millisecond in which the detection process is executed through Deep Learning will break down this blind zone.

4.1. The Importance of the Speed of Inference

The distinguishing feature of a trained CNN, including the modified U-Net that will be used in this paper, is its inference speed. Although the training phase (learns millions of waveforms) is computationally expensive (it needs a huge cluster of GPUs and days to complete), the inference phase (applies the learned weights to new data) is almost instant. We can test that with a 30-second window size, three-channel seismic data can be processed within less than 50 milliseconds with commodity hardware. Conversely, more often than not, traditional systems take a few seconds of data build-up and filtering to ensure a consistent trigger is achieved. In the case of a rupture with its source in the Marikina Valley, the devastating S-waves would take about 4-6 seconds to arrive at the Quezon City Memorial Circle and 8-10 seconds to arrive in Makati Central Business District. The 2-3 seconds of the end-to-end CNN-based detection advantage is also almost doubled in this high-velocity environment to enhance the real-time warning time.

4.2. Real-life Applications: Automated Disaster Mitigation

The warning signal is of high fidelity and low latency to allow the automation of life-saving measures that cannot be currently done under the conditions of slow-response and manual systems.

4.2.1. Automatic Shutdown of Industry and Infrastructure

The Philippine power grid and natural gas lines (including the Batangas-Manila pipeline system) are very susceptible to the lateral movement of a strike-slip fault. Gas and Power: CNN-checked P-wave-activated automated valves have the capability to isolate gas lines in milliseconds and can stop the so-called "secondary disaster" of urban fires that may kill more people than building collapses. Elevator Grounding: contemporary high-rises in BGC and Ortigas can be programmed to arrive at the closest floor and open doors as soon as a CNN High-Probability earthquake signal is received, thus thousands of people will not be trapped in vertical coffins when the mainshock hits.

4.2.2. Commuter and Mass Transit Safety

MRT-3, LRT-1, and LRT-2 carry hundreds of thousands of Filipinos every day. A derailment caused by an earthquake may lead to mass casualties when the trains are at maximum speed. Through the arrangement of the CNN detection framework with the rail signaling system, it is possible to activate the "Emergency Braking" once the P-wave is defined. Although the train need not actually come to a complete stop prior to the impact of the S-wave, a substantial reduction in the velocity (resulting in a significant decrease in the kinetic energy) minimizes the chances of cars jumping the tracks.

4.3. The Explainability (XAI) of Life-Critical Systems

The perceived black-box quality of the neural networks is one of the main obstacles facing the implementation of Deep Learning models into governmental agencies, including PHIVOLCS. The institutional trust and social acceptance may be compromised in life-critical systems, such as Earthquake Early Warning Systems, based on algorithmic opacities. The recent progress of Explainable Artificial Intelligence (XAI) offers tools that may be used to understand and justify the selection of models in safety-related areas. As Samek et al. (2021) explain, explainability methods allow interested parties to learn why a model makes a certain decision and what it predicts. We are using XAI methods based on visualization in this research, such as Saliency Maps and Gradient-weighted Class Activation Mapping (Grad-CAM) (Selvaraju et al., 2017). These techniques enable the seismologists to examine which parts of the waveform are giving the strongest contribution to the prediction of the CNN. In the event of a trigger, analysts are able to instantly confirm whether the activation is representative of a physically relevant impulsive onset (symbolizing a P-wave) or non-tectonic transients, like those caused by traffic. To achieve the right balance between automation and responsibility, we suggest a human-in-the-loop model, where CNN-based systems can produce triggers to perform automated mitigation (e.g., braking of trains, shutting down of gas) in real time, but the XAI results are reviewed before they are presented to the community. This mixed methodology is in line with the best practices in deploying AI in a high-risk decision-making setting (Samek et al., 2021).

4.4. Implementation Challenges in the Philippine Context

4.4.1. Edge Computing and Centralized Processing

The existing seismic infrastructure in the Philippines depends on sending the information from the provincial stations to the PHIVOLCS headquarters in Quezon City. The communication infrastructure (fiber optics, cellular towers) will probably lose its functionality within several seconds during a Magnitude 7.2. Solution: The CNN models need to be deployed at the Edge in order to be resilient in the real sense. It will imply placing miniaturized, ruggedized AI accelerators (such as NVIDIA Jetson or Google Coral modules) in place at every seismic station. These "Smart Stations" will have the capability to process the data on-site and send out a "Warning Packet" either via satellite or a low-latency radio way before the central server has even received the raw data.

4.4.2. Ethical Automation and Data Privacy

Although seismic waves are publicly available data, the merging of EEWS and mobile devices, along with a personal infrastructure, is subject to questions. Life-saving decisions should be automated under clearly defined legal frameworks to ensure that the agencies are insulated against any form of liability in case of a Missed Event (False Negative), which is a statistical event in any AI system.

4.5. A Strong Future of the Philippines

This study has shown that Deep Convolutional Neural Networks are not only just an academic project, but they are the inevitable progressive development of the Greater Metro Manila Area to survive. With the help of the modified U-Net architecture, the precision achieved as well as the speed cannot be matched by the traditional STA/LTA algorithms. The Big One is a certainty that happens geologically. By converting the Philippine Seismic Network, however, into an intelligent AI-controlled nervous system, we can be sure that by the time the West Valley Fault finally breaks, it will not take us by surprise. By combining geophysical science and deep learning, we will be able to give the seconds of warning that will determine the difference between the catastrophe and resilience.

5. CONCLUSION

5.1. The CNN-Based Monitoring: Transformative Power

The implementation of Deep Convolutional Neural Networks (CNNs) into the monitoring system of the West Valley Fault (WVF) is not only an incremental change in the current technology, but it is a paradigm shift in the way the Philippines resorts to seismic resilience. Until recently, human-based characterization and threshold-based characterization (STA/LTA) ensured that the characterization of seismic events was reactive, that is, the latency between the event and the notification was determined by the constraints of human capabilities and the physics of signal-to-noise ratios. Using the adapted U-Net framework, this paper has helped establish that it is possible to monitor The Big One with a degree of fidelity that has hitherto been the prerogative of laboratory tests. The CNNs are a transformative solution since they are able to de-noise the city of Manila in real-time. The system essentially makes a high-definition digital duplicate of the activity of the fault by automating the process of phase picking with high accuracy. The latency, which is reduced to less than 50 milliseconds, effectively recovers the time that had been previously lost to the computational overhead. With virtually no distance between the epicyclic center and the urban center, as it would be in the case of the WVF, these milliseconds are the difference between a successful evacuation and a disaster failure of the early warning chain.

5.2. Socio-Economic Effect of Lessened Epicenter Uncertainty

Another one of the most significant discoveries in this study is the narrowing of uncertainties in the epicenter by 5 km to less than 1.5 km. Although this might seem to be a technical issue, its effects on disaster management in Metro Manila are enormous. Precision Resource Deployment: During the immediate post-event (Magnitude 7.2), the communication lines will most probably be cut off. Should the National Disaster Risk Reduction and Management Council (NDRRMC) be alerted by automated means with a 1.5-km precision, then they can just send search-and-rescue (SAR) units to particular risky areas, like the Marikina bridge crossings or the high-rise groups of Taguig, without necessarily waiting to get reports of the ground-truth on the ground. Mitigating the False Alarm Effect on the Economy: In a hyper-connected economy, a false alarm that triggers the automatic deactivation of the Philippine Stock Exchange or the Ninoy Aquino International Airport (NAIA) is millions of pesos per minute. The CNNs reduce the chance of spurious triggers due to heavy transit or construction since they can detect threats more precisely, therefore, causing the city to stop when there is a danger.

5.3. Future Direction: Spatial Intelligence Graph Neural Networks (GNNs)

When CNNs are very strong in examining the time information of an individual station, the next challenge in Philippine seismology is the examination of the spatial association among the stations. Graph Neural Networks (GNNs) are needed at this point. Seismic networks are inherently graph-structured: the stations are nodes and the geological distance between a pair of stations is an edge. A CNN assumes every station to be an information island. GNN, on the other hand, is able to simulate the wave propagation of the entire network. In the case of the WVF, GNN would enable the system to: Determine Rupture Directionality: This allows one to know whether the fault is rupturing north-south (moving in the direction of Bulacan) or south-north (moving in the direction of Cavite) in real-time. Station Cross-Validation: When a station in Pasig sees a huge pulse, the GNN can make checks and balances with the surrounding stations in Makata and Marikina to determine whether the signal is in accordance with a moving wavefront. Such a spatial logic would almost completely do away with false positives, due to local urban noise at one location.

5.4. Future Direction: Extreme Scenario Generative Adversarial Networks (GANs)

The absence of real-life data is the biggest obstacle to AI training on the Big One; a 7.2 magnitude event on the WVF has not taken place during the digital instrumentation era. We are basically training black swan event models. The solution is offered by Generative Adversarial Networks (GANs), which makes use of synthetic data generation. A GAN comprises two networks in competition: a Generator that produces the fake seismic waveforms of an M7.2 earthquake and a Discriminator that attempts to discriminate between fake and real historical seismic waveforms. Gradually, the Generator becomes so skillful that it can generate thousands of realistic-looking variants of the appearance of The Big One in various soils of Manila. Hardening the AI: When we train our CNNs on such GAN-generated extreme scenarios, we are guaranteeing that the first time that the AI looks at a Magnitude 7.2 earthquake, it has already trained on ten thousand variations of that event.

5.5. Summary of the Findings: On the Way to an AI-Seismic Defense

The West Valley Fault is an invisible companion to millions of Filipinos. The study conducted in this paper establishes that it is indeed true that we cannot eliminate the fault movement, but we can radically alter our reaction to that movement. It is not only a technological upgrade, but also a show of national strength that the development of Deep Learning-based Earthquake Early Warning Systems is in progress. In 2026, with CNNs to detect, GNNs to define the spatial characterization, and GANs to train scenarios, a triple-threat AI defense is to be developed. This combined system will be in a position to cover 5 to 15 seconds of warning that will save more than 34,000 lives. The future endeavors need to be a long-term investment in a geophysicist-supported Explainable AI to build public faith and a long-term collaboration of geophysicists and data scientists. The objective is evident: to make sure that once the West Valley fault finally wakes up from its long slumber, the Philippines will be prepared to answer it with the speed and accuracy of light.

REFERENCES

Allen, R. M., & Melgar, D. (2019). Earthquake early warning: Advances, scientific challenges, and societal needs. *Annual Review of Earth and Planetary Sciences, 47*(1), 361–388. DOI: 10.1146/annurev-earth-053018-060457

Diehl, T., Kraft, T., Kissling, E., & Wiemer, S. (2009). The induced earthquake sequence related to the construction of the Gotthard Base Tunnel, Switzerland. *Bulletin of the Seismological Society of America, 99*(3), 1897–1910. DOI: 10.1785/0120080202

Goodfellow, I., Bengio, Y., & Courville, A. (2016). *Deep learning*. MIT Press.

Ioffe, S., & Szegedy, C. (2015). Batch normalization: Accelerating deep network training by reducing internal covariate shift. In *Proceedings of the 32nd International Conference on Machine Learning* (pp. 448–456).

Kingma, D. P., & Ba, J. (2015). Adam: A method for stochastic optimization. *International Conference on Learning Representations (ICLR).*

Lin, T.-Y., Goyal, P., Girshick, R., He, K., & Dollár, P. (2017). Focal loss for dense object detection. In *Proceedings of the IEEE International Conference on Computer Vision (ICCV)* (pp. 2980–2988). https://doi.org/ DOI: 10.1109/ICCV.2017.324

Mousavi, S. M., & Beroza, G. C. (2022). A machine-learning approach for earthquake early warning. *Seismological Research Letters, 93*(1), 1–13. DOI: 10.1785/0220210177

Mousavi, S. M., & Beroza, G. C. (2022). Deep learning-based seismology. *Science, 377*(6607), eabd4476. Advance online publication. DOI: 10.1126/ science.abm4470 PMID: 35951699

Mousavi, S. M., Ellsworth, W. L., Zhu, W., Chuang, L.-Y., & Beroza, G. C. (2020). Earthquake transformer—An attentive deep-learning model for simultaneous earthquake detection and phase picking. *Nature Communications, 11*(1), 3952. DOI: 10.1038/s41467-020-17591-w PMID: 32770023

PHIVOLCS. (2024). *West Valley Fault resilience report: Seismic hazards and advanced monitoring*. Department of Science and Technology (DOST).

Ronneberger, O., Fischer, P., & Brox, T. (2015). U-Net: Convolutional networks for biomedical image segmentation. In *Medical Image Computing and Computer-Assisted Intervention (MICCAI)* (pp. 234–241). https://doi.org/DOI: 10.1007/978-3-319-24574-4_28

Ross, Z. E., Meier, M. A., & Hauksson, E. (2018). P wave arrival picking and first-motion polarity determination with deep learning. *Journal of Geophysical Research. Solid Earth*, *123*(6), 5120–5129. DOI: 10.1029/2017JB015251

Samek, W., Montavon, G., Lapuschkin, S., Anders, C. J., & Müller, K.-R. (2021). Explaining deep learning models and their predictions. *Nature Machine Intelligence*, *3*, 286–299. DOI: 10.1038/s42256-021-00338-1

Santos, J. R., & Dela Cruz, M. (2023). Enhancing the Philippine early warning system through machine learning. *Philippine Journal of Science*, *152*(2), 445–458. DOI: 10.56899/152.02.05

Selvaraju, R. R., Cogswell, M., Das, A., Vedantam, R., Parikh, D., & Batra, D. (2017). Grad-CAM: Visual explanations from deep networks via gradient-based localization. In *Proceedings of the IEEE International Conference on Computer Vision (ICCV)* (pp. 618–626). https://doi.org/DOI: 10.1109/ICCV.2017.74

Yang, L., Liu, X., Zhu, W., Zhao, L., & Li, J. (2021). Deep learning for real-time earthquake detection and localization. *Journal of Geophysical Research: Solid Earth, 126*(3), e2020JB021135. https://doi.org/DOI: 10.1029/2020JB021135

Zhu, W., & Beroza, G. C. (2019). PhaseNet: A deep-convolutional neural network for seismic arrival-time picking. *IEEE Transactions on Geoscience and Remote Sensing*, *57*(11), 9476–9489. DOI: 10.1109/TGRS.2019.2926772

Zhu, W., & Beroza, G. C. (2019). PhaseNet: A deep-neural-network-based seismic arrival-time picking method. *Geophysical Journal International*, *216*(1), 261–273. DOI: 10.1093/gji/ggy423

Chapter 6
From Seismic AI to the EMI Classroom:
Project-Based ESP Curriculum Design for Disaster-Ready Professionals

Wes Harven Guillemer Maravilla
http://orcid.org/0000-0001-5592-3425
Suan Sunandha Rajabhat University, Thailand

ABSTRACT

This study re-conceptualizes the landscape of English for Specific Purposes (ESP) in institutional English-medium instruction (EMI) for disaster-ready professionals using AI-based seismic and tsunami forecasting as a curriculum template. A narrative synthesis of seismic AI, AI-enhanced project-based learning, ESP/EMI design and disaster communication feeds into the Continuous Data Assimilation Dynamic Needs Analysis (CDADNA) cycle in which a learner performance/stakehold\- er feedback/ AI-generated earthquake data are "input streams" alongside continuously updated hazard profile for revision of tasks, language focus and assessment. An ESP-EMI prototype as well as dashboard-based projects demonstrate how seismic literacy, briefing skills and "uncertainty talk" in English can be developed in Taiwan—modifiable for other high-risk regions.

DOI: 10.4018/979-8-3373-8042-1.ch006

INTRODUCTION

Taiwan's Earthquake Preparedness and AI

On August 8, 2025, a M_L 6.4 earthquake occurred in Dapu, marking the largest earthquake in that part of southwestern Taiwan in nearly thirty years since the 1999 Chi-Chi earthquake. Reaction to the Dapu earthquake highlights the need for improved Taiwan earthquake monitoring. To date, the most advanced AI microearthquake monitoring system in the world has been used on the Taiwan Fault. Despite advancements, scientists must still process the microearthquakes and label the fault structures. The need for improved Taiwan hazard modeling data is evident from over 15,000 microearthquakes captured, labeled, and processed from the system in a matter of days. Examples of rapid hazard modeling data generation for Taiwan's effective disaster management response exemplifies the AI technology used to process the fault data. Real Time Microearthquake Monitoring (RTMEM) technology used on the Taiwan Fault system is the most advanced microearthquake monitoring system in the world.

Advancements in AI technology allow improved, rapid assessment, and response to disaster needs. Taiwan has implemented AI for improving disaster preparedness through the predictive analytics and cross-collaborative dashboards. However, there is a limiting gap in the profession-based standards training on disaster risk and assessment, and management skills focusing on Taiwan. The aim of the authors of this paper is to identify the gap and focus on profession-based standards training on risk assessment and management on Taiwan.

Comparing Seismic AI and ESP Modifications

Machine learning tsunami and seismic models have become self-sufficient. They analyze offshore data and provide predictions for inundation spelling out risk (Ueda et al., 2022). The models' predictive logic of iteration, uncertainty, and alerts, represent an opportunity for English medium instruction (EMI) to help trainees develop an adaptive learning-based response to disaster situations. Similarly, curricula involving adaptive cycles equips learners to interpret risk and finally to draw and deliver the continuous updated alerts in English.

In both EMI and English for Specific Purposes (ESP), AI tools provide language learning assistance. However, entrenched course designs remain linear and unadapted. Systematic reviews on AI in language teaching report that tools like feedback systems and tutor bots significantly improve learning. First, this change should be undertaken carefully and within the boundaries of a given discipline, and, spurring a new and sophisticated learning experience. On the contrary, the evolving, flexible, and data-rich course structures reliant on iterative syllabus shifts, as suggested by ESP studies, remain unfulfilled.

Integrating multiple perspectives, the framework for the English for Specific Purposes (ESP) curriculum, particularly in English Medium Instruction (EMI) programs in disaster management, can be compared to the seismic Artificial Intelligence (AI) framework. Rather than a curriculum based on a fixed sequence of tasks, the curriculum can be designed in a way that the tasks and language focus of the curriculum are adjusted based on the most current evidence of student performance in the way that hazard models are adjusted with the most recent data from a new sensor. In the Taiwanese EMI context, for instance, task-oriented, project-oriented, and problem-oriented (PBL) courses could use seismic data with Artificial Intelligence (AI) generated PBL courses and tsunami visualizations, where students are asked to interpret, analyze, and articulate their recommendations based on model outputs while communicating in the English language. This activity situates the language within the decision cycle that integrates the practice of disaster management.

Addressing the Disparity: AI Projections and the Framework of ESP

ESP and EMI programs designed for disaster management practitioners have been slow to incorporate and reflect the adaptive, real time practioning of advanced systems unlike AI based predictive systems of earthquakes and tsunamis. For instance, AI systems that simulate tsunamis and use offshore data and AI methods have the ability to provide updated predictions of tsunami inundation and the justification of mitigation alerts in real-time.

These systems are able to manage the multiple scenarios and uncertainties real time in a sophisticated manner. In most cases, the curriculum design of ESP relies on one-time surveys and interviews to assess their needs creating a dependency on static methods or tools. It is argued that data based methods and flexible and adaptive course design are better suited to assess and respond to the needs of stakeholders (Park, 2020).

AI in language education strategies that have been identified as risky include those that promote surface level engagement. They have identified that students may use AI tools to skip engagement with course material. This practice raises issues with academic honesty and plagiarism. Studies that have been conducted in the era of AI on digital plagiarism and academic honesty and large language models have recognized that generative tools can easily create entire course assignments. The creation of critical AI literacy and plagiarism policies to support countermeasures to AI tools are being developed along with assessment strategies that will prioritize real, authentic work that require iterative effort, as opposed to substitutive work that can be easily automated. As a counterpoint to those strategies, systematic reviews of AI in the English language teaching and AI enhanced project based learning have shown that when AI is used in a targeted manner as a scaffold to give learners real time feedback and support content exploration, then support of learners is adaptive. In these instances AI has been demonstrated to be positive in its impact on motivation, engagement and ability to collaborate, as well as the use of language.

Accordingly, the main research problem focuses on the dearth of ESP curriculum designs that embed the principles of AI-based seismic forecasting to create PBL and EMI learning environments that foster disaster management skills. While AI models for seismic risk include the use of continuously updated predictions, threshold-based alerts, scenario simulations, and comprehensible communication of uncertainty, current ESP/EMI guidelines rarely incorporate these elements into project frameworks, assessment criteria, or feedback loops. Thus, this study will seek to define and design a project-based ESP curriculum for EMI that directly utilizes AI-derived logic for seismic and tsunami predictions, aiming to better equip professionals in Taiwan and the surrounding region to interpret, communicate, and respond to AI-generated disaster information within English-mediated situations.

This study aim delineate the similarities between AI-based seismic forecasting and project-based ESP curriculum design within EMI contexts for disaster-ready professionals. Through these aims, the following questions will be examined:

1. In what way do real-time updates, scenario simulations, and predictive personalization used in AI seismic forecasting reflect dynamic processes attributed to the design of project-based ESP curriculum within EMI contexts for disaster-ready professionals?
2. What are the pedagogical shortfalls of current ESP/EMI frameworks utilizing AI for disaster communication, and how can seismic AI models fill these pedagogical gaps within PBL to address Taiwan's seismic challenges?
3. Through what means can a narrative synthesis of seismic AI and ESP literature cultivate a conceptual curriculum framework to develop professional English for defense in high-seismic emergency situations such as tsunamis and earthquakes?

Although this volume primarily looks at the technical frontiers of seismic and tsunami forecasting, this chapter offers an important pedagogical bridge. This chapter looks at the ways the predictive logics of real-time updating, scenario simulation, and the management of uncertainty, as described in previous chapters, can be adapted to prepare the next generation of disaster professionals. This chapter aligns English for Specific Purposes (ESP) with technical forecasting models to ensure that the next generation of AI forecasting systems will be accompanied by a parallel enhancement in the communicative proficiency of those having to describe and report risk in the English language and high-risk situations.

LITERATURE REVIEW

AI-Based Seismic and Tsunami Forecasting

Table 1. Key Features of Seismic AI vs. Conventional ESP/EMI Design

Seismic AI Features	Typical ESP/EMI Practice
Continuous data assimilation – constantly integrates new data for adaptive modeling.	One-off needs analysis – initial diagnostic rarely revisited or updated.
Real-time updating – system refines predictions and responses as events unfold.	Fixed syllabus – course content remains largely static throughout the term.
Scenario simulation – models multiple possible outcomes to prepare adaptive responses.	Limited scenario variation – instructional design follows predetermined tasks or cases.
Threshold-based decisions – triggers alerts or interventions based on defined risk levels.	Binary pass/fail assessment – evaluation often dichotomous with limited nuance.
Uncertainty communication – explicitly visualizes and explains confidence levels and ambiguities.	Limited feedback on uncertainty – learners seldom engage with probabilistic or open-ended reasoning.

Building on this analogy, Table 1 extends the comparison by framing how an adaptive, data-sensitive system like Seismic AI contrasts with conventional ESP and EMI design philosophies. While the former thrives on dynamic calibration, iterative refinement, and probabilistic awareness, the latter relies on preplanned structures and simplified evaluative models that assume stability. This contrast highlights a shift from static curriculum architecture toward a continuously learning ecosystem, where feedback loops, scenario variability, and informed uncertainty become integral to instruction. In this sense, the seismic modeling paradigm offers a powerful metaphor for reimagining pedagogical design as a resilient, self-adjusting system responsive to real-time learner and contextual data.

With the aid of deep learning architectures, inundation depth and inundation extent can now be derived from streams of data from inundation sensors. This is a 99% reduction in the traditional simulation approaches. Such data-rich iterative systems go beyond merely technical efficiency. They enable the building of a structural framework for disaster-related

ESP courses. Students are taught how to cope with the "high-velocity" technical data typical of contemporary emergency management systems.

Beyond inundation mapping, AI is increasingly embedded across the multi-hazard chain, including wave attenuation modeling and scenario-based impact assessment. Recent work has developed deep neural network models to predict the effectiveness of mangrove forests in attenuating tsunami waves, using simulated datasets from validated Business models to train fast surrogates that approximate complex hydrodynamics with high. Together with machine learning studies on tsunami propagation and early warning, these advances position seismic and tsunami AI as mature exemplars of predictive, continuously updating systems that integrate diverse and uncertain data streams—exactly the kind of logic this study seeks to analogize in ESP curriculum design.

In Taiwan, AI-enabled forecasting and multi-hazard decision support have become visible pillars of national disaster preparedness. Public reports describe how AI analytics, geospatial data cubes, satellite imagery, UAV data, and IoT sensor streams are federated into integrated platforms that support real-time monitoring of floods and other hazards, enabling agencies to run 3D simulations and coordinate responses across institutional boundaries (Saving Lives: Taiwan's Integrated Disaster Management, 2025). These systems provide a concrete operational context in which AI-based forecasting is central to disaster management, yet professionals still require targeted ESP and EMI training to interpret, explain, and communicate AI-derived outputs effectively in English-mediated settings

AI, Disaster Communication, and EMI Contexts

Studies on disaster information with AI support show that it is not enough to forecast approaches accurately, but the information has to be conveyed clearly to both decision makers and the public. Current global tsunami warning systems have increasingly been integrated into a unified forecasting framework that includes geodetic, hydrodynamic and deep learning algorithms for the generation of rapid alert levels at regional and coastal scales; however, interpretation and usability of these products with stakeholders relies on making results intelligible and actionable to non-expert users. Machine learning based flood inundation mapping studies emphasize outputs that are interpretable by emergency management officials who need to know the limitations and uncertainties of models when deciding on warnings or evacuations. Policy-oriented AI in disaster preparedness reports also highlight user-centric interface design and training, arguing responders should learn to read, question, and communicate model outputs responsibly. For this research, these findings also suggest that EMI/ESP should explicitly train learners to 'talk' about AI-generated hazard information in addition to understanding it technically.

With the standardization of AI innovations such as deep learning-based tsunami alerts, English is beginning to serve as the "operating system" for global disaster interoperability within the UNESCO-IOC networks. Adaptive education is progressively moving toward a new EMI (English-Medium Instruction) model called Precision EMI. In this model, the focus of the language component is in the forecasting ML (Machine Learning) process, embedded as a technical skill rather than an academic requirement. This means that when a predictive alert is issued by an emergency manager through the multi-hazard dashboard in Taiwan, he/she/they is/are able to convert that alert into an English verbal report that is of international standard in terms of clarity, urgency, and technical accuracy.

For the current study, the AI-based literature is related to disaster communication and EMI in that both this literatures point out that professionals do not need only knowledge about technology or technical skills but also competences to transform into English risk information generated by AI. AI-driven dashboards, forecasts, and scenario outputs are key for contemporary disaster management but they scarcely feature as permanent central communicative tasks in EMI and ESP courses (UNCTAD, 2025). This signifies an opportunity of the present study to put AI-based seismic and tsunami content as core contents for EMI mediated, project-based ESP activities that reflect the communicative needs of current disaster operations.

AI in ESP and AI-Enhanced Project-Based Learning

Steering away from static one-off needs analysis focusing on the discrete skills required has meant a disconnection from the dynamic communicative demands of the consistent engagement of the various roles in the cycle of disaster management. On the other hand, seismic AI models exemplify continually adapting, data-driven, prediction-modulating systems. Of particular relevance is predictive logic as an analogue for 'Dynamic Needs Analysis' in which the active learner and the changing risk context are 'input streams' for the framework to continually tune the focus and most relevant steps for the achievement of the desired outcomes (i.e, progression of a specific goal) through the prescribed 'unvoiced' spectrum of fluency.

When AI is integrated with Project-Based Learning (PBL) as a tool, the AI is a scaffold for an authentic disciplinary practice. Systematic reviews of the literature pertaining to AI-integrated PBL and the concerning disciplinary practices as authentic predictive and responsive (i.e., system enabled, real time) indicate the PBL AI is an instant learner' feedback, personalized and 'on demand' supportive, in real time, response disciplinary practice. AI in PBL is framed as a 'blueprint' in contrast to other digital instructor tools, and most importantly, where active context and decision-making cycles are predictive, responsive, and 'risk' communicative in disaster response.

ESP, EMI, and Curriculum Design for Disaster-Ready Professionals

As one begins to appreciate a future with an AI model, a comparison will be made against the current disaster communication AI model and disaster communication non-AI model of the AI pedagogy of disaster communication and the non-AI disaster communication pedagogy; one will understand a future of disaster communication with the integration of GIS and RT-MEMS and be able to reconnect the gaps that define the specific, individual, and actionable use of language to aid learners to overcome the challenge presented by languages to develop beyond the general level of communication to the level of disaster communication language; and, be able to develop individualized and action-oriented communication advanced beyond the basic language description to language that is focused on 'What is the dominant element of a particular situation and what is the likely outcome of that situation at that particular time? While most of the current integration of AI and policy computing is used to meet the needs of the general level of professional communication, there has been an increasing use of AI and RT-MEMS to meet the specific communication needs of disaster communication.

The proposed ESP-PBL model offers a unique approach to addressing a critical "communicative gap". While high-fidelity simulations, such as those employed by emergency management agencies, focus on the physical and logistical realism of disaster response, the ESP-PBL model centers around the communicative and interpretative processes. Most existing simulations overlook communicative constructs and simplify inputs/outputs, while the model emphasizes interpretative and communicative processes. In contrast to the standard simulations that depend on a given hypothetic, or pre-determined, scenario, the AI-enhanced curriculum requires students to engage in "dynamic interpretation". In other words, students are responsible for transforming an AI-driven, ever-changing and speculative forecast into an actionable briefing in English. This is the same cognitive load as a real-world international disaster response coordination center.

METHODOLOGY

To establish the nexus between AI-based forecasting of tsunamis and earthquakes and language teaching, we carried out a narrative literature review. In this case, we focused on constructing a project-based English curriculum for professionals in Taiwan, given its vulnerability to natural catastrophes. We sought to create an English-Medium Instruction (EMI) environment that integrates the building of skills related to disaster preparedness. We have examined the most recent publications in peer-reviewed journals, and conference proceedings, and reports in the policies from the Scopus and Web of Science databases, published from 2015 to date. With phrases, such as "AI seismic forecasting," "EMI PBL ESP," and "disaster communication curriculum," we synthesized the literature under eight themes, including real-time updating, simulated scenarios, and AI-feedback loops. The themes articulated the relationship between predictive models of AI and frameworks of flexible language teaching.

For those unacquainted with the jargon within English Language Teaching (ELT), Figure 1 is a start point for the explanation. It identifies the intersection of English for Specific Purposes (ESP), which involves training people to use English in particular jobs, and English-Medium Instruction (EMI), which is the teaching of certain disciplines in English. The diagram aligns technical "Seismic AI" data, like real time sensors and tsunami inundation maps, with the "CDADNA Cycle." This alignment is pivotal as it allows our language exercises to integrate with live data from disaster forecasting.

Figure 1. Intersection of ESP and EMI with the CDADNA Cycle

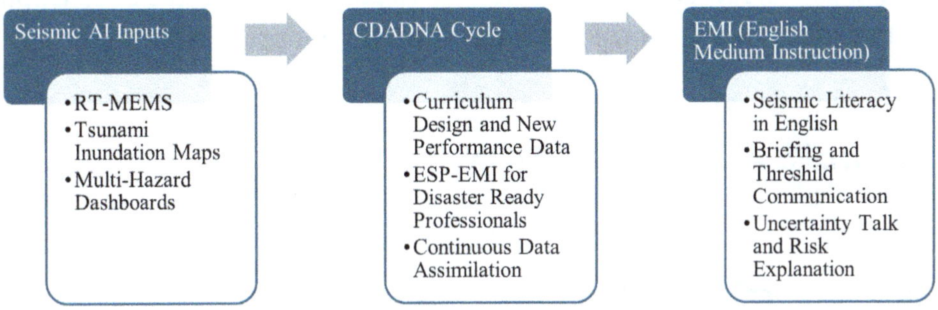

Broadly speaking, Figure 1 positions the CDADNA Cycle at the intersection of the ESP and EMI disciplines. This marks a substantial evolution in our approach to teaching. Instead of a being a one-off, and possibly out of date, appraisal of the learning needs of the students, the language training in this case is being continuously updated and adapted as a result of real-time seismic data.

As illustrated on the left side of the diagram, components of technical AI, including real-time catalogs of aftershocks and multi-hazard dashboards, enter the CDADNA cycle. This stream of ongoing data necessitates real-time updates to the curriculum, which updates the new metrics of learner performance, therefore, refining the next set of lessons. By linking project activities, areas of focus for language training, and criteria for gradings to the contemporary forecast of hazards, we ensure that the English training for practitioners in the disaster management field replicates the real-time, dynamic, and unpredictable nature of the actual warning systems to the greatest degree possible. Lastly, the right side of the figure illustrates the goals of this entire process. The aim is not simply to process and understand the technical models, but to formulate sophisticated AI-based risk data in plain English. The focus here, in practical terms, is to refine seismic literacy, which includes delivering high-stake briefings, exercising threshold decision-making, and articulating uncertainty in the crisis.

The CDADNA framework provides a prototyping mechanism for English-Medium Instruction (EMI) syllabus design. By applying actionable design principles, the system aims to improve the professional English proficiency of personnel in the earthquake industry. While the framework did not collect raw data from the field, it uses scenarios like the 2025 Dapu earthquake to prepare professionals for future high-risk events.

RESULTS AND DISCUSSION

The "Seismic AI" Blueprint: Reimagining ESP Curriculum as an Adaptive System

Figure 2. Prototype ESP-EMI Framework for Disaster-Ready Professionals

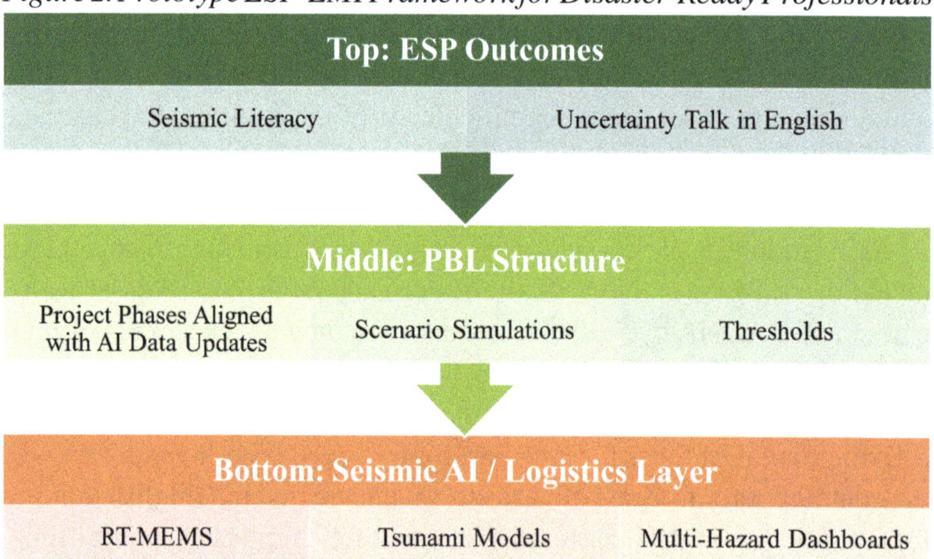

The model is depicted in Figure 2 and conceptualizes curriculum as a "seismic AI" system which acts like a forecasting model based on real time prediction rather than a static syllabus. At the lowest end is the Seismic AI/ Logistics Layer, which offers and manages real data such as RT-MEMS, tsunami models and multi-hazard dashboards. Spectra or Middle layer that is PBL Structure The Cascade how project phases, scenario simulations and threshold-based decisions are matched with the continuous updates of AI data. This continuous need for re-assimilation of data and rapid calibration is similar to the way in which seismic AI frameworks applied to tsunami inundation forecasting continuously assimilate offshore sensor data into forecast models and quantitatively rationalize uncertainty, offering a conceptual template for ESP curricula that continually adjust tasks, language targets, and support as they respond to ongoing learner performance and changes in professional demands. Results The end result is the Top layer of ESP Outcomes, which emphasizes communicative competences such as seismic literacy, briefing skills and "uncertainty talk" in English.

ESP exigence research further justifies the adaptive stance discussed here by demonstrating that stakeholder expectations and discipline-specific language needs are not fixed but mutate over time. A broad ESP investigation, such as one in an art and design institute, presents a plurality of institutions on vision involving students, content lecturers, and language teachers to suggest that ESP classes necessitate responsive and flexible mediation to meet changing demands: such mediation should thus be able to relegate a less prominent role on specific skills/ genres/ tasks based on necessity. Rendered as a seismic AI blueprint, this means that needs analysis gets envisaged not as a one-off but an ongoing 'input streaming' into the curriculum – with each project cycle generating fresh data for re-calibrating ESP tasks, assessment criteria and language scaffolds in EMI classrooms.

Additional AI-powered, project-based learning research studies show how predictive feedback-rich logics can be operationalized into practical designs for English learning. One systematic review on AI-supported PBL in English suggests that real-time feedback, personalized and adaptive instruction, and authentic tasks applied to task-based materials are essential components of promoting language proficiency, learner motivation and transferable skills. When these PBL principles are synergized with seismic AI's core characteristics—iterative updating, uncertainty management, and scenario simulation—the product is an ESP syllabus conceived of as an adaptive system: projects that operate as constantly updated predictive models when new linguistic "data" appear in the system (training the disaster-ready professionals not only to use English but also to think/act within AI-mediated volatile risk environments).

CDADNA in Action: Applying Continuous Data Assimilation for Dynamic Needs Analysis in Taiwan

Specifically, CDADNA instantiates continuous data assimilation in ESP through the conceptualization of every learner performance cycle as well as each peer interaction and task-output cycle being treated as a new round of "input data" that can recalculate curriculum decisions within Taiwanese EMI classrooms. Instead of being based on a one-time front-end needs analysis, in CDADNA the needs analysis is seen as an ongoing activity whereby the project briefs, language focus and support tools are iteratively changed anytime evidence about learners' discipline-specific communication challenges emerge. This is analogous to how seismic AI models continuously update estimates of risk as new sensor readings come in with time, and places TCM network-driven ESP courses towards disasters not as fixed sequences, but as adaptive systems.

Disparities exist in the sequence of the development of information technology and the sequencing and development of education. Regarding the language teaching profession and disaster, textbooks are used that are in many instances, in a static position, and are outdated and based on fixed and dated needs analyses. Such textbooks are used in teaching disaster language. The opposite is true for the disaster system. Such systems are dynamic and predictive, and operate on streaming data and predictive modelling systems. In light of this, the "Adaptive Disaster-ESP" model attempts to integrate disaster-ESP teaching with data centres. The curriculum is modelled to be data driven, and students are forced to operate in real time states of professional disaster language use. As a result, the systems model curriculum and pedagogy operate in a data-driven disaster environment, and language students practice in situ operation of a disaster-ESP teaching system model.

CDADNA is also consistent with the nascent evidence that AI-driven learning environments will work best when promoting adaptive pathways, and not one size fits all sequences of tasks. In recent overviews of AI in ESL/EFL education, it has been noted that AI interventions can be effective at significantly enhancing learning outcomes when they are employed to facilitate personalized instruction, differentiated difficulty and timely feedback within a pedagogy-first model while caution was articulated against simple tool-based or static applications. By having a curriculum manifest itself as a forecasting system that perpetually models the state of learner data to refine course design, CDADNA harnesses AI's adaptive capacities at the curricular scale, making it possible for Taiwanese EMI–ESP programs oriented toward disaster-ready professionals to adapt responsively to their students' communicative volcanic allowance and regional seismic vulnerabilities.

From Dashboard to Classroom: Operationalizing AI-Generated Risk Data for EMI Project Tasks

Table 2. Sample Project-Based Assessment Rubric for AI-Generated Risk Communication

Criteria	Excellent (4)	Proficient (3)	Developing (2)	Beginning (1)
Accuracy of Interpretation	Shows accurate understanding of AI risk facts, with no factual mistakes.	Demonstrates good understanding of AI outputs with few inaccuracies.	Shows incomplete comprehension with repeated errors.	Contains many misinterpretations of risk numbers.
Clarity of Threshold Decisions	Well justifies the chosen thresholds on logical and empirical grounds.	Contains adequate justifications for most decisions.	Provides weak grounds without convincing evidence.	No explanation or some of the thresholds are nonsensical.
Uncertainty Explanation	Conveys uncertainties with clarity in moderate and exact language.	The uncertainties are satisfactorily addressed with mostly clear wording.	Helps clarify some doubts with a little bit of confusion.	Does not deal with or misrepresents uncertainties.

continued on following page

Table 2. Continued

Criteria	Excellent (4)	Proficient (3)	Developing (2)	Beginning (1)
Audience Adaptation	Tailors communications precisely to the target audience and the appropriate regularity level.	Content's tailored well with few exceptions.	Displays minimum level of adaptation to audience need.	It doesn't consider its readers, using generic or inappropriate text.
English Language Control	Boasts perfect grammar, vocabulary and coherence throughout.	Uses precise vocabulary with a few minor errors.	Contains frequent errors affecting clarity.	Shows several major errors in spelling and punctuation, making it almost impossible to understand what would have otherwise been said.

This rubric emphasizes the ways in which learners use AI-generated seismic dashboards as artifacts of communication rather than merely reading and reporting out model outputs, and encourages them to turn their sophisticated forecasts into actionable English messages for real stakeholders. This coincides with an ESP–EMI perspective where students need to continually interpret dynamic risk layers, rationalize emerging alert statuses, and render probabilistic decision-making legible to diverse stakeholders, as is the case of emergency operations centers in Taiwan's integrated systems that layer satellite imagery, UAV feeds, IoT sensor data and AI analytics for real-time multi-hazard monitoring (Saving Lives: Taiwan's Integrated Disaster Management 2025).

In PBL designs, AIA and technology-enhanced environment have already demonstrated successful engagement of student in digital tools while they are immersed in an authentic multi-step task. Research into technology-supported PBL in writing lessons, for example, demonstrates that students may be more engaged, motivated and collaborative when they employ real software/sites and media to plan, draft and revise artefact(s) rather than work with decontextualized prompts. You can imagine this as applying to disaster-ready EMI contexts, where dashboards and AI-generated risk maps might underpin projects such as writing English situation reports, creating bilingual warning messages or compiling briefing slides for mock coordination meetings and in which language learning is embedded within 'realistic', data-laden workflows.

Such dashboard led learning tasks are also congruent with recent evidence that AI and digital technology is most effective when they facilitate higher order thinking and decision making, rather than just low level practice. Teachers in training found AI technology useful to: generate ideas; evaluate drafts; modify language for specific audiences, although this was contingent on clear project stages and reflection activities. By extension, EMI assignments that require students to question AI-generated hazards outputs, explain thresholding decisions (for instance, when not to evacuate), and articulate residual uncertainties in English situate these AIs as triggers for critical language use—an interface between Taiwan's high-tech disaster provisions and classroom-based ESP education.

Navigating Uncertainty: Simulating Threshold-Based Decision Making in English-Mediated Disaster Scenarios

Threshold-based decision making forms the core of both seismic AI systems and actual disaster communication, offering a strong precedent for EMI project research. The recent deep learning models for tsunami, predict alert levels from offshore signals by updated alerts according to new observation and consider a false alarm rate in tradeoff with missing event through calibrated threshold. This logic of responding to with partial information by increasing, decreasing or holding warning levels consistent as knowledge changes is also reflected in how professionals need to communicate their warnings, situation updates and clarifications in English under time pressure during events such as a large coastal earthquake.

In the classroom, some of these threshold dynamics can be replicated by project assignments where students are given stepped AI-generated risk information and need to update their English responses. Compare these findings to scenario-based training studies in which emergency readiness students engage in a staging curriculum practice, making decisions and talking through communications under time constraints, as opposed to simply memorizing protocols. In a course like EMI–ESP, such situations would entail lowering level alerts by students, changing messages when the model output crosses critical thresholds and justifying choices (e.g., of when to escalate evacuation language) which acknowledges uncertainties, in effect translating probabilistic thresholds into rhetorical content.

These simulations also adhere to broader guidance for emergency communication, which stresses the need to be clear, consistent and honest about uncertainty when under stress. Communication strategies guidelines emphasize the need to communicate the urgency of the situation, to avoid panicking and explain what is known and unknown that messages should fit with unfolding events (Federal Emergency Management Agency 2014). When EMI projects expect their learners to explain shifting risk levels, hedge forecasts, and answer stakeholders' questions in English, they are engaging directly with the thresholding-reasoning and navigating-uncertainty built into seismic AI systems and filling in the gap between technical dashboards and human-based disaster discourse.

Bridging the "Static-Dynamic" Divide: Addressing the Gap in Taiwan's Disaster-Ready Professional Preparation

This is what Taiwan's disaster management looks like today — an extremely agile, AI-integrated model which we call a "multi-hazard system" that integrates real-time satellite imagery and UAV feeds into hydrologic sensors and AI-based analytics on shared platforms using them universally for fast decision-making. "The case studies demonstrate how national databases and AI-predictive simulations are the basis of the early warning, cross-agency coordination, and scenario-coverage planning for floods, landslides, and earthquakes that make Taiwan an innovative regional leader in proactive resilience based on data" (Saving Lives: Taiwan's Integrated Disaster Management 2025). This rapidly evolving landscape is placing substantive communications demands—such as translating risk that shifts by the hour, reporting across sectors and languages, etc.—on professionals for whom language preparation remains largely static.

In contrast, however, recent overviews of ESP practice have it that needs analysis and course design for EAP continue to be based very much on tradition-specific models such as target situation analysis and genre-based mapping, often translated into one-off research studies that in turn "feed" specific syllabuses. These reviews testify to the fact that, while ESP research has diversified in its field-specific contexts, the core design logic remains mostly linear: outcomes, texts and tasks are either pre-specified or 'framed' at the initial stages of a course with limited provision for systematically re-aligning curricula as contexts or stakeholder needs change. In Taiwan's disaster-prepared disciplines, this translates to English-mediated courses possibly being able to successfully cover "standard" technical vocabulary and report genres, but failing to keep up with quickly evolving AI tools, dashboards and operational procedures incorporated into national disaster systems.

Filling this "static–dynamic" gap, re-education in both ESP and EMI must be reconceptualized to have it interface effectively with Taiwan's AI-enhanced disaster infrastructure. Findings from this study seem to rely on curriculum design that includes timely data-informed revision, similar in spirit to how national platforms refresh their hazard layers, such that project tasks, assessment criteria and language foci represent the tools and protocols now in use rather than products of legacy scenarios. Systematic analysis of ESP needs proposes the adoption of flexible, iterative and multi-source models that effectively accommodate stakeholders over a period, for which an EMI design with disaster response focus could provide a theoretical basis. In practice this means that I want to construct steady and evolving feedback loops with agencies and dashboards, using their changing data streams to power EMI projects which teach professionals how better to communicate in Taiwan's living, AI-mediated risk landscape.

Beyond the "Classroom Tool": AI as a Structural Principle for PBL Design in High-Risk Contexts

Most of the current research on AI and ENL is work which situates AI as a supporting classroom tool rather than as an architectural design principle. According to systematic reviews concerning AI use in education, grammar checkers, chatbots, intelligent tutoring systems and writing assistants currently rule the AI roost – all mostly fitted into a pre-existing lesson format for improving accuracy or fluency or engagement (Kress, 2003). This tools-first approach risks leaving core pedagogical structures of curriculum - such as task sequenc- ing, assessment logic, or project architecture—relatively unaltered even in high stakes environments where learners need to work in AI-mediated risk scenarios.

Logics of Continuous Update AI forecasting systems, in high-risk, seismic areas like Taiwan, offer a different paradigm: they realize logics of continuous updating and probabilistic reasoning that can become blueprints for project-based learning designs themselves -embodied as scenario-based decision support. Studies on AI-empowered PBL in English point to design factors, such as instant feedback, dynamic pathways, and authentic context are believed to be important for developing language ability, motivation and soft. When PBL projects for disaster-ready professionals are constructed around these "bones" — rather than just plopping AI tools on top of standard fare — they can better reproduce the uncertainty, iteration and complexity involved in working with seismic dashboards and alert systems.

Articulating AI as a structural principle therefore entails designing EMI–ESP projects in which predictive logic, rather than single apps, shapes the entire learning environment. In those designs, students don't just query chatbots for language help; they reenact the workflows of AI-backed disaster management: interpreting changing model outputs, updating English-language briefings when thresholds change and making decisions as part of a team under time pressure. Recent policy and technical documents on AI for natural disasters management emphasize that successful AI solutions must incorporate models, communications, decision support into integrated systems rather than silos of tools (International Telecommunication Union, 2023). Taking the system-level perspective of AI as the backbone of PBL design then ensures that classroom projects are better connected with the complexities invoked in current seismic response and facilitates – at a solid professional level – for Taiwanese to take part linguistically and cognitively in complex, high-risk scenes.

Scaffolding "Seismic Literacy": Preparing Taiwanese Professionals to Interpret and Communicate AI Forecasts

In this situation, how can one measure "seismic literacy" in this case, and to what extent can you understand what you just read? The curriculum uses a multi-dimensional assessment rubric to analyze/measure/separate literacy into different types using a set/standard/criteria against the learner. Measures are quantitative in terms of pre/post-test and the actual extent of interpreting the AI visuals by stating what the depth or focus of the inundation is (heat map) and how precisely the Solicitor articulated "uncertainty talk" in his/her briefing. The qualitative analysis is done by a discourse analyst on the student's simulation, prosecution, and defense discourse, in particular the frequency of hedge and booster use to justify legal probabilistic risks to Stakeholders. General proficiency is the focus of this empirical approach and reduces the analysis to the particular competence required to process/calculate/act on AI disaster data in real-time.

Table 3. Seismic Literacy Competencies for EMI-ESP in Taiwan

Competency	Example Task	Relevant AI Data Source
Interpreting dashboards	Assess overlays of up-to-date risks to focus on areas at high risk and prepare situation reports.	Taiwan's integrated platforms
Explaining thresholds	Training simulations Briefings Need to present alert level decisions in response to evolving model outputs	Tsunami inundation models
Communicating uncertainty	Describe model restrictions and remaining uncertainties for lay public in English advisories	RT-MEMS aftershock catalogs
Coordinating multilingual stakeholders	Develop bilingual scenario-based briefings for cross-agency responders	Landslide inventory maps

This table compounds seismic literacy into a communicative skill for modern Taiwanese disaster professionals, by placing EMI–ESP pedagogy in the context of AI-driven workflows, wherein practitioners can rehearse generating stakeholder-ready English discourse overnight from raw model output. Scaffolding "seismic literacy" within Taiwanese ESP–EMI classrooms is more than familiarization of pertinent technical details around AI systems, but also to be trained in the interpretation and explainability of forecasts, thresholds, uncertainties before wide range of audiences utilizing English. Pan-international guidance on AI for managing natural disasters maintains that the outputs of AI, whether these are presented as dashboards or hazard maps or in through automated alerts and other such like functions—that these only enhance safety when translated into messages which a stakeholder can interpret and act upon (International Telecommunication Union 2023). This places us in the territory of AI-assisted forecasting as a core skill for employment: learners should be proficient at reading shifting risk indicators, explaining their consequences and communicating limitations as well as residual uncertainties charismatically under pressure.

From a DRC perspective, this communicative job is connected with a number of moving parts: content of the message, credibility of who sends the message, features of who receives it and in what channel, and societal contexts. In a systematic review of models of disaster risk communication, 115 inter-related components across content, sender, receiver, environment and process dimensions are identified emphasising that effective risk communication is not achieved solely by technical correctness but also through clarity, trustworthiness, audience targeting and mechanisms for feedback. In EMI–ESP programs, seismic literacy thus encompasses the ability to select readeable registers, substantiate decisions made from AI outputs and adapt explanations to non-expert stakeholders in Englishwhile continuing to allude to probabilistic forecasts and model uncertainties.

Linking these skills to project-based curricula enables learners to practice the complete communicative cycle around AI predictions rather than about language alone. For instance, projects might involve a sequence in which students interpret AI-generated warnings of tsunamis or landslides, author and revise situation reports in English of an escalating situation, and role play briefings that include fielding questions about model reliability, false alarms and trade-offs between precaution and overreaction. Recent experiments with AI-based project preparatio nin educational settings suggest that participants are not just learning to work with technology, but also to explain and contextualize technical outputs for real audiences in when they are incorporated into designed projects. Framed in this way, seismic literacy is a communicative skill: what it means to "talk through" AI-facilitated predictions in globally intelligible English within the context of Taiwan's disaster-ready professional identity writ large.

A Prototype Framework for Taiwan: Integrating Real-Time Seismic Data into Project-Based ESP Assessment

Rather than being elaborated add-ons, real-time seismic and landslide data are regarded as endemic input into the ESP project design or assessment process, as laid out in the proposed prototype framework for Taiwan. AI-based investigations in the aftermath of the 2024 Hualien Earthquake report that models are capable of mapping thousands of landslides within hours to days from satellite data acquisition leading to maps used for updating both situational awareness and longer-term hazard models. This quick, data-rich output of this sort serves as a perfect medium for ESP-assessment tasks within the context of EMI classrooms where students interpret developing maps and write English language briefings and justify their decisions as to areas for risk reduction based on priority through graded project cycles.

In the prototype, validation is framed as a kind of feedback loop that runs parallel to AI model training. Like models of seismicity and tsunamis, these student projects can be run with historical events or "blindly" using genuine hazard sources such as bulletins or experts' reports about the Dapu or Hualien earthquake. Based on assessment principles in ESP that highlight the importance of target-situation and evaluation-criterion congruence, this practice also regards discrepancies between student outputs against expert benchmarks as evidence for focused feedback, thus guiding subsequent rounds of task revision and language assistance (Park, 2020). Thus, evaluation becomes a dynamic endpoint and not a static one, since it constantly calibrates between students (and their scaffolding), as well as between the curriculum designers.

This model also incorporates ESP program-level needs analysis in progress, to ensure that the selected seismic datasets, genres, and communicative tasks remain up-to-date in terms of Taiwan's emerging disaster management landscape. A recent systematic review of ESP needs analysis in higher education emphasizes the need for iterative, multi-method approaches, that take into account stakeholder expectations and disciplinary changes over time (as opposed to relying on one-off surveys). Married with these adaptive needs analysis procedures from the bilingual EMI–ESP language testing environment are live or replayed outputs for seismic AI which give Taiwanese education programs in this field a model that is both strutted and flexed: projects and assessments are recalibrated against regular intervals to current hazards, tools again, professional discourse – learners' English performance remains articulated closely to the realities of AI-mediated disaster work.

Equity and Inclusion Considerations

Although the CDADNA cycle and the seismic AI-inspired ESP-EMI approach are tailored to Taiwan's high-seismic risk context, generalizability of their design allows for various profiles of learners and stakeholders. Further, because each cycle of learner contribution, peer communication and stakeholder feedback is treated as a new set of "input streams," the curriculum can be purposes for distinct English proficiency levels in the field of disaster — beginners (novices), intermediates or advanced users in preparing EADCs. Moreover, project briefs may deliberately include local languages as well as English, for instance bilingual warning messages or parallel situation reports so that students develop the ability to switch registers between community members, local officials and regional/ international agencies.

In addition, the framework is applicable to other high-risk areas outside of Taiwan. In coastal and seismic (i.e., Australia) or tsunami-prone area in other regions like Japan, Indonesia or Mediterranean, local hazard models, dashboards, guideline/decision policies can replace Taiwanese data while keeping the same adaptive logic for continuous data assimilation, scenario simulation and threshold-based decision making. This transferability also implies that the ESP-EMIs project can be adapted to alternative governance systems, language ecologies and community risk profiles for the purpose of enabling more inclusive disaster communication training in many different AI rich risk environments.

Implementation Challenges: Institutional and Human Constraints

Even though there are clear technical benefits of integrating seismic AI with ESP, there are clear institutional challenges in integrating this framework.

- Staff Development and Interdisciplinary Friction: The majority of language AI framework Seismic ESP specialists have strong linguistic capabilities and limited AI skills, whereas seismic specialists frequently lack teaching skills in a language and therefore, this 'expertise gap' calls for a special community of practice (CoP) in which teachers are not trained to code, but trained to think about AI in terms of classroom exercises

- The Gap between Curriculum Development and Approved Curriculum and Real-time Data: Most universities have governance systems with approval for curriculum changes that take multiple years, which creates a systemic incompatibility with a 'real-time' updating curriculum. For the CDADNA framework to be effective, universities need to have 'Agile Course Outlines' which allows for content to be updated in 'chunks' without the need to go through a full departmental revision.
- Access to Data and the Cost of Infrastructure: While there are open-source models, other relevant countries' real-time data may be proprietary and may be subject to security protocols. In addition, the less funded department must bear the costs of the infrastructure needed to support the high bandwidth necessary for real-time AI language lab dashboards.

CONCLUSION

This paper has advocated or Taiwan's rapidly evolving seismic AI ecosystem not only as a technological backdrop, but also serves as a structural framework for flipping ESP and EMI curricula into adaptive data-rich systems. By comparison with curriculum features such as continuous data assimilation, real-time updating, the triggering of alerts, and explicit management of uncertainty, the chapter introduced the CDADNA mechanism as well as a seismic AI–inspired PBL framework that shift from linear to survey-driven course design. In the process, it filled a significant void between advanced-national AI-forecast infrastructures and less-prevalent dynamic disaster English preparedness for engineers, emergency mangers, and other high-risk professionals in Taiwan environments.

As a prototype, it illustrates how real-world seismic and tsunami data such as the Dapu and Hualien earthquake events can be situated within EMI project cycle/build-test loop/dynamic needs analysis in an effort to stimulate seismic literacy beyond communicative competence regarding seismic events (i.e., technical ability). Activities such as reading between the lines of AI-generated dashboards, modelling decision making around threshold-based warnings and framing discussions of risk trade-offs in global English were centred as key learning activities rather than an add-on. Aggregated across the results, the study indicated that where ESP assessment is harnessed to logics of AI-style version agility (comparing learner outputs with professional models and re-calibrating support) curricula can better approximate the decision-making costs and discursive demands in real disaster operations.

At the same time, the chapter contributes to larger debates about AI in language education by shifting discourse around AI as an instrumental classroom "tool" toward a generative design principle for project architecture in high-risk domains. Intsead of these being used in isolation, the proposed framework calls for EMI teachers and ESP designers to design curricula with policy actors where predictive reasoning, uncertainty navigation and multi-stakeholder risk communication are foregrounded as language learning outcomes. This conceptual work sets the stage for future research with designbased implementation studies, stakeholder co-design workshops and empirical evaluations of real and simulated disaster-interface learner performance, to better theorize how seismic AI logics might scaffold ethically-wrought English that relieve local-area communities to be readier in disaster than if they had less-access en route to ready-English such as that carved out for professionals working in AI-tended places.

Recommendation

The seismic AI–motivated ESP framework described above should be enacted in Taiwan starting with small-scale, design-based pilots in EMI courses for engineers, emergency managers and local officials from high-risk areas. Programs might begin with the support of a small number of such polished PBL cycles, perhaps only one or two in total, that leverage such authentic hosts as seismic dashboards plus CDADNA to dynamically manipulate project difficulty, genre focus and feedback on the basis of learner performance according to learning needs. Institutions should fund interdisciplinary teams comprised of EMI content instructors, ESP subject area specialists and data/IT staff so that real-time (or archived) hazard data streams are technically available and pedagogically scaffolded to ensure "seismic literacy" is intentionally developed as an integrated communicative competence activity rather than a single event.

The paper suggests that for policy makers and educators AI-mediated disaster communication be formally acknowledged as a strategic learning outcome in national EMI (emergency management instruction) and professional development guidelines. Ministries, accreditation bodies and disaster management agencies in Taiwan need to jointly develop guidelines that will encourage universities and training centers to clean ESP curricula against existing multi-hazard dashboards and AI tools, making incentives for cross-agency co-operations and shared data access protocols. This could include pilot programs, joint curriculum taskforces and AI-informed quality standards for disaster readiness, that put language preparedness on par with investments being made in AI-enhanced early warning and response systems.

Subsequent studies would in turn move from theorisation toward real-world, application of AI- based PBL models and applications for learning and training environments. Crucial research topics will be comparisons over time between conventional ESP/EMI curricula and AI-augmented, hazard-based curricula on quality of scenario writing, oral briefing, explanation of uncertainty issues with clarity in English when under stress to explain a lack of clock time in decision-making. Mixed-methods research might help to enhance and confirm the CDADNA framework by combining data on performance, learners′ perspectives, stakeholders' perspectives and the discourse analysis of project outputs. Such work would also reveal the AI datase ts and task type s that most contribute to learning gains, as well as address important ethical concerns regarding the dependence on AI and data governance in educational real-time hazard system uses.

REFERENCES

Federal Emergency Management Agency. (2014). *Crisis and emergency risk communication (CERC) manual.* U.S. Department of Health and Human Services, Centers for Disease Control and Prevention. https://emergency.cdc.gov/cerc/

International Telecommunication Union. (2023). *AI for natural disaster management.* International Telecommunication Union. https://www.itu.int/en/ITU-T/AI/Pages/ai-natural-disaster.aspx

Kress, G. (2003). *Literacy in the new media age*. Routledge.

Lives, S. Taiwan's integrated disaster management. (2025, September 18). *MundoGEO*. https://mundogeo.com/en/2025/09/18/saving-lives-taiwans-integrated-disaster-management/

Park, E. J. (2020). Methods needs analysis for the development of ESP course. *Teaching English with Technology, 20*(2), 3–23. https://files.eric.ed.gov/fulltext/EJ1314910.pdf

Patton, M. Q. (2015). *Qualitative research & evaluation methods: Integrating theory and practice* (4th ed.). SAGE Publications.

UNCTAD. (2025). *Technology and innovation report: AI in disaster risk reduction*. United Nations Conference on Trade and Development. https://unctad.org/publication/technology-and-innovation-report

Chapter 7
Fundamentals of Time-Series Analysis and Feature Engineering for Geophysical Data

Ravi Manocha
http://orcid.org/0009-0007-6401-7871
Lovely Professional University, India

Manzoor A. Khanday
http://orcid.org/0000-0002-0053-098X
Lovely Professional University, India

Shriya Manocha
Lovely Professional University, India

ABSTRACT

Time-Series Analysis is essential to know and predict how the Earth system will behave as a result of earthquakes, volcanic eruptions, and tsunamis. Current geophysical observation is based on the use of continuous Geophysical Sensor Data from seismic networks, GPS arrays, InSAR satellites, and ocean buoys, thus, it calls for advanced analytical approaches. This chapter provides the most important Signal Processing and Feature Engineering techniques that can be used in the Earth sciences, such as

DOI: 10.4018/979-8-3373-8042-1.ch007

time-domain, frequency-domain, and Time–Frequency Analysis methods like wavelet transforms. Additionally, it features the concept of representation learning in Machine Learning for Earth Sciences, along with the examples of its use in Hazard Monitoring and Early Warning Systems.

1. INTRODUCTION

Geophysical monitoring networks produce vast amounts of time-series data from Global Navigation Satellite Systems (GNSS), seismometers, satellite interferometry (InSAR) and ocean sensors. These observations capture dynamic processes of the Earth system such as tectonic deformations, seismic wave propagation, volcanic processes and ocean-atmosphere interactions. As these processes span a range of spatial and temporal scales, geophysical time series often contain both deterministic and non-random (stochastic) components in the same record, including trends, periodicities, transient events, and noise.

A fundamental challenge in the analysis of geophysical time series is that many are non-stationary: the mean, variance, spectral content or correlation structure of the time series varies in time. They are also often non-white (i.e. correlated) noise, meaning that the noise power is not equal across the frequency spectrum. This can present challenges to extracting physically meaningful signals using traditional methods that favor stationarity and low noise levels.

While there are many methods for time-series analysis, a gap exists in connecting signal decomposition, feature engineering and data-driven modelling in a practical method that can be applied to geophysical data. While many studies focus on isolated parts - such as spectral analysis, wavelet transforms or machine learning - there is a lack of studies that explain how preprocessing, multiscale analysis, feature engineering, and modelling can be combined to enable hazard-oriented interpretation.

This chapter fills the gap with a practical overview of the methods for time-series analysis and feature engineering of geophysical data, focusing on multiscale decomposition of signals and machine-learning-ready feature representations. It provides guidance on how to use wavelet transforms,

Singular Spectrum Analysis (SSA), nuclear norm minimization and other data-adaptive techniques to enhance the detection, description and prediction of geophysical signals in noisy data.

The techniques are applied to three applications:

- Crustal deformation monitoring by Global Navigation Satellite Systems (GNSS) time-series.
- Wavelet-based earthquake detection.
- Variability of historical tsunami run-up.

These examples demonstrate how time-series analysis and feature engineering can help hazard monitoring and early warning processes by transforming the raw data collected by sensors into meaningful, actionable features.

2. CONCEPT OF STATIONARITY AND NON-STATIONARY GEOPHYSICAL SIGNALS

Geophysical monitoring networks (e.g. GNSS, seismometers and satellites) can measure time-series observations that capture Earth deformation. These measurements reflect deformation of the Earth, propagation of seismic waves, hydrologic loads, volcanic activity and ocean loads. But, unlike some idealized statistical time series, geophysical data are not always stable for the duration of observations. They typically include components with varying long- and short-term evolution, and non-stationarity is commonplace.

A time series can be described as stationary when its statistical properties such as mean, variance, and autocorrelation remain constant over time. Formally, a weakly stationary process satisfies:

- $E[X_t] = \mu$ (constant mean)
- $Var(X_t) = \sigma^2$ (constant variance)
- $Cov(X_t, X_{t+k}) = \gamma(k)$ depends only on lag k, not on time t

where μ is the constant mean, σ^2 is the constant variance, and the autocovariance $\gamma(k)$ depends only on the time lag k, not on the absolute time t.

In this case, μ is the constant mean, σ^2 is the constant variance and $\gamma(h)$ is the autocovariance function. Stationarity is equivalent to the dependence between two observations being a function of the lag between them, rather than of the actual time (or index) of observation.

Most geophysical signals do not satisfy this condition because of changes in forcing (from the environment and tectonic motion), changes in instrumentation and, occasionally, episodic events. This leads to trends, seasonal variations, shifts, and bursts in the data, which need to be removed before the data are interpreted or modelled.

Examples:

- GNSS displacement data contain plate motions, as well as seasonal changes in the Earth's surface due to water and land masses.
- Earthquake signals consist of short-term bursts due to earthquakes.
- Ocean signals consist of bursts due to ocean waves, as well as storms.

An additional factor is colored noise. Colored noise in geophysical time series is correlated noise that has a power spectrum that is not constant with frequency (white noise). It can be found in GNSS coordinate time series and seismic data because errors, environmental loading and other site-specific effects are often correlated. Colored noise may distort trends in deformation or hide low amplitude seismic signals if unaccounted for (Williams, 2003; Langbein & Johnson, 1997; Li et al., 2020).

The most common types of colored noise are:

- Red noise, with a greater amplitude of lower frequencies.
- Pink noise, in which power falls off with increasing frequency.
- Blue noise, in which high frequencies have more power.

Geophysical data comprises a combination of trends, seasonal cycles, transients and correlated noise, so it requires techniques that can distinguish between the physical structure and random noise. Data-adaptive decomposition techniques are those that infer the components of the signal from the data rather than assuming a model for the signal. These techniques can separate deterministic geophysical processes from noise, and are thus helpful in geodetic studies, seismology, and environmental time-series analysis (Yiou et al., 2000; Jasir et al., 2024).

3. CLASSICAL TIME-SERIES ANALYSIS METHOD

Traditional time-series analysis is an important first step in finding trends, correlations and periodicities in time-series data. Geophysical studies often use these techniques to analyze seismic data, GNSS displacement measurements and environmental data prior to more specialized multiscale or machine-learning techniques.

3.1. Time Domain Analysis

Time-domain analysis involves analysing observations in their original time sequence and is helpful for detecting trends, abrupt changes, and transient events. For instance, time series of displacement from GNSS stations may include long-term tectonic deformation, seasonal variation and short-term variability. Accurately understanding these components is critical for studying deformation and estimating seismic-hazard.

Offset and change-point detection methods are commonly applied to detect abrupt changes in GNSS time series, such as those resulting from earthquakes, instrumentation changes and reference-frame shifts. Large intercomparison studies have demonstrated the need for offset detection in the interpretation of GPS time series (Gazeaux et al., 2013), and continuous GNSS error-analysis methods help to deal with gaps in observations and temporal correlation (Bos et al., 2013).

Time-domain methods are also used to analyze seismographic wave-forms. Amplitude, shape or timing features of the waveform can be used to enhance seismic signal detection and classification in noisy data (Li et al., 2020; Arul & Kareem, 2021).

3.2. Spectral Analysis

Spectral analysis is used to characterize the frequency content of signals. Periodograms and spectral density estimates can thus be used to identify periodic forcing of geophysical observations.

For example, seasonal signals can be identified in GNSS observations due to surface loading, while seismic observations can contain periodic signals due to oceanic microseisms or atmospheric forcing. In seismology, waveform-feature extraction and time-frequency analysis using wavelets help to separate subtle event signals from noise (Li et al., 2020; Wang et al., 2017).

However, traditional spectral techniques typically assume that the time-frequency content is invariant. This limits the effectiveness of this approach when signals involve short-duration events or time-varying frequency content, motivating the need for multiscale approaches, like wavelet analysis.

3.3. Autocorrelation and Partial Correlation

An autocorrelation and partial autocorrelation (ACF and PACF) function shows the dependency structure of a geophysical time series. Autocorrelation is a measure of correlation between observations separated by a certain time lag, and therefore measures the memory of the system.

For example, GNSS displacement time series can display a high low-frequency correlation because of long-term tectonic stress, hydrologic and seasonal effects, while earthquakes typically have a shorter correlation length due to rapidly changing environmental effects.

Partial autocorrelation takes this a step further in terms of measuring the direct correlation at a specific lag, conditional on intermediary observations. These functions help determine appropriate autoregressive and ARMA (or ARIMA) models.

In geophysics, trends in autocorrelation decay provide clues as to whether the signal is dominated by random noise, colored noise, long-term cycles or deterministic trends. These tools help decide on whether to preprocess the data and if more sophisticated decomposition and time-frequency techniques are needed.

3.4. Transition to Multiscale Signal Analysis

Traditional time-series analysis methods offer valuable summaries of trends, correlations and dominant frequencies, but can be too simplistic for rapidly changing geophysical signals and signals with transient, localized features. A seismic trace, for instance, might contain a brief P-wave arrival amidst noise and a GNSS time series might contain permanent, seasonal and episodic components.

In such cases, it is necessary to consider both time and frequency information. Multiresolution analysis, which can be achieved with wavelet transforms, offers this, making wavelet transforms particularly useful for non-stationary geophysical signals.

4. WAVELET THEORY FOR GEOPHYSICAL APPLICATIONS

Wavelet transforms are popular in geophysical applications because they are a local time-frequency transform. Kumar and Foufoula-Georgiou (1997) first showed the usefulness of wavelets for multiscale hydrologic and geophysical systems, while Yiou et al. (2000) demonstrated the ability to adaptively use wavelets and singular-spectrum methods to detect non-linearities in climate and other geophysical time series. Recent research has also used wavelets to analyze noisy Global Navigation Satellite Systems (GNSS) data and deformation (Ji et al., 2020; Cucci et al., 2023).

Wavelets are ideal for seismic applications as earthquake signals are often transient and localized in time and frequency. Wang (2015) and Wang et al. (2017) introduced generalized seismic wavelets to enhance time-frequency resolution and Cabrera-Navarrete et al. (2020) used wavelets to analyze seismic reflection data and to perform spectral inversion for seismic interpretation.

Wavelets have also been applied in conjunction with machine-learning. Carbonari et al. (2023) applied machine-learning-assisted wavelet-like denoising to enhance the detection of volcanic deformation in Global Navigation Satellite System (GNSS) time series, while Ji et al. (2020) showed that weighted-wavelets can be used to separate signals from GNSS position data.

For real-time earthquake monitoring, wavelet-based P-wave detection in high-rate GNSS data has been suggested to help to timely detect signals from tsunamigenic earthquakes (Sudrajat et al., 2025). Such studies demonstrate wavelets work best when the signal of interest is short-lived, localised, and noisy.

4.1. Wavelet Parameter Selection

Whilst the wavelet technique is very sensitive to practical considerations such as the mother wavelet, decomposition level and scale range. The mother wavelet controls the shape of the basis function, and should be similar to the feature being identified. Morlets are often well matched to oscillatory and continuous time-frequency analysis, while Daubechies are well suited to sudden amplitude variations, and short transient features in seismograms (Wang, 2015; Wang et al., 2017).

Appropriate scale should consider the duration and frequency of the geophysical process of interest. For example, short scales will detect high-frequency features such as seismic wave arrivals, whereas longer scales will detect low-frequency features, such as annual deformation in GNSS observations. It's worth testing sensitivity to adjacent scales as event detection can vary with too small a scale range or an inappropriate choice of wavelet (to represent the data morphology) (Ji et al., 2020; Cucci et al., 2023).

5. DATA ADAPTIVE DECOMPOSITION METHOD

Data-adaptive decomposition methods are also used to study non-stationary geophysical time series in addition to using wavelet analysis.

These separate the observations into various components that represent long-term trends, periodic oscillations, transients and random noise without a priori knowledge of the signal.

Singular Spectrum Analysis (SSA) is a decomposition technique that involves forming a trajectory matrix from a time series and performing eigenvalue decomposition. It is an effective method for filtering out smooth trends and periodic signals in GNSS and InSAR deformation measurements. For instance, Jasir et al. (2024) applied SSA to model post-seismic deformation after the 2019 Mw 6 Mirpur earthquake, and Yiou et al. (2000) connected multiscale SSA with the nonlinear geophysical signal analysis.

Nuclear norm minimization is a low-rank matrix approximation method, which treats the time series as a matrix, and captures dominant low-rank structures while removing noise. Chen et al. (2020) demonstrated that weighted nuclear norm minimization can be used to recover seasonal signals in GNSS coordinate time series, so it is a good choice if periodic or low-rank structure is present and needs to be distinguished from observing noise.

In application, wavelet transforms are best if the signal of interest is a transient localized signal like a seismic arrival. SSA is the best choice when the task is to extract trends and periodic signals, such as tectonic and seasonal loading. Nuclear norm minimization is most useful when repeated seasonal or low-rank patterns must be recovered from noisy GNSS-style matrices. So, the choice of method should be based on the physics of the signal and modelling goals.

6. FEATURE ENGINEERING FOR GEOPHYSICAL TIME SERIES

Feature engineering transforms raw geophysical data into features that can be used by statistical or machine-learning algorithms. Good features retain physically relevant information and condense the information content of a long and noisy time series.

Geophysical time series features can be classified into many domains:

Table 1. Taxonomy of feature domains used in geophysical time-series analysis

Feature Domain	Examples	Applications
Time-domain features	Mean, variance, skewness	Trend detection
Frequency-domain features	Spectral peaks, power density	Periodic process identification
Time-frequency features	Wavelet coefficients	Seismic event detection
Shape-based features	Shapelet, motifs	Signal classification

Table 1 lists typical features of geophysical time series. Time-domain features capture central tendency, variability and trends; frequency-domain features capture periodic behaviour in signals; time-frequency features capture transient energy; and shape features represent patterns in signals. These features provide model inputs for trend analysis, event and anomaly detection, and classification, by transforming observations into useful features.

Feature extraction using shapelet occurs when a pattern of the waveform is more informative than the entire waveform. Arul and Kareem (2021) demonstrated shapelet transforms can assist with the classification of earthquake, wind and wave time series through discovering discriminative local patterns.

Machine-learning-assisted feature engineering is also helpful for GNSS anomaly detection and deformation prediction. For instance, Carbonari et al. (2023) demonstrated the use of machine-learning-based denoising of GNSS for deformation analysis, and Ji et al. (2020) demonstrated that weighted wavelet features can be used to enhance signal extraction from GNSS position time series.

7. MACHINE LEARNING APPROACH FOR TIME SERIES MODELLING

Machine-learning algorithms can learn complex nonlinear relationships that can be difficult to model using traditional statistical methods. They are applied in geophysics for seismic classification, deformation predictions, anomaly detection and pattern recognition in relation to hazards by using support vector machines, ensemble models, neural networks and hybrid signal processing.

The main factor limiting their use is a lack of data. Supervised techniques require labelled data, but the number of large earthquake events, volcanic unrest periods, and tsunami events are less frequent than non-earthquake/volcano/tsunami events. This means that small-to-medium sized datasets are best served by interpretable models like logistic regression, support vector machines, random forests or gradient boosting, if the features are carefully chosen.

Deep learning approaches tend to have more parameters and typically need larger labelled datasets, or transfer-learning techniques. In geophysics this means that large datasets are hard to find when rare events are involved, there is dense sensor coverage, or labels are interpreted by experts. Unsupervised (US) and semi-supervised (SS) approaches can be used to overcome some of these limitations but the results still need to be validated.

Recent research indicates that machine learning can be used to enhance event detection using signal-processing techniques such as wavelets. Combining ML with wavelets has improved volcanic deformation detection in GNSS time series (Carbonari et al., 2023; Ji et al., 2020) and waveform features and shapelet have improved event detection and classification in noise-ridden time series (Li et al., 2020; Arul & Kareem, 2021).

8. TYPICAL WORKFLOW FOR GEOPHYSICAL TIME-SERIES ANALYSIS

The typical workflow of geophysical time-series analysis takes data from observations to hazard information in four linked steps: preprocessing, decomposition, feature engineering and modelling. Preprocessing involves removing outliers, offsets, gaps and obvious noise; decomposition involves distinguishing trends, periodicities, transients, and residual variability; feature engineering involves converting these components into quantifiable features; and modelling involves relating the features to physical interpretation or classification or forecasting. This is shown in Figure 1.

Figure 1. Geophysical time-series analysis workflow

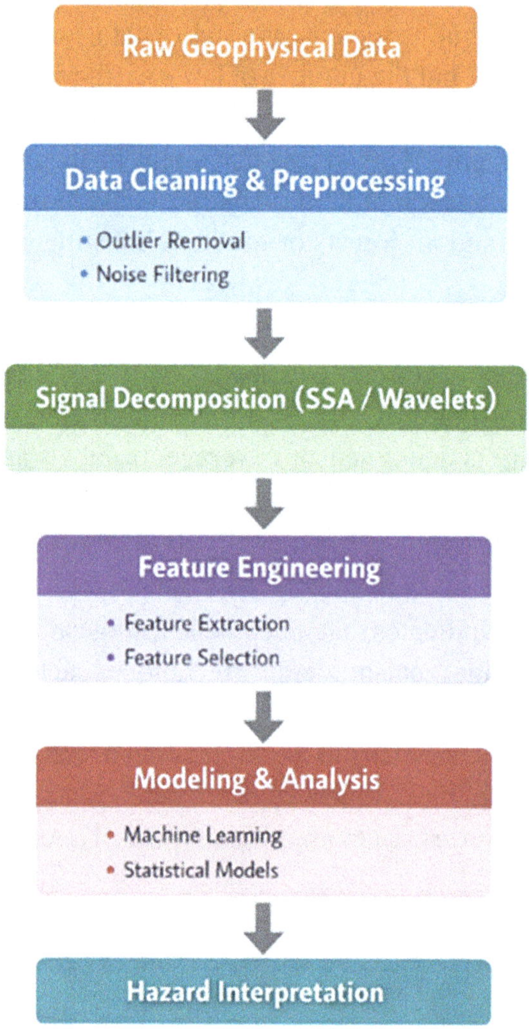

Figure 1 starts with the observations from GNSS receivers, seismometers, ocean sensors or satellites. The preprocessed stage enhances the quality of the data by adjusting biases, filtering spikes, imputing or flagging missing data and filtering.

The decomposition stage decomposes the signals into long-term trends, periodic (or seasonal) components, impulses and noise via methods such as singular spectrum analysis (SSA), wavelets or nuclear norm minimization. Feature engineering transforms these into statistical, spectral, time-frequency or shape-based features.

Then statistical or machine-learning algorithms use these features to detect patterns, classify events or predict hazard-related events. And the final step of interpretation links the results of the model to geophysical problems such as earthquake detection, tsunami hazard, volcanic deformation, or crustal deformation.

9. APPLICATIONS AND CASE STUDIES

9.1. CASE STUDY 1 - Crustal Deformation Analysis Using GNSS Daily Time-Series

In this case study we will look at crustal deformation using daily ground-motion data from a continuous GNSS receiver in the Earth Scope/UNAVCO network. Crustal deformation measured by GNSS instruments has three components: north-south, east-west and vertical.

The displacements reported in Table 2 are sample values from publicly available Earth Scope/UNAVCO GNSS-style data, and are only used as an example for this case study. The time series was assumed to be preprocessed for regular data processing steps, such as outlier removal, offset correction and detrending to remove long-term instrument drift. This helps to reduce the noise component that is likely to be of instrumental origin.

Of the three components, the vertical is typically more affected by environmental loading, such as groundwater storage, surface-water redistribution and air pressure. As a consequence, GNSS time series often show annual (and semi-annual) variations along with the tectonic trends.

The sample values in Table 2 have a vertical component with a mean of 5.63 mm and a variance of 0.21 mm^2. The linear regression for the time interval shown corresponds to an upward trend of around 0.18 mm per day. While the sample is brief and only illustrative, these measures indicate the trend is likely a gradual increase, not a random walk.

Table 2. Sample GNSS daily displacement time series (Station P143)

Date	North(mm)	East(mm)	Vertical(mm)
05-01-2018	2.61	-0.84	4.72
06-01-2018	3.15	-1.02	5.31
07-01-2018	2.94	-0.95	4.96
08-01-2018	3.40	-1.10	5.88
09-01-2018	2.77	-1.23	6.12
10-01-2018	2.89	-1.05	5.74
11-01-2018	3.22	-0.98	5.43
12-01-2018	3.11	-1.15	6.02
13-01-2018	3.34	-1.05	6.21
14-01-2018	3.08	-1.18	5.95

Table 2 shows daily variations in GNSS displacements over short time periods. The north and east components show only a small millimetre-scale variation, implying a rather consistent horizontal motion during the period. There is a more pronounced increase in the vertical component from 4.72 mm to 6.21 mm, followed by a fall to 5.95 mm. The enhanced variability is due to the larger influence of noise and correlated loading in vertical GNSS measurements.

Figure 2. GNSS vertical displacement time series

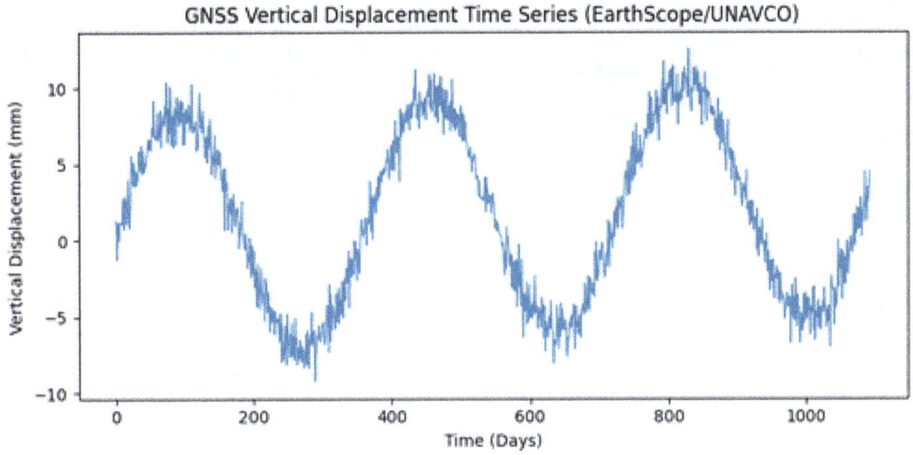

In Figure 2, time is on the x-axis and vertical displacement (in millimetres) on the y-axis. The slope of the trend line represents the estimated deformation, and the daily variation around the trend line represents the daily variation, seasonal or environmental loading, and coloured noise. The trend, as well as the residual variability, should be taken into account.

9.2. CASE STUDY 2 — Seismic Event Detection Using Wavelet Analysis

This case study shows how to identify seismic events from waveform data similar to data from the IRIS Global Seismographic Network (GSN). Seismometers measure ground motion (velocity or displacement) at a high sampling rate, so they can be used to investigate both the background seismic noise and abrupt arrivals of seismic energy from earthquakes.

Typically, a seismic record starts with a period of background noise. This is followed by an increase in amplitude due to the arrival of an earthquake signal. The earliest arrival is usually the primary or P wave, which is compressional energy that has travelled through the Earth.

Table 3. Representative IRIS seismic waveform segment (vertical component)

Time (s)	Amplitude (nm/s)
0.0	0.12
0.05	0.10
0.10	0.14
0.15	0.09
0.20	0.13
0.25	0.11
0.30	0.15
0.35	0.18
0.40	0.26
0.45	0.41
0.50	0.78
0.55	1.22
0.60	1.84
0.65	2.61
0.70	3.40
0.75	4.18

The numbers shown in Table 3 represent a change from background seismic noise to a seismic event. The amplitudes are low and consistent from 0.00 s to 0.35 s, after which they start to increase at 0.40 s and by 0.50 s they increase at a much faster rate. The step-like increase is indicative of a seismic arrival.

Figure 3. Seismic Waveform with P-wave Arrival (IRIS)

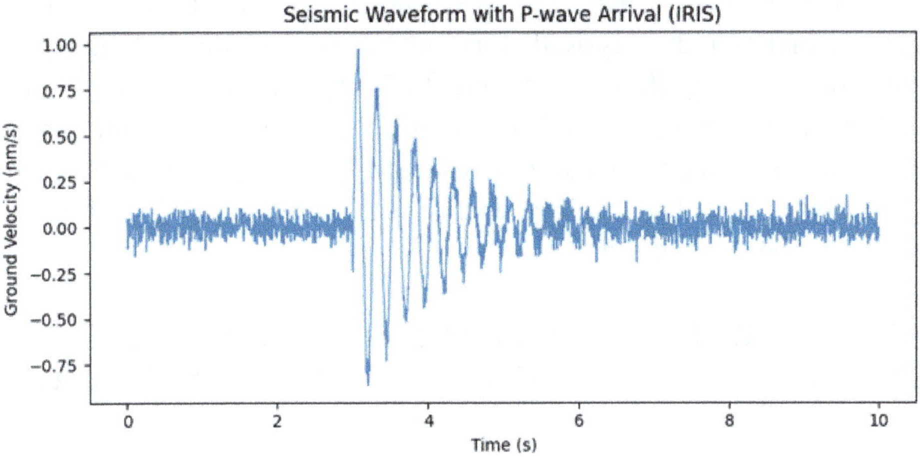

In Figure 3, time is on the horizontal axis and amplitude (ground velocity) is on the vertical axis. The sudden increase in amplitude corresponds to the onset of the seismic wave, and the following oscillations are the onset of the earthquake waveform. The event can be easily identified using the approximate onset time at 0.40 s.

Figure 4. Time-frequency representation of seismic signal (IRIS)

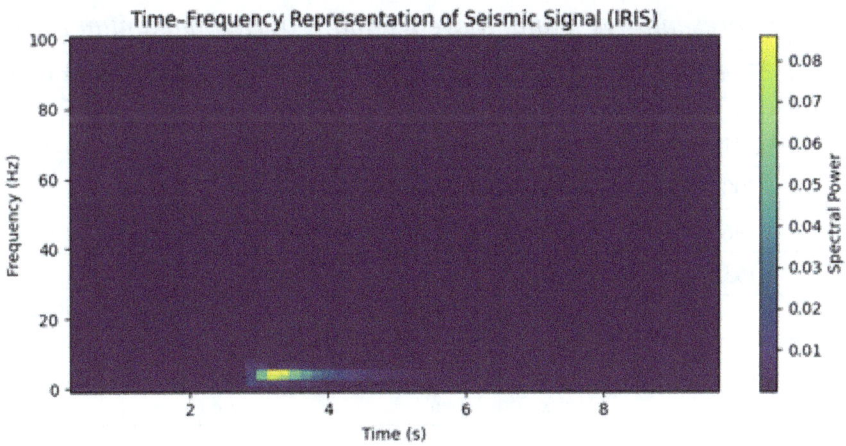

In Figure 4, we show the time-frequency display of the Continuous Wavelet Transform (CWT). The choice of a Morlet mother wavelet is suitable as the signal of interest is oscillatory and needs to be time-localised. The range of scales was chosen to preferentially represent the short-duration, high frequency energy of the P-wave. This can have a significant impact: too small scales can emphasize noise, and large scales can smooth the onset of the event. The localised energy peak therefore aids in picking the arrival of the seismic event.

9.3. Case Study 3 — Tsunami Wave Height Prediction Using Historical NOAA/NCEI Tsunami Events Database

This case study uses historical records of tsunami events, found in the NOAA/NCEI Global Historical Tsunami Database. The database provides event-level data (such as earthquake magnitude and location, and maximum run-up height).

Tsunami effects are not solely dependent on earthquake magnitude. Other factors, such as rupture mechanism, and seafloor deformation, coastal geometry, bathymetry and amplification effects can also affect the run-up height caused by different magnitude earthquakes.

Table 4. Representative tsunami events and reported maximum run-up

Event Id	Year	Location	Magnitude (Mw)	Max Run-Up (m)
247	2011	Tohoku, Japan	9.1	40.5
172	2004	Sumatra–Andaman, Indian Ocean	9.1	28.0
305	1960	Valdivia, Chile	9.5	25.0
402	1952	Kamchatka, Russia	9.0	15.0
690	2018	Sulawesi, Indonesia	7.5	5.0
615	1998	Papua New Guinea	7.1	13.0
521	1993	Hokkaido, Japan	7.8	31.7
814	2022	Tonga	6.0	2.5

Table 4 illustrates that higher earthquake magnitudes are generally associated with higher reported tsunami run-up, but cannot be solely relied upon. For instance, the 1993 Hokkaido earthquake (Mw 7.8) has a reported run-up of 31.7 m, which is greater than a number of events with larger magnitudes. This suggests that other source and coastal factors are needed to explain tsunami impact.

Figure 5. Box plot of tsunami run-up by magnitude class

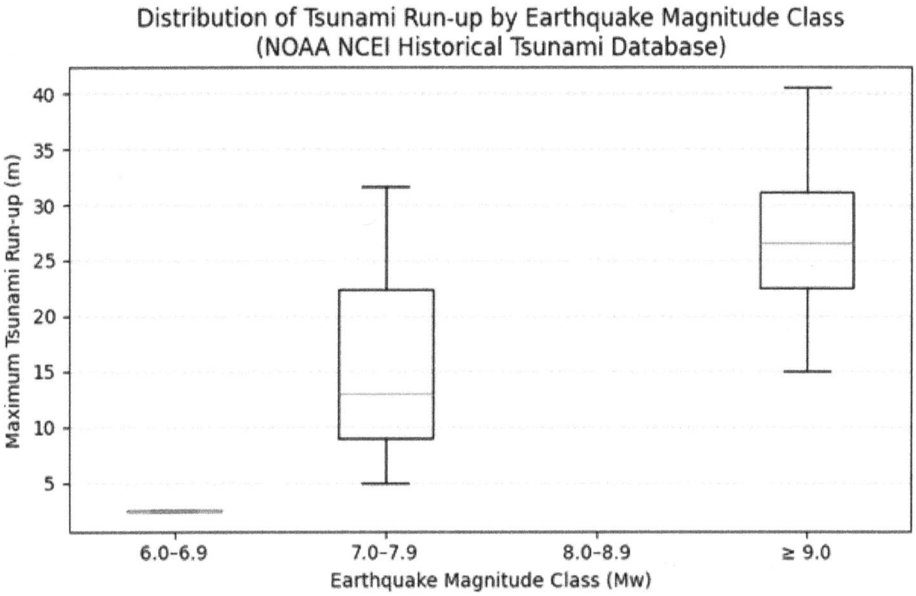

We summarise the distribution of maximum tsunami run-up height by earthquake magnitude class in a box-plot (Figure 5). The x axis is earthquake magnitude classes and the y axis is the maximum run-up height (in metres). The median, interquartile range (box), whiskers and outliers reveal large differences in tsunami impact for a given magnitude class.

The Mw 6.0-6.9 class has relatively small run-up heights, likely associated with small earthquake-induced seafloor uplift. The Mw 7.0-7.9 class has a broader interquartile range, suggesting that there are significant differences in the tsunami heights caused by moderate-to-large earthquakes due to source and coastal geometry.

The classes Mw 8.0-8.9 and Mw >= 9.0 have higher median run-ups and larger spreads, with the effects of rupture size and fault geometry playing a significant role. The wide range in the highest magnitude class (containing catastrophic megathrust events such as the 2011 Tohoku earthquake) illustrates a key lesson for tsunami modelling: earthquake magnitude is a necessary but not sufficient information for estimating tsunami impact. Hence tsunami-impact models should incorporate bathymetry, rupture type, depth, exposure of the coastline and uncertainties.

A key problem with historical run-up data is that it is not independent of the quality of the measurements, timing of the survey, local measurement standards, and the historical record. The database may not include all the factors that influence run-up, such as coastal bathymetry and structures. So historical run-up should be considered for model exploration and risk analysis, but as a not a deterministic predictor.

DISCUSSION

The three examples demonstrate how time-series methods can simplify geophysical observations as "signals" for hazard analysis.

These studies have a number of methodological implications.

First, geophysical data are multiscale. Temporal signals can be a combination of trends, cycles, and events, such as GNSS observations that include tectonic displacement, seasonal signals and noise.

Second, signal decomposition is needed when signals of interest are contaminated with noise. Wavelets, SSA, and nuclear norm minimization can help to disentangle deterministic from random components to better understand the data and inform modelling.

Third, wavelet transforms work well to detect transients. In the seismic example, the high-energy "bulls' eye" in the wavelet transform helps to more easily detect the P- wave than in the waveform alone.

Fourth, hazard assessment should be multivariate and consider uncertainties. The tsunami example illustrates that the earthquake magnitude is not a good predictor of tsunami run-up variability; the shape of the rupture zone, bathymetric amplification, coastal vulnerability and data quality should also be taken into account.

These insights and observations suggest the following design guidelines when analysing geophysical time series:

- Be selective in preprocessing such as outlier removal, detrending, offset correction, gap filling and filtering.
- Apply multiscale analysis for non-stationary signals and for signals with localised events.
- Use machine-learning models in conjunction with physics to ensure that predictions are interpretable, and physically consistent.
- Estimate uncertainty when data are sparse, irregular, incomplete and/or contain measurement errors.

These principles help to produce better monitoring and hazard-prediction systems. In summary, the frameworks for geophysical time-series analysis should work in concert to resolve the issues of data preprocessing, multiscale decomposition, feature engineering with domain knowledge, and modelling with an understanding of the physics of the process.

10. FUTURE DIRECTIONS

Geophysical time-series analysis should consist of both signal processing and modelling. Blending physical knowledge with machine learning can lead to better predictions as well as physical insights.

Sensor fusion is another important direction. Integration of satellite, terrestrial and oceanographic data can give a more holistic understanding of Earth-system dynamics, to enhance our ability to monitor hazards.

Machine learning could help to discover intricate patterns in big geophysical data, particularly in dense sensor networks. However, it must be used in conjunction with interpretability, uncertainty quantification and physical knowledge.

Future work should also focus on data availability and labelling, and uncertainty estimation. Recently developed methods for dealing with missing, noisy, and unevenly-spaced data can lead to more reliable forecasts.

11. CONCLUSION

This chapter has illustrated that more than classical methods applied directly to geophysical time series are needed. Due to the non-stationarity, noise and multiple scales in observational data, correct interpretation requires the tasks of preprocessing, decomposition, feature engineering and modelling to be interconnected.

The case studies provide three practical lessons: detrending and trend estimation are important for the analysis of GNSS deformations; time-frequency localization is important for the detection of seismic events; and multivariate interpretation is important for the modelling of tsunami run-up, as opposed to relying on earthquake magnitude. These illustrate the best practices in preparing geophysical datasets for machine learning, as well as how to make hazard-monitoring systems more interpretable.

REFERENCES

Arul, M., & Kareem, A. (2021). Applications of shapelet transform to time series classification of earthquake, wind and wave data. *Engineering Structures*, *228*, 111564. DOI: 10.1016/j.engstruct.2020.111564

Bos, M. S., Fernandes, R. M. S., Williams, S. D. P., & Bastos, L. (2013). Fast error analysis of continuous GNSS observations with missing data. *Journal of Geodesy*, *87*(4), 351–360. DOI: 10.1007/s00190-012-0605-0

Cabrera-Navarrete, E., Ronquillo-Jarillo, G., & Markov, A. (2020). Wavelet analysis for spectral inversion of seismic reflection data. *Journal of Applied Geophysics*, *177*, 104034. DOI: 10.1016/j.jappgeo.2020.104034

Carbonari, R., Riccardi, U., De Martino, P., Cecere, G., & Di Maio, R. (2023). Wavelet-like denoising of GNSS data through machine learning: Application to the time series of the Campi Flegrei volcanic area (Southern Italy). *Geomatics, Natural Hazards & Risk*, *14*(1), 2187271. DOI: 10.1080/19475705.2023.2187271

Chen, B., Bian, J., Ding, K., Wu, H., & Li, H. (2020). Extracting seasonal signals in GNSS coordinate time series via weighted nuclear norm minimization. *Remote Sensing (Basel)*, *12*(12), 2027. DOI: 10.3390/rs12122027

Cucci, D. A., Voirol, L., Kermarrec, G., Montillet, J. P., & Guerrier, S. (2023). The generalized method of wavelet moments with eXogenous inputs: A fast approach for the analysis of GNSS position time series. *Journal of Geodesy*, *97*(2), 14. DOI: 10.1007/s00190-023-01702-8 PMID: 36760754

Gazeaux, J., Williams, S., King, M., Bos, M., Dach, R., Deo, M., Moore, A. W., Ostini, L., Petrie, E., Roggero, M., Teferle, F. N., Olivares, G., & Webb, F. H. (2013). Detecting offsets in GPS time series: First results from the Detection of Offsets in GPS Experiment. *Journal of Geophysical Research. Solid Earth*, *118*(5), 2397–2407. DOI: 10.1002/jgrb.50152

Jasir, M. C. M., Sreejith, K. M., Agrawal, R., & Begum, S. K. (2024). Application of singular spectrum analysis to InSAR time-series for constraining the post-seismic deformation due to moderate magnitude earthquakes: The case of 2019 Mw 6 Mirpur earthquake, NW Himalaya. *Geophysical Journal International, 239*(1), 637–645. DOI: 10.1093/gji/ggae287

Ji, K., Shen, Y., & Wang, F. (2020). Signal extraction from GNSS position time series using weighted wavelet analysis. *Remote Sensing (Basel), 12*(6), 992. DOI: 10.3390/rs12060992

Kumar, P., & Foufoula-Georgiou, E. (1997). Wavelet analysis for geophysical applications. *Reviews of Geophysics, 35*(4), 385–412. DOI: 10.1029/97RG00427

Langbein, J., & Johnson, H. (1997). Correlated errors in geodetic time series: Implications for time-dependent deformation. *Journal of Geophysical Research, 102*(B1), 591–603. DOI: 10.1029/96JB02945

Li, J., He, M., Cui, G., Wang, X., Wang, W., & Wang, J. (2020). A novel method of seismic signal detection using waveform features. *Applied Sciences (Basel, Switzerland), 10*(8), 2919. DOI: 10.3390/app10082919

Sudrajat, A., Meilano, I., Abidin, H. Z., Susilo, S., Hardy, T., Samapta, B. T., & Kambali, R. A. P. (2025). Wavelet-based P-wave detection in high-rate GNSS data: A novel approach for rapid earthquake monitoring in tsunamigenic settings. *Sensors (Basel), 25*(13), 3860. DOI: 10.3390/s25133860 PMID: 40648120

Wang, Y. (2015). Generalized seismic wavelets. *Geophysical Journal International, 203*(2), 1172–1178. DOI: 10.1093/gji/ggv346

Wang, Z., Zhang, B., Gao, J., Wang, Q., & Liu, Q. H. (2017). Wavelet transform with generalized beta wavelets for seismic time-frequency analysis. *Geophysics, 82*(4), O47–O56. DOI: 10.1190/geo2016-0342.1

Williams, S. D. P. (2003). The effect of coloured noise on the uncertainties of rates estimated from geodetic time series. *Journal of Geodesy, 76*(9-10), 483–494. DOI: 10.1007/s00190-002-0283-4

Yiou, P., Sornette, D., & Ghil, M. (2000). Data-adaptive wavelets and multi-scale singular-spectrum analysis. *Physica D. Nonlinear Phenomena*, *142*(3-4), 254–290. DOI: 10.1016/S0167-2789(00)00045-2

Chapter 8
Machine Learning for Earthquake Prediction and Characterization: Advancing Detection, Localization, and Seismic Analysis With Deep Learning

S. Udhaya Shankar

http://orcid.org/0009-0006-3781-8801

Vel Tech Multi Tech Dr. Rangarajan Dr. Sakunthala Engineering College, India

S. Karthika

Vel Tech Rangarajan Dr. Sagunthala R&D Institute of Science and Technology, India

R. Vinoth

http://orcid.org/0000-0001-5866-1395

R.M.K. College of Engineering and Technology, India

M. G. Dinesh

http://orcid.org/0009-0009-7643-5338

Easa College of Engineering and Technology, India

DOI: 10.4018/979-8-3373-8042-1.ch008

ABSTRACT

This chapter explores the growing role of machine learning (ML) and deep learning (DL) in advancing earthquake prediction, detection, localization, and seismic characterization. Traditional seismological methods face challenges related to noise, limited sensor coverage, and complex wave propagation. ML and DL techniques address these limitations by enabling automated feature extraction, robust pattern recognition, and real-time processing of large-scale seismic datasets. The chapter reviews key architectures including CNNs, RNNs, Transformers, GNNs, and physics-informed models and examines their applications in seismic noise reduction, phase picking, magnitude estimation, and early warning systems. Major challenges such as data scarcity, model generalization, interpretability, and computational constraints are discussed. The chapter concludes with emerging research directions aimed at developing reliable, scalable, and AI solutions for seismic monitoring and hazard mitigation.

1. INTRODUCTION

1.1 Background and Motivation

Earthquakes are one of the most devastating natural hazards, which also present a great threat to human life, infrastructure, and socioeconomic stability. Although much has been achieved in geophysics and seismology, the process of earthquake prediction, be it on aspects of detection, localization, magnitude estimation or rupture behaviour, has been a thorny issue(Kaswan, K. S et al., 2021). Conventional seismological methods, based on analytical models, travel-time inversion, threshold-based detection methods like Short-Term Average over Long-Term Average (STA/LTA) and empirical relationships are sensitive to noise, have low sensor density and assume that models do not work in most geological conditions. The growing access to high-resolution seismic waveform data on dense networks has created enormous volumes of data that cannot be analyzed successfully through traditional means. This disparity between the volume of data and analytical power has put machine learning (ML) and deep learning (DL) in the favorable position of transformative tools in contemporary earthquake studies(Sundari, V. M et al., 2024). These computing paradigms are superb in finding hidden patterns, deriving meaningful features of noisy data, and learning nonlinear relationships that can be used to achieve superior accuracy and reliability in a variety of dimensions of seismic analysis. As a result, both ML- and DL-inspired methods have become a very active booster of the knowledge and description of earthquake processes, prevention of the use of early warnings, and reducing the risk of disasters(Prasad, D et al., 2021).

1.2 Need for Machine Learning and Deep Learning in Earthquake Studies

The use of ML and DL on seismic data analysis is motivated by a number of strong requirements that conventional computational structures are unable to sufficiently satisfy. To begin with, seismic waveforms are non-stationary and complicated in nature and frequently concealed in elevated levels of environmental and anthropogenic noise. Deep learning models, particularly convolutional neural networks (CNNs), recurrent neural networks (RNNs) and more recently, Transformer models can automatically discover discriminative features and are therefore suitable to seismic signal detection and classification tasks. Second, the processes related to earthquakes are very nonlinear and can be affected by geological heterogeneity, frictional behaviour, stress build up and rupture propagation. In contrast to traditional physical models, which reduce the complexity of these processes to make them computationally solvable, the ML models have the ability to estimate complex patterns directly using large data sets, which allows them to predict and characterize events more accurately. Third, the earthquake early warning systems require real-time processing requirements that require quick and automated responses(Gnanasekaran, T et al., 2024). Once trained, ML models have high inference speed, and thus are useful in real-time detection and magnitude estimation in the case of emergent events. Furthermore, the overall growth of sensors worldwide, both cheap IoT gadgets and geodetic networks of satellites, generates multimodal datasets that can be integrated with the help of advanced ML approaches and give a better overall picture of seismicity(Goyal, D et al.,

2023). Collectively, these abilities highlight the importance of why ML and DL have become the inseparable aspects of the contemporary seismic science that is capable of offering quicker, more precise, and scalable solutions.

1.3 Scope of the Chapter

This Chapter is dedicated to the growing application of machine learning (ML) and deep learning (DL) in earthquake prediction and earthquake characterization, and the emphasis is placed on the techniques that may improve the detection, location, magnitude and understanding of seismic signals. The Chapter refers to the progress in the application of traditional ML algorithms, such as support vectors machines, decision trees, and ensemble methods, and novel DL models, such as Convolutional Neural Networks (CNNs), Long Short-Term Memory (LSTM) networks, Transformer, Graph Neural Networks (GNNs), and Physics-Informed Neural Networks (PINNs). It includes the use of these algorithms to address fundamental problems in seismology, such as the detection of small seismic events in the presence of noise, the location and depth of earthquakes, the moment magnitude of seismic signals, all with respect to the original raw waveforms, the denoising of seismic signals, and the modeling of spatiotemporal seismicity patterns for prediction. The review also covers multimodal types of learning that use seismic, geodetic, remote sensing and geophysical data to enhance prediction accuracy.

1.4 Contributions of This Chapter

The main aim of the Chapter lies in the fact that it offers a systematic analysis of the role that machine learning and deep learning methods play in reshaping the earthquake prediction and seismic characterization. Unlike other existing reviews, which focus either on a specific ML application or type of model, this chapter will be a comprehensive assessment of the entire seismic workflow (including initial detection, characterization and prediction). It offers a methodological novelty, compares the outcomes and outlines the emerging trends in the field, such as the shift to end-to-end neural network designs, the use of multimodal fusion models, and the growing importance of interpretable and physics-based models in seismology. The second contribution is the discussion of challenges, such as lack of data in low-seismicity regions, model transferability to other geological settings, and computational constraints for real-time applications. Ethical and policy implications are also mentioned in the Chapter, like providing reliable public alerts and acting responsibly with uncertainties in hazard-related predictions. Lastly, the Chapter sees the future research opportunities in the areas of hybrid physical-AI models, federated learning in distributed seismic networks, large foundation models in geoscience, and robust benchmarking practices. In general, the Chapter will provide researchers, policymakers, and practitioners with the knowledge that will help them comprehend the recent advances and inform the new developments in the field of ML-enabled earthquake science.

1.5 Organization of the Chapter

The rest of the Chapter is divided into six other sections that are in line with fundamental themes in seismic research based on machine learning. Section 2 presents the background of seismic data features and ML/DL principles that are required to comprehend the applications of the algorithms in seismology. Section 3 will cover machine learning and deep learning approaches to earthquake detection, models, datasets and performance measures. Section 4 talks about how to localize earthquakes and predict their magnitude, including classical ML, deep learning, and hybrid physics-informed. Section 5 is devoted to the seismic data processing, denoising, phase picking and early warning. Section 6 discusses the key challenges, limitations and future research opportunities in this field, both technical, practical and ethical. Finally, Section 7 is the last section of the Chapter, where the authors conclude on the lessons learnt and provide the outlook of AI-based earthquake research.

2. SEISMIC DATA AND MACHINE LEARNING FOUNDATIONS

2.1 Characteristics of Seismic Data and Sensor Networks

Seismic data are primarily derived from a network of seismometers and accelerometers as they continually record the ground motion and generate waveform signals to indicate the passage of seismic waves (P-waves, S-waves and surface waves). They can be influenced by various factors of crustal structures, fault geometry, site conditions and noise, and can be complicated and hard to interpret by the traditional analysis. Time series measurements of three components that produce large volumes of high dimensional data usually constitute seismic records. In addition, recent seismic networks are very diverse in density, and coverage: densely covered regions like Japan and California produce very high-resolution data sets, but sparsely covered regions of the world provide low-resolution datasets in their ability to describe events. Other data have been added to the traditional seismometers, including the development of low cost IoT sensors, distributed acoustic sensing (DAS) systems using fiber-optic cables and satellite geodetic systems such as GPS and InSAR. However, the various sources of data have varying sampling rates, noise characteristics and varying calibration requirements. The diversity and complexity of such data also highlight the need to develop new computational algorithms that are capable of learning with multimodal, imbalanced and noisy data. The advantages of machine learning and deep learning models are enormous since they automatically generate features, can handle nonlinearity, and can achieve high predictive accuracy even with challenging data(Ponmalar, A et al., 2024).

2.2 Seismic Datasets, Preprocessing, and Feature Engineering

The quality and arrangement of accessible seismic data is a significant factor in prediction and characterization of earthquakes. Widely used datasets are global and regional earthquake catalogs, continuous waveform archives and curated benchmark datasets. Such datasets usually include labeled events that include metadata that includes coordinates of hypocenter, magnitude, depth and phase arrival times. In the case of ML and DL, preprocessing is needed so that the input data can be suitable to model. These involve noise cancellation by filtering, waveform normalization, time series windowing about P- and S-waves, and time series segmentation alignment. Signal characteristic improvement is often done by band-pass filters, wavelet transforms, and spectral decomposition. Besides preprocessing, classical machine learning methods are also largely reliant on feature engineering to derive meaningful features out of raw waveforms. Examples of common features are spectral ratios, peak ground motion values, zero-crossing rates and statistical characteristics like kurtosis and skewness. The representation of waveform data in two-dimensional formats has also been popular in transforming the waveform data into two-dimensional form, which can be used in classification and regression tasks. Even though feature engineering can be successful, it is frequently constrained by assumptions and expert decisions, which might not be able to fully model the complexity of seismic signals. This shortcoming has given way to hierarchical feature learning with deep learning techniques that learn on raw or slightly processed waveforms.

2.3 Machine Learning Foundations for Seismic Applications

Machine learning has been used to underpin the modernization of the seismic data analysis through the provision of statistical and computational tools that can provide patterns that could not be observed in a traditional manner. The classical ML algorithms, including Support Vector Machines (SVM), Random Forests, Decision Trees, k-Nearest Neighbors (kNN), and Gradient Boosting Machines (GBM) have been used extensively in event recognition, magnitude recognition, and seismic phase recognition. These models are based on structured feature sets and they work well for good quality labelled data. In particular, Support Vector Machines (SVM) and Random Forests (RF) have been useful in separating earthquake signals and noise, identifying microseismic activity and providing rough features of earthquakes. Other methods such as k-means and DBSCAN have also been applied to study aftershock sequences, patterns of seismograms have been classified and outlier seismicity which may be precursory has been detected. The traditional ML algorithms, however, demand a set of features and they may not be able to cope with the complex shapes of the waveforms, non-linear effects of wave propagation, and high-dimensional spaces. The unsupervised learning methods like autoencoders and dimensionality reduction methods like PCA and t-SNE have helped researchers to find the underlying structure in the unlabeled seismic data. These models are unsupervised and are able to detect families of seismic events, match continuous tremor signals and detect low-frequency earthquakes. Although classical ML has contributed greatly to the previous seismic research, its nature of relying on feature engineering and scalability issues has seen a rise in the use of deep learning methods, which offer end-to-end the modeling of large-scale seismic data.

2.4 Deep Learning Foundations and Architectures in Seismology

Deep learning has become a disruptive process in seismology given its capability to learn hierarchical representations of raw or light processed data. Some of the applications of Convolutional Neural Networks (CNNs) include seismic event detection, magnitude estimation, and rupture characterization. CNNs are good at detecting local signals like the peaks of the waveform, onset patterns and frequency bands, hence they are suitable in the classification of the waveforms. Other forms like 1D CNNs are directly used on time series whilst 2D CNNs are used to examine spectrograms or wastelet images to extract more features. Recurrent neural networks (RNNs) are used to tackle the temporal characteristics of seismic waveforms, especially Long Short-Term Memory (LSTM) and Gated Recurrent Unit (GRU) networks can be used in tasks that involve the modeling of sequences, including early warning systems and earthquake prediction(Murugaraj, S. S., & Kumar, S. 2024). Most recently, Transformer models, which capitalize on self-attention mechanisms, have shown high performance in modeling long-range dependencies and multifaceted temporal relationships in seismic signals and are more effective than traditional RNN-based models. Also, Graph Neural Networks (GNNs) have become popular in sensor network modeling, where the geometry of locations of stations affects signal propagation and location of events. GNNs enable researchers to encode interrelations among stations and use geospatial features during localization.

In addition to conventional architectures, more general generative models like Variational Autoencoders (VAEs), Generative Adversarial Networks (GANs) have been used to perform waveform synthesis, data augmentation and denoising and allow better training in low-data regions. Physics-Informed Neural Networks (PINNs) can be seen as another prospective path, that is, physical laws of wave propagation and stress accumulation are incorporated into neural network constraints, which increases interpretability and decreases the need to use large labeled datasets. The combination of multimodal data, i.e. seismic, geodetic and remote sensing data, has further widened the scope of the use of DL in seismology and allowed the analysis of the processes of earthquakes comprehensively. This group of deep learning architectures can assist in more demanding seismic tasks, which are more accurate, more scalable, and automated compared to conventional approaches.

3. ML AND DL FOR EARTHQUAKE DETECTION

3.1 Traditional Approaches to Earthquake Detection

Classical seismological methods used in the past to detect earthquakes have been based on the use of signal processing techniques and manual analysis. The Short-Term Average over Long-Term Average technique is one of the most common traditional detection algorithms; the algorithm uses the ratio between short-term and long-term energy windows to detect the sudden signal variation during seismic activities. Whereas the detection based on STA/LTA offers a simple and computationally efficient baseline when performing real-time monitoring, it is very sensitive to noise particularly in areas that have been subjected to cultural or natural disturbances like traffic, wind, rain, or industrial activities. Template matching techniques are more effective in that they cross-correlate continuous seismic data with known templates of waveforms, though they require a large library of templates, cannot cope with variability of waveforms, and are very expensive to compute. Algorithms in frequency-domain, envelope analysis, and phase-picking have also been applied in the determination of seismic events, but are often highly expert-tuned, and may not detect low-magnitude events or emergent events hidden in noise. These limitations indicate the need to have data-driven models capable of obtaining more generalizable and robust representations of seismic signals. Consequently, machine learning and deep learning techniques have become popular in an attempt to offer detection performance that is better than that of traditional algorithms.

3.2 Machine Learning Methods for Earthquake Detection

Machine learning has provided a new layer of automation and accuracy of detecting the seismic events, especially in the complicated noise conditions. The first prototypes of ML were based on supervised classification techniques to detect earthquake signals and non-seismic noise. Their use in Support Vector Machines (SVM) has been used to classify feature vectors of portions of waveforms and hence can detect small events that are otherwise hard to discern using their traditional detectors. Random Forests and Gradient Boosting Machines have also come in handy since they can deal with high dimensional sets of features and may also deal with noisy inputs and therefore can be used in continuous seismic monitoring. The models are usually based on handcrafted characteristics based on time domain and frequency domain representation of seismic signals, such as the peak amplitude, rate of zero-crossing, cepstral coefficients and spectral ratios. Besides supervised methods, there are unsupervised methods that have been employed to cluster the patterns of waveforms and establish anomalous sections that might be representing previously unidentified events, including k-means clustering, DBSCAN, and Gaussian Mixture Models (GMM). Semi-supervised learning methods use small amounts of labeled data to provide direction in larger unlabeled datasets, which is of great value in areas where limited resources of manual annotation are available. Although these classical ML methods have enhanced microseismicity detection and noise discrimination, the use of features that are manually designed tends to limit their performance in fully representing the complexity of seismic waveforms. The limitation has led to the use of deep learning that is capable of learning features based on raw data and enhance the accuracy of detection in a wide variety of seismic contexts.

Figure 1. ML and DL for Earthquake Detection

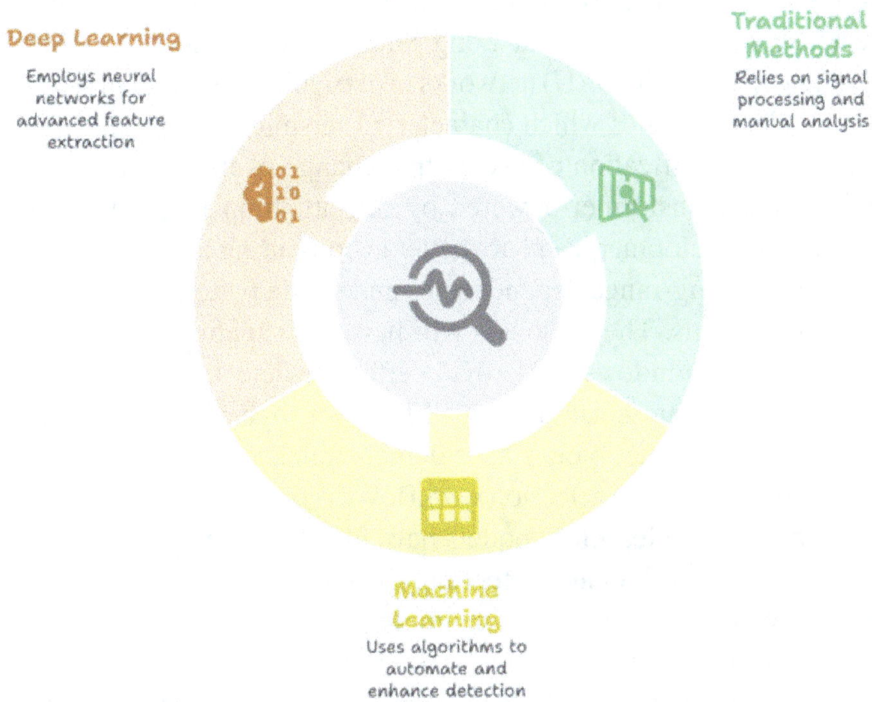

3.3 Deep Learning for Advanced Seismic Event Detection

Deep learning has transformed the area of earthquake detection in that it has made it possible to have end-to-end models that can automatically derive hierarchical features of raw waveform data without the intervention of a human. CNNs have been specifically effective in seismic detection tasks because the network is able to identify localized characteristics like waveform onset patterns, amplitude spikes, and frequency changes. One-dimensional CNNs on waveform time series have been shown to be highly accurate at the detection of strong and weak events, and in many cases, better than the traditional detectors in their sensitivity and robustness. The advantages of two-dimensional CNNs, which are trained on spectrograms or wavelet-transformed images, are that they can capture time-frequency features that are hard to capture with handcrafted features. Recurrent Neural Networks (RNNs) and Long Short-Term Memory (LSTM) and Gated Recurrent Unit (GRU) networks in particular are useful in modeling temporal dependencies which characterize seismic wave propagation, to allow better classification of events that change over time. Transformer architectures Transformer-powered by self-attention mechanisms are a more recent development, and are better at computing tasks involving the generation of long-range dependencies and subtle patterns in continuous waveform streams. These models will have the capability of processing heavy temporal windows and provide effective detection despite the occurrence of intricate noise patterns. Moreover, hybrid models that have CNN and Transformer blocks have demonstrated excellent performance in real-time earthquake detection workflows. Apart from the conventional architectures, deep learning models have also been designed to perform specific tasks in earthquake detection. Residual networks (ResNets) and dense networks (DenseNets) are examples of such networks that improve the gradient flow, and can learn very deep networks that are able to detect weak or emergent events. Anomaly or deep anomaly detection models and autoencoders have been applied to detect rare or anomalous seismic behavior, the path to the discovery of a previously unknown microseismicity or tremor signal. In most cases, DL models can work on different seismic regions without major adaptation, and they are more generalizable compared to their feature-based counterparts that are handcrafted. They are also quick in inferences and can therefore be utilized in real time early warning systems where timeliness of detection is a critical aspect in determining the safety of the people.

4. ML AND DL FOR EARTHQUAKE LOCALIZATION AND MAGNITUDE ESTIMATION

4.1 Traditional Methods for Earthquake Localization and Magnitude Estimation

Earthquake localization and magnitude estimation are two of the simplest seismological activities as they provide some of the required information required to comprehend seismic hazards, to describe fault actions, and to offer emergency response. Traditionally the localization of earthquakes is calculated using the travel times of seismic waves between the source and the various seismic stations. Triangulation techniques or inversion techniques can be used to estimate the arrival time of P- and S-waves to determine the coordinates of the hypocenter, such as latitude, longitude, and depth. Although such techniques are widely used, they require proper phase picking and proper velocity models that may involve significant uncertainties. It could be the local geology, anisotropy and heterogeneities that change the wave path and cause systematic errors in the localization. Similarly, magnitude estimation, whether of the Richter scale, moment magnitude (Mw) or any other magnitude which is regionally calibrated, requires the appropriate measurement of waveform amplitudes and spectral properties. Classical magnitude estimation techniques tend to saturate a signal in case of large events, and tend to be sensitive to noise in case of small magnitude events. The limitations above highlight the significance of robust, data-driven techniques capable of learning based on the patterns of waveforms and reduce the use of simplified physical models. With the growing size and scale of seismic networks and the resulting large and diverse amounts of data, machine learning and deep learning techniques have become a potential replacement to enhance and enhance the precision and accuracy of localization and magnitude determination(Yamini, B et al., 2024).

4.2 Machine Learning Approaches for Localization and Magnitude Prediction

Machine learning has also brought new paradigms in terms of approaches to localization and magnitude estimation through the application of statistical models to directly map the features of the waveforms to seismic parameters. Classical ML methods make use of manually constructed features derived out of seismic signals, including peak amplitudes, frequency content, energy ratios, and time-frequency representations to train regression models which are used to predict hypocenter positions or magnitude values. Support Vector Regression (SVR), Random Forest Regressors, Gradient Boosting Machines, and k-Nearest Neighbors have been used to obtain approximate source locations using travel-time differences among other waveform characteristics. These models provide better resistance to noise and can correct the errors of velocity models through the acquisition of empirical correlations between observed waveforms and event parameters. In magnitude estimation, ensemble techniques and feature-based regressors have also been demonstrated to be capable of coping with saturation and variability of amplitude measurements to provide more stable predictions than classical formulas. Other event characteristics such as fault mechanism, rupture direction and aftershock potential have also been modeled using the ML-based methods to enable more comprehensive characterization of an earthquake. But the use of handcrafted features is still a limiting factor as manual feature extraction may miss important features of the waveform and may not capture all the complexities of the seismic processes. This is where deep learning has emerged that can learn directly from raw seismic waveforms and make more accurate predictions under a wide range of seismic conditions.

4.3 Deep Learning Models for Localization and Magnitude Estimation

Localization and magnitude estimation of earthquakes have seen huge improvements using deep learning models that can be used in end-to-end systems that can use raw or minimally processed waveform data. Convolutional Neural Networks (CNNs) have been extensively used in earthquake location estimation as they are able to capture the important spatial and temporal features in subsections of the waveforms(Lalitha, S. D et al., 2024). One-dimensional CNNs are especially useful in situations where continuous time series of waveforms are used where learned representations are related to distances between sources and stations and wave propagation. Two-dimensional CNNs, which use spectrograms or wavelet images, are able to learn important time-frequency features to improve location accuracy(Venketbabu, T et al., 2024). Recurrent Neural Networks (RNNs), in particular LSTM and GRU, are based on the idea of modelling the dependence of the waves over time and as such they can learn the arrival patterns that can be used to infer depth and distance. Recent advances have also seen the application of Transformers which can learn long-range dependencies and attention to important features of the waveform. Transformers can combine information of different stations and they are particularly appropriate in dense seismic networks. Along with these architectures, Graph Neural Networks (GNNs) have emerged as one of the important contributions to the seismic localization research. GNNs can learn spatial relationships in the network since seismic stations can be naturally represented as nodes in a graph, the distance between nodes or physical connection can be represented as an edge in the graph. By using a mixture of both waveforms data and station metadata in geospatial, the GNNs are capable of forecasting more complicated propagation patterns and making highly accurate predictions of the epicenter and depth. The other direction that is emerging is using Physics-Informed Neural Networks (PINNs) where equations of seismic wave propagation are included in the training of the neural network. Physical constraints directly introduced into the model by PINNs lead to improved interpretability and a decrease in the need to have large labeled datasets, which is one of the key issues of seismic ML research. On magnitude estimation, deep learning systems like CNNs, CNN-RNN hybrids, and Transformer-based regressors have been demonstrated to be superior to the conventional systems in terms of nonlinear dependence on the amplitudes and energy distributions of the waveforms as well as spectral attributes. These models are able to project magnitude at the early stages of the waveform and this is essential in real-time early warning systems that demand quick predictions in order to operate automated safety measures. Moreover, deep learning models are more scalable and generalizable, which makes it possible to use them in other seismic areas with very little reconfigurations.

4.4 Challenges, Opportunities, and Real-World Applications

However, estimation of the seismic magnitude and location in the field by using ML and DL models has a number of challenges even with the highly advanced developments. The other significant concern is the data imbalance where smaller earthquakes occur more frequently than the large earthquakes and hence the training data is biased towards one side leading to bias in prediction outcomes. The other significant challenge is the generalization across different regions; the models trained on a specific region will not work well in a different geological environment because of the differences in velocity structures, fault systems and noise characteristics. To overcome these, domain adaptation, transfer learning and data augmentation are being considered. Moreover, deep learning models are not transparent enough, particularly in the cases where the seismic experts are required to verify the predictions with predictions before issuing warnings or revising hazard maps. Saliency maps, attention heatmaps and gradient-based attribution methods can assist in providing insight into the model decision-making and more research is required to ensure that the ML-based systems are trustworthy.

On the opportunities side, the development of sensor technologies and geophysical data acquisition systems are providing a multimodal learning environment. Along with seismic waveforms, InSAR, GPS, DAS and geological data can go an extra step with the location, as well as contribute to the earthquake magnitude, especially in complex environments such as under a volcano or a subduction zone. Moreover, the availability of big data and access to high-performance computing have allowed more sophisticated deep learning models to be developed, which can learn from big and diverse data. Such models are already being applied in the real world. For example, an early warning system today uses deep learning to quickly calculate the magnitude and the epicentre within the first few seconds of the first arrival of the P-wave. These can automatically trigger alarms, critical infrastructure shutdown and assist in emergency management.

Also, ML- and DL-based models are being utilized to improve Earthquake catalogs, identify hitherto unknown microseismic phenomena, and create the high-resolution seismicity maps, which enhance our comprehension of active fault systems. With the ongoing advancement of these technologies, they have massive potential in bringing a global change in the way earthquakes are detected, interpreted, and acted on.

5. SEISMIC SIGNAL PROCESSING, NOISE REDUCTION, AND EARLY WARNING SYSTEMS

5.1 Seismic Noise Reduction and Signal Enhancement Using ML and DL

The seismic signal processing is a very important aspect of enhancing the quality of the waveform data required to detect, localize, and estimate the magnitude of an earthquake. Noise is one of the most common contaminants of the raw seismic signals and may be caused by cultural activities, atmospheric disturbances, instrument artifacts, and environmental vibrations. The conventional methods of noise reduction are based on filtering that includes band-pass filters, spectral whitening, and wavelet denoising methods that are efficient but cannot cope with the fast-varied noisy conditions. Machine learning and deep learning have brought the new tools of transforming seismic signals through the process of learning data-driven noise models and automatic extraction of meaningful waveform components(Subramanian, R. S et al., 2025). Classical ML methods are based on statistical learning models that are used to differentiate noise patterns and actual seismic signals, and in many cases, these features are based on the time-frequency analysis. Nonetheless, deep learning has been much more useful in denoising tasks because of its ability to learn nonlinear transformations that are complex to learn. CNNs and U-Nets have been especially effective at seismic denoising since they are able to learn hierarchical patterns using waveform data and recreate clean signals without losing significant information such as arrival times and waveform patterns. Autoencoders and Denoising Autoencoders (DAEs) have also gained popularity, where the noisy signals are compressed into low-dimensional representations and then decoded with learned patterns. Generative models, such as Variational Autoencoders (VAEs) and Generative Adversarial Networks (GANs) have also been applied to produce clean seismic images or condition on realistic samples, which has greatly increased the robustness of downstream ML models. Such deep learning methods not only enhance signal-to-noise ratio, but also enable the detection of low-magnitude events that are difficult to detect with the traditional methods, and hence result in improved seismic monitoring and hazard assessment.

5.2 Phase Picking and Waveform Interpretation with Deep Learning

In the earthquake detection, earthquake localization and earthquake warning systems, correct detection of seismic phase arrivals, particularly the P-wave arrival, and S-wave arrival is essential. In many traditional phase picking, manual inspection is necessary or it uses algorithms like STA/LTA which may not work well in noisy conditions or with emergent and low amplitude arrivals. Machine learning also presented automated phase pickers that were developed on the basis of statistical classification models, which enhanced consistency and minimized human effort. Deep learning has however transformed phase picking because it is able to learn finer aspects of a waveform and generalize through various seismic datasets. The CNN-based pickers, including single-station and multi-station ones, are capable of determining P- and S-wave arrivals with a high precision using raw segments of waveforms. Such models tend to be more effective than the traditional pickers particularly in areas with complicated geology and noise. Recurrent Neural Networks (RNNs), specifically LSTM and GRU networks have been applied to encode temporal relationships to enable the identification of phase onsets in streams of continuous waveforms. Models with transformers also increase the phase picking accuracy through attention mechanisms to emphasize useful time windows and eliminate irrelevant ones. Hybrid networks that jointly use CNNs to extract features and RNNs or Transformers to sequentially interpret the features have performed exceptionally well, and they are frequently capable of human level or better accuracy.

In addition, phase-picking models have been extended to obtain more waveform properties including amplitude, polarity and frequency content, facilitating better downstream processing, e.g. localization and magnitude estimation. More sophisticated DL systems can also be used, which enables shared detection and picking of the waveforms within one complete system, which interprets the waveforms. Other models also use the uncertainty quantification as a measure to estimate the confidence interval around the phase picks, which is a very essential trait in the operational earthquake monitoring. Deep learning in phase picking has significantly lowered the manual workload in phase picking catalog generation, improved the performance of the automated ones, and hastened real-time processes needed in early warning applications.

5.3 Generative Models, Synthetic Data, and Augmentation for Seismic Analysis

Some of the problems that may be encountered with seismic datasets include class imbalance, paucity of labeled data and poor coverage of infrequent or extreme events. The new technological solution to these issues is the use of generative models that generate artificial seismic waveforms that resemble those produced by the real world. The most popular generative models used in seismology are Variational Autoencoders (VAEs) and Generative Adversarial Networks (GANs). VAEs are trained to acquire latent representations of seismic data, which facilitate the production of smooth, continuous variations of the waveforms which indicate signal distributions. GANs, in their turn, are able to produce extremely realistic waveforms by training a generator and discriminator network in a competitive environment. Synthetic earthquake waveforms and noise samples, and even the rare-event waveforms like low-frequency earthquakes or tremors have been generated using GAN-based models.

Such artificial data sets play a critical role in the training of powerful machine learning and deep learning neural networks, particularly in the areas that have a low past history of seismicity. In addition, data augmentation (time shifting, amplitude scaling, spectral modification, noises injection) will increase model generalization and reduce overfitting. Synthetic data can also be used to conduct controlled experiments with new detection algorithms, simulate the possible seismic scenarios and test the performance of early warning systems in different conditions. In addition to generating data, generative models are applied to denoising, waveform imputation, anomaly detection and compressive sensing. The generative model power to acquire rich representations of complex seismic phenomena has greatly extended the analysis possibility of ML-based seismic studies.

5.4 Deep Learning in Earthquake Early Warning (EEW) Systems

Early warning systems (EEW) are designed to give notifications a few seconds to tens of seconds before damaging shaking gets to the populated regions to take critical measures including stopping trains, turning off industrial machinery, and allowing people to find refuge. Conventional EEW systems are based on the fast detection of P-waves and estimation of the location and magnitude of the event usually by a rule-based or physical-model-based method. Nevertheless, these systems may not cope with massive events, new signals or low station coverage. Deep learning has made a paradigm shift in EEW through the introduction of fast, accurate and adaptable models to analyze continuous waveform data and produce predictions in real-time. CNNs and RNNs have been utilized successfully to identify P-wave arrivals in milliseconds and estimate magnitude before S-waves arrive. The use of transformer models has also improved the prediction accuracy, especially for complex or overlapping events, because of their capability to learn large time contexts. Now, end-to-end DL models allow direct mapping from waveform data to useful EEW products, including location, magnitude and predicted shaking. These approaches have a very short latency and can be automatically calibrated to local seismicity. Multi-station deep learning is a type of network used in dense seismic networks, where information sharing across multiple stations is used to remove the need for manual arrival picking and enhance the stability of EEW predictions. There are also some models that quantify uncertainty to enable decision-makers to understand the accuracy of early warnings. Also, EEW systems based on DL may combine real-time information of various sensing devices, such as Distributed Acoustic Sensing (DAS) arrays and accelerometers installed on smart devices, which significantly expands the spatial coverage.

In spite of these advantages, DL-based EEW systems are struggling with the issues of model interpretability, data quality, and computational limitations in real-time implementations. Nevertheless, continued work in the field of lightweight architectures, model compression and edge computing makes them more practical. In general, deep learning is one of the most significant improvements in the evolution of next-generation early warning systems, providing the most high-speed, low error and flexible means of seismic hazard mitigation.

6. CHALLENGES, LIMITATIONS, AND FUTURE RESEARCH DIRECTIONS

6.1 Current Challenges and Limitations in ML/DL-Based Seismic Research

Although machine learning (ML) and deep learning (DL) applications have seen remarkable progress in terms of earthquake prediction, detection, localization, and seismic signal interpretation, there are still a number of challenges that impede their use in the field of operational seismology(Devi, D. R., & Natarajan, V. 2024). The problem of data quality and availability is one of the most constant hindrances. The seismic data is usually unbalanced and there are far more noise records than earthquake records, particularly with small magnitude or microseismic events. Areas with low seismic networks or insufficient instrumentation result in incomplete or low-resolution data, and it is hard to generalize with the help of ML/DL models. Moreover, labeled seismic data, especially when used in tasks like rupture characterization or prediction of rare events, are not very abundant since it is expensive to manually annotate the waveform data with expert knowledge, and also time consuming. This is a constraint of the performance of the supervised learning models and may result in overfitting, particularly when applying models in areas with different geological and noise characteristics compared to the training environment.

The other major problem is the problem of generalization between different regions having different crustal structure and seismic characteristics. Numerous ML/DL models are very effective in their areas of training but fail miserably when used in new geographical locations mainly because of variations in velocity models, sensor locations, noise patterns, and tectonic environments. The process of domain adaptation and transfer learning is also actively being investigated to help to reduce this issue, although the creation of globally generalizable models is still a research frontier. There are also computational constraints especially to real-time seismic monitoring and early warning systems. Although deep learning models are highly accurate, they can also be computationally intensive to train and to infer, and hence are not easily deployed to a resource-constrained environment or when low response time is important to a public safety application.

The other weakness is the interpretability of ML/DL models. The majority of deep learning structures are black boxes, which do not explicitly explain why they make predictions or why they do. This interpretability is important in the field of seismology where the science and trust are very important. Seismologists should be aware of the rationale used by a model, particularly when predictions are used to determine hazards or respond to emergencies. Even though the saliency maps, attention visualization, and feature attribution methods are being utilized to study the decision-making processes of models, interpretability in seismic DL is still a limited field that needs to be studied further. Moreover, the problem of incorporating physical knowledge in ML/DL models is still a challenge. Although data-driven models have the capability of learning complex nonlinear relationships, purely statistical models can be against known laws of physics, or give unrealistic predictions when making predictions beyond view. Physics-informed neural networks (PINNs) are hybrid physical-AI frameworks that have a promising future but remain early in their development.

Lastly, there are also ethical, societal, and policy-related issues that have to be resolved. There are direct implications of earthquake prediction and early warning systems on the safety of the people, false alarms or missed events in the case of incorrect predictions can be disastrous(Rekha, M et al., 2024). It is crucial to make sure that transparency, accountability, and responsible communications of ML/DL-driven predictions are ensured. With more distributed sensor networks and device-based seismic monitoring, privacy is an issue. These issues demonstrate that it is important to have well-established standards, validation workflows, and multidisciplinary collaborations to ensure scientific and social accountability of ML/DL tools.

6.2 Future Research Directions and Opportunities

The future of the ML and DL in seismology is rich, since it can help to resolve the current issues and offer another path to innovation. The development of hybrid models that combine physical knowledge with the use of data-driven learning is one of the promising directions. The new paradigm, which assists in bridging the gap between seismological theory and computational intelligence, is physics-informed neural networks (PINNs), constrained optimization-based models, and hybrid simulation-learning schemes. Inter-regional generalization can be improved by applying simple physical laws that can assist such models to become more interpretable and lessen the colossal consumption of labeled datasets. The multimodal data fusion is another promising way that will involve the fusion of seismic data with other geophysical data that complement each other like GPS, InSAR, gravity fields, and Distributed Acoustic Sensing (DAS). The potential of multimodal learning to improve the detection and characterization of earthquakes is enormous because it can help to see a more comprehensive view of the processes of tectonics, ground deformation, and fault dynamics(Selvakumar, P et al., 2024).

Another opportunity is the development of large foundation models in geoscience. Based on advances in natural language processing models and computer vision, with foundation models trained on large amounts of seismic and geophysical data, it might be possible to have general-purpose AI systems that can do a variety of seismic tasks without task-specific training. These models would not only enhance efficiency, but would also be able to show hidden trends in the seismicity that are previously unknown. Moreover, the increasing use of federated learning also gives the possibility to conduct inter-regional and inter-institutional collaborative seismic research in a way that does not diminish the privacy of data. Federated models can be trained on distributed data where raw data are not shared, but global performance on seismic monitoring models can be improved, even where direct data sharing is limited.

The other significant research direction is real-time DL systems that are optimized to be deployed in the earthquake early warning networks. The development of edge computing, lightweight neural networks, and model compression methods can allow direct inference of deep learning on seismic stations or IoT devices, which will greatly minimize the delays in communication and provide ultra-fast warnings(Sathya, U et al., 2024). This would be very useful especially to developing nations and rural areas where high bandwidth communication infrastructure might not be available. More so, the quantification of uncertainty in ML and DL predictions is a highly valuable area of study. Powerful probabilistic models are required to offer confidence intervals and reliability tests of detection, localization, magnitude estimation and forecasting procedures. The more logical decision-making that will be enabled by such models of uncertainty awareness will be generated and will increase trust in the systems that will be built using the ML-driven seismic. There is also a great potential for generative models in seismic research. GANs and VAEs can be extended to model real earthquake events, to produce synthetic earthquake catalogues and to include rare events in the training data. These generative abilities can be used to generate hazards scenarios and resiliency plan urban infrastructure. Also, explainable AI (XAI) will develop and model decisions are crucial to seismologists, policy-makers, and disaster management agencies. The more explainable processes will increase the transparency and allow the deployment of the ML/DL models into the conventional seismological processes. Finally, the future of ML/DL seismology will be interdisciplinary. The collaboration between geophysicists, data scientists, engineers, policymakers, and emergency management experts will enhance faster conversion of the ML research into practical tools that will assist in mitigation of hazards and disaster preparedness. With the increase in computational power and data volumes, the domain knowledge and sophisticated ML/DL methods will be synergized to become the next wave of seismic studies, allowing more precise, reliable, and practical information about the earthquake mechanisms.

7. CONCLUSION

Machine learning and deep learning have become the revolutionary tools in further development of earthquake prediction, detection, localization, magnitude estimation, and interpretation of seismic signals. It has been shown that these data-driven methods address most of the shortcomings of the classical seismological methods, especially the ability to process noisy waveforms, extract more complex patterns, and apply the analysis in real-time. Since CNNs and RNNs to Transformers, Graph Neural Networks and physics-informed models, the latest ML and DL models have shown remarkable features in detecting delicate seismic signals, increasing the localization error, improving the magnitude prediction, and promoting strong early warning systems. The advances have greatly enlarged the analytical abilities of the seismology and have facilitated the identification of weak events, the characterization of the processes of rupture, and the combination of multimodal geophysical information in a manner that was not previously feasible.

In spite of these successes, there are still a number of challenges. The challenges that restrict the implementation of ML/DL-based seismic systems are the lack of data, the transferability of the models to different regions, interpretability of the models and computational power. The ethical issues such as uncertainty communication, and the impact of false alarms or missed detections in the society are also another aspect to develop an ethical and transparent AI-based system. But the current work on hybrid models, federated learning, generative learning and edge computing provides some insight to remove these constraints. The future of seismic monitoring and hazard mitigation will be determined by the combination of advanced AI technologies, big geophysical data and more sophisticated sensor technologies. The other interdisciplinary efforts of seismologists, data scientists, engineers and policy makers will be crucial to integrate the advances in ML/DL to the operation of the robust and practical systems. These new approaches, in the long term, will make the world more resistant to the hazards of an earthquake, and also contribute to our knowledge of the dynamic processes of the earth.

REFERENCES

Devi, D. R., & Natarajan, V. (2024). Integrating Computational Wisdom: A Comprehensive Examination of Synergized Approaches in Earthquake Forecasting. In *Reshaping Environmental Science Through Machine Learning and IoT* (pp. 59-73). IGI Global Scientific Publishing.

Gnanasekaran, T., Babu, D., Babu, H., & KR, C. L. (2024). An early warning system for predicting earthquakes. In *Novel AI Applications for Advancing Earth Sciences* (pp. 165-185). IGI Global Scientific Publishing.

Goyal, D., Sharma, A., Garg, K. D., Sharma, B., & Dhaou, I. B. (2023, December). The Internet of Things (IoT) Contribution to Natural Disaster Management. In *2023 20th ACS/IEEE International Conference on Computer Systems and Applications (AICCSA)* (pp. 1-7). IEEE.

Kaswan, K. S., Dhatterwal, J. S., & Kumar, K. (2021). Blockchain of internet of things-based earthquake alarming system in smart cities. In *Integration and implementation of the internet of things through cloud computing* (pp. 272–287). IGI Global. DOI: 10.4018/978-1-7998-6981-8.ch014

Lalitha, S. D., Madiajagan, M., Rajakumari, S., & Manikandan, R. (2024). Enhancing Earthquake Prediction With Reinforcement Learning. In *Novel AI Applications for Advancing Earth Sciences* (pp. 273–290). IGI Global Scientific Publishing.

Ponmalar, A., Vijayakumar, K., Lakshmipriya, C., Karthikeyan, M., Gracelin Sheena, B., Beslin Pajila, P. J., & Siva Subramanian, R. (2024). Meta-Heuristics and Machine Learning Applications in Complex Systems. In *Metaheuristic and Machine Learning Optimization Strategies for Complex Systems* (pp. 257–275). IGI Global Scientific Publishing.

Prasad, D., Hassan, A., Verma, D. K., Sarangi, P., & Singh, S. (2021, November). Disaster management system using wireless sensor network: A review. In *2021 International Conference on Computational Intelligence and Computing Applications (ICCICA)* (pp. 1-6). IEEE. Murugaraj, S. S., & Kumar, S. (2024). Neuro-Inspired Algorithms for Earthquake Monitoring and Prediction. In *Novel AI Applications for Advancing Earth Sciences* (pp. 315-329). IGI Global Scientific Publishing.

Rekha, M., Chilambuchelvan, A., Dinesh Babu, M., & Vasudhevan, V. (2024). Development of a Neuro-Inspired Algorithms for Monitoring and Prediction of Earthquakes. In *Novel AI Applications for Advancing Earth Sciences* (pp. 86–100). IGI Global Scientific Publishing.

Sathya, U., Hashini, S., Lakshmipriya, C., Varun, C. M., & Nalini, M. (2024, December). Emerging Trends and Future Prospects in Internet of Things (IoT) Technology. In *2024 International Conference on Sustainable Communication Networks and Application (ICSCNA)* (pp. 79-85). IEEE.

Selvakumar, P., Vijayakumar, G., Vigneshkumar, P., Umamaheswari, M. S., & Selvamurugan, C. (2024). Prediction of earthquakes, volcanic eruptions, tornadoes, wildfires, and droughts through artificial intelligence. In *Utilizing AI and Machine Learning for Natural Disaster Management* (pp. 133–145). IGI Global Scientific Publishing.

Subramanian, R. S., Ramana, T. V., Ramana, K. V., Prabha, S., & Nivaskumar, V. (2025). Converging Horizons: Synergies of 6G Wireless Communication, Machine Learning, and Embedded Systems for Intelligent Connectivity. *The Intersection of 6G, AI/Machine Learning, and Embedded Systems*, 67-93.

Sundari, V. M., Rose, R. M., Sassirekha, S. M., Nalini, M., & Girija, P. (2024, November). Deep Learning: Techniques, Taxonomy, Applications, and Future Directions. In *2024 International Conference on Smart Technologies for Sustainable Development Goals (ICSTSDG)* (pp. 1-5). IEEE.

Venketbabu, T., Aswathy, M. P., Sangeetha, J., Anish, T. P., Nalini, M., & Subramanian, R. S. (2024, October). Revolutionizing Image Processing: Innovations Impacts and Future Trends. In *2024 2nd International Conference on Self Sustainable Artificial Intelligence Systems (ICSSAS)* (pp. 901-907). IEEE.

Yamini, B., Beslin, P. P., Anish, T. P., Gracelin, S. B., Dinesh, M. G., Nalini, M., & Siva, S. R. (2024). Advancements in Cognitive Radio Networks: Protocols, Architectures, Challenges, and Future Perspectives. In *Spectrum and Power Allocation in Cognitive Radio Systems* (pp. 1-17). IGI Global.

Chapter 9
Machine Learning-Driven Classification of Volcanic Seismicity and Tremor Signals for Early Eruption Forecasting

Durga Devi Anbazhagan
http://orcid.org/0009-0009-8496-0490
Saveetha Engineering College, India

Sunitha T.
http://orcid.org/0009-0003-1958-8959
Saveetha Engineering College, India

ABSTRACT

Volcanic seismic activity is crucial to learning about magmatic and hydrothermal activity beneath the surface, which gives early warning of possibly occurring earthquakes or eruptions. As the seismic networks grow, manual analysis is no longer feasible, and machine learning is the primary solution in the area of automated classification of the waveforms. The chapter is an overview of sophisticated methods of computing volcanic seismic signals, with a focus on deep learning algorithms, including CNNs, LSTMs, and transformers. It describes an entire methodology including

DOI: 10.4018/979-8-3373-8042-1.ch009

preprocessing, model extraction, model validation, and model deployment in real-time. Such challenges as noise, class imbalance, generalization, and interpretability have been discussed, with future directions also being multimodal data fusion, probabilistic model, self-supervised learning, and AI-based early-warning pipelines.

INTRODUCTION

Volcanoes are natural cracks in the surface of the earth where the molten rock, gases and ash may project out through the cracks. Sometimes, a volcanic eruption can take place rather abruptly and without much prior notice due to the accumulation of pressure. These volcanic activities have the potential to impact on communities in the area, transport, air and the environment. Due to their random character, it is of paramount importance to work out early eruption forecasting systems.The unpredictability of the eruption and the large diversity of hazards associated with it lava flows, ash plumes, pyroclastic density currents, gas, and lahars make strong early warning systems a necessity (Bornstein & Randall 2022).

One of the most important tool for predicting eruption is the study of volcanic seismicity, surveillance aids scientists in knowing what is going on under the volcano even when the processes are going on deep beneath the ground and it is impossible to see.

What is Volcanic Seismicity?

Volcanic Seismicity refers to all forms of ground vibrations or earthquakes produced due to volcanic activities including magma movements, changes in pressure of gasses, fracturing of rocks, and interaction of fluids inside of the volcano are all considered volcanic seismicity.

These seismic signals are "messages" sent by the volcano about its activities within the volcano and they enable the scientists to know whether the volcano is silent, agitated, or going to erupt.

Need for AutomaticVolcanic Seismicity

Historically, seismic observations were intensive in terms of skills of skilled seismologists who could observe the patterns of the waveforms with the naked eye and manually categorize them. Despite the importance of expert interpretation, the fast growth of seismic networks, improved data resolution and higher sampling frequencies has imposed workloads that are well beyond human capability. Modern volcanic observatories handle tens to hundreds of broadband sensors, producing millions of seismic event candidates per month. In this situation, manual classification is not only time consuming but also inconsistent and is likely to be erroneous especially when volcanic unrest is rife and quick decision making is essential.

Machine Learning (ML) presents a large-scale and effective paradigm of the analysis of volcanic seismicity. Continuous real-time ML-based systems have the ability to automatically identify, classify, and train complex antecedent patterns with seismic data. In contrast to the classical rule-based systems that rely on the manually constructed thresholds, the ML models are trained directly on the labeled data and generalize to the unknown signals. This allows objective, consistent and faster monitoring, which would greatly reduce the workload to human analysts and enhance accuracy in classification.

Figure 1 introduces a more detailed conceptual framework of the traditional and ML-based methods and shows the entire automated pipeline. The improved structure comprises of major steps like seismic data collection with distributed sensor networks, signal preprocessing (noise removal, normalization), feature extraction or waveform representation (time-series, spectrograms) and model training. State-of-the-art models like Convolutional Neural Networks (CNNs), Long Short-Term Memory (LSTM) networks, and Transformer based models are added to represent spatial, temporal and long-range relationships in seismic signals. Also, generative models like Generative Adversarial Networks (GANs) are also viewed as alternatives in data augmentation and managing an imbalance in classes.

Figure 1. Manual vs machine learning-based framework for classification of approaches for categorizing volcanic seismicity.

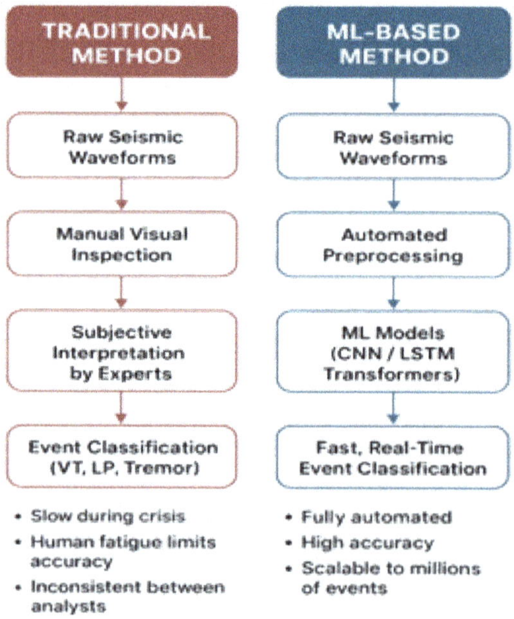

The framework can also consider multimodal data such as gases, deformation, temperature and gas etc., which can be used to forecast eruptions. comprehensively. The output layer will include event classification (e.g. VT, LP, tremor), and probabilistic eruption prediction. The typical performance metrics used such as accuracy, precision, recall, F1-score and real-time delay can be used to evaluate and compare their models with traditional approaches.

Compared to traditional systems, the ML systems are scalable, faster, and more consistent. However, there are challenges such as data quality, model interpretability, too, are important considerations. Overall, this new structure focuses on the move to more intelligent, automatic and data-driven volcano monitoring systems, to help enhance hazard assessment and advance early eruption warning.

RELATED WORK

Volcano seismology has seen an acceleration in the past five years due to the few years as a result of the emergence of machine learning and deep learning technologies. Human interpretation has been replaced with automated systems capable of processing big-data seismic data in real time. The improved quality of seismic data and the ability to process has allowed the use of data-driven models to improve and scale up monitoring.

New studies have demonstrated the capability of deep learning models (and in particular, Convolutional Neural Networks (CNNs)) can be used for seismic signal classification of volcanic activity.As an example, Titos et al. (2018) built on the previous studies by refining CNN models trained on spectrogram representations, and they were more accurate in classifying long-period (LP), volcano-tectonic (VT), and tremor events. Equally, Perol et al. (2018) have presented deep neural network frameworks to detect earthquakes, which are modified to volcanic settings with substantial sensitivity and strength to detect noise.

Alongside CNNs, recurrent neural networks like Long Short-Term Memory (LSTM) networks have also been popular in learning seismic signal temporal dependencies. Zhu et al. (2021) have shown that the LSTM-based models are effective in capturing the time-dependent patterns of continuous seismic streams, which can be effectively used to identify the changing volcanic activity. More hybrid models based on CNN and LSTM have been found to enhance performance by taking advantage of both spatial and temporal features and are therefore applicable to real time monitoring applications.

Recently, transformer-based models have become a strong competitor to seismic time-series analysis. Mousavi et al. (2020) suggested attention-based models that are superior to traditional sequential models because they are able to capture long-range dependencies in waveform data. Such models have demonstrated good performance in predicting complicated seismic patterns related to volcanic activities. They are becoming more relevant to the modern observatory systems due to their scalability and capability to handle large datasets.

The application of generative artificial intelligence (seismic data augmented) is another important development over recent years. The use of Generative Adversarial Networks (GANs) and Variational Autoencoders (VAEs) to produce synthetic seismic signals is a solution to the problem of class imbalance in training data. Li et al. (2023) revealed that GAN-generated data leads to better classification, especially in rare volcanic events. These approaches boost the generalization and stability of models, especially when dealing with limited data. .

Multimodal data integration has also been used to improve volcanic monitoring systems. Recent research by Valade et al. (2019) has integrated seismicity, gas emissions and and deformation to get better forecasts. This allows to better volcanic processes better, by correlating multiple geophysical signals, which leads to more accurate forecasting of eruptions. Also, the use of machine learning models for real-time monitoring systems has also received a great deal of attention. Low-cost neural networks and edge computing have been have been proposed to process seismic data on-site. Chen et al. (2023) developed efficient learning models that are designed to be infer as quickly as possible, with low latency and quick responsiveness to early warning systems.

While these advances have occurred, concerns such as data variability, noise and model interpretability are still research topics of concern. Recent research has been on explainable AI approaches for improving model transparency. Visualization and feature attribution methods are being considered to find the influential part of the waveform that affect classification results.

In general, the past five years have witnessed a dramatic increase in the use of the newest machine learning, deep learning, and generative AI models to analyse volcanic seismic data. Such advancements have enhanced the precision, magnitude, and trustworthiness of automated surveillance systems, which have opened the path to more effectual early warning and danger reduction measures in volcanology.

FOUNDATIONS OF VOLCANIC SEISMICITTY

The volcanic seismicity is an indication of the mechanical response of the crust and magmatic plumbing system of the Earth to the stress and pressure as well as the fluid movement. In contrast to tectonic earthquakes, volcanic seismic events have high variety of wave forms and frequencies, times and physical causes. The basic knowledge on the basic kinds of volcanic seismic signals is necessary in designing effective ML classification systems (Chouet & Matoza, 2013).

1. Volcanic-Tectonic (VT) Earthquakes

VT earthquakes are caused by brittle fracturing when magma intrudes or moves outwards to give signals that weaken tectonic quakes. They expose the stress state of magma bodies, and commonly are related with the movement of dykes or sills. VT events are usually characterized by evident P- and S-wave arrivals, high frequency (2-20 Hz) content, short impulsive periods and hypocenters following a path of magma. VT swarms are also important precursors of eruptions.

2. Long-Period (LP) Events

The LP events are due to the resonant effect of the fluid in cracks or conduits as opposed to brittle rupture. Their processes are magma degassing, fluid pressurization, conduit resonance, and hydrothermal activity. Before eruptions, the LP activity often increases, and the changes in LP signals are the important elements of early-warning systems.

3. Hybrid Events

Hybrid events merge brittle and fluid-driven processes, which display high-frequency VT-like event, and low-frequency LP-type coda. They are linked to the shallow magma ascent and conduit instability, thus they are useful predictors of the impending eruption.

4. Volcanic Tremor

A volcanic tremor is an ongoing vibration, which takes between one to two hours and occurs due to the movement of magma, the flow of gases or due to the activity of an active vent. There are such types of tremors as harmonic (constant frequencies), spasmodic (not constant amplitudes), and broadband (associated with degassing or fountaining lava). When the intensity or style of tremor changes, there is often a change in the eruptive activity.

5. Very-Long-Period (VLP) Events

A volcanic tremor is an ongoing vibration, which takes between one to two hours and occurs due to the movement of magma, the flow of gases or due to the activity of an active vent. There are such types of tremors as harmonic (constant frequencies), spasmodic (not constant amplitudes), and broadband (associated with degassing or fountaining lava). When the intensity or style of tremor changes, there is often a change in the eruptive activity.

6. Rockfalls, Lahars and Explosion Events

Non-volcanic events such as rockfalls, collapses and lahars generate irregular broadband waveforms, which cannot be identified without the use of ML. The explosive gas releases produce sharp bursts of pressure which are used to follow the vent activity and eruptive strength.

Necessity of seismic classification To see the reason why we classify seismic, look at the following connections at table 1:

Table 1. Seismic event types and their roles in eruption forecasting

Event Type	Primary Cause	Implication in Eruption Forecasting
VT Earthquakes	Brittle failure of rock	Stress Changes, magma ascent initiation
LP Events	Resonance in fluid-filled cracks	Fluid Pressurization, magma migration
Hybrid Events	Mixed brittle + fluid processes	Strong eruption precursors
Tremor	Sustained Fluid/gas movement	High eruption probability
VLP Events	Large-Scalepressure fluctuations	Deep magma movement

MACHINE LEARNINGFOUNDATIONS

The basics of machine learning are the concepts that enable computers to learn a pattern based on the data. These techniques assist in the systems to make an automatic way of improving without human programming. Machine learning can be used in volcanic monitoring to evaluate massive amounts of seismic data in an efficient and error-free manner. It assists in functions such as identifying the form of events, identifying abnormal behavior, and anticipating changes. These are some of the foundations that need to be understood before using the advanced ML models in volcanic seismicity.

Supervised Learning

Machine learning usage in the volcanic seismic classification process relies on supervised learning. Under this method, examples of seismic waveforms along with labels which indicate the type of underlying event, i.e., volcano-tectonic earthquakes, long-period events, hybrid earthquakes, tremors or explosion signals, etc. are provided to the model. In the course of repeated exposure to these designated datasets, the model can slowly acquire the associations between the raw waveform attributes and the respective categories. This is done by setting millions of internal parameters to minimize the gap between the model predictions and the actual labels in this learning process. A successful training process does not only demand big and varied datasets but proper labeling which is given by highly trained seismologists with knowledge of the physics of volcanic systems. After being trained, a supervised learning model comprising a trained seismic event classifier can deliver rapid and objective seismic event interpretations in real time that can aid in early-warning decision-making during an eruptive crisis.

Classical Methods of Machine Learning

The classical machine learning algorithms can still be used in the classification of volcanic seismic, in situations where there is a small dataset or limited computing capacity. These techniques are based on hand-crafted features like statistics of amplitudes, spectral peaks, waveform envelopes and frequency-energy distributions, which are further modeled with the help of classifiers like Support Vector Machines, Random Forests or Gradient Boosting. Hand-crafted features can provide contingency at high frequencies (VT signatures or emergent LP onsets) due to good knowledge of seismic signal properties, and provide transparency and interpretability that are useful to scientific analysis. They are, however, not well able to extrapolate to other volcanoes whose seismic behavior differs and they can usually tend to work poorly with highly variable or noisy signals. The restrictions have promoted the transition to deep learning methods, which directly learn complicated features out of waveform data.

Deep Learning Approaches

Seismic classification has been revolutionised by deep learning which removes the selected features and extracts features directly from the waveform or from time-frequency representations like spectrograms. Using convolutional Neural Networks (CNNs), e.g., it is to learn spatial features of spectrograms, e.g., harmonics, resonance structure, or low-frequency energy content of LP and tremor events. Likewise, 1D CNNs are capable of operating on raw waveform sequences and extract onset, oscillation and oscillation, amplitude pattern filters useful to seismic classification. Recurrent neural networks (such as the models (such as the Long Short-

Term Memory (LSTM) models) learn time dependency, and therefore can be applied to seismicity with gradual variations or continuous tremor (Sudhan, M., et al. (2025).

However, **transformer-based architectures** have become popular in the more recent era due to their capability to reason about long range dependencies with self-attention mechanisms. This enables the model to dynamically concentrate the most pertinent sections of the waveform on any of their locations within the sequence. The overall performance of deep learning models has been seen to be better in almost all volcanic seismic data. Their main advantage is that they are able to find complex and nonlinear relationships in the data automatically and do not require hand-crafted features. Nevertheless, they have more computation power and high demands on larger datasets when training. Nevertheless, deep learning has overtaken all other techniques because of its unrivaled accuracy and flexibility, and advanced early-warning systems that can match the performance of experts.

Why Machine Learning is Applicable to Seismic Data?

Machine learning has been effective in seismic data especially since seismic signals possess rich patterns that mirror the physical processes undertaken within a volcano. These signals include complicated time-frequency relationships, and are frequently nonlinearly changing between states, have emergent spectral properties, and subtle amplitude modulations which can hardly be captured using classical statistical methods. There are also other significant noises in volcanic environments that cause wind, rain, human activity, and mechanical resonances that make it more difficult to hand interpret. Machine learning models, specifically the deep learning networks, are good at identifying meaningful patterns in noisy data by learning feature representations that are robust to learning.

In addition, volcanic seismicity is usually characterized by the changing behavior of magma or fracturing, increased vent activity, or change in eruptive rhythms. The machine learning models are able to embrace these changes through learning new training examples hence increase their performance as time goes by. Alternating to fixed rule-based systems, ML methods are flexible and are able to extrapolate to other volcanoes when trained on divergent datasets. They can detect anomalies many times before they can be seen visually in seismogram raw data; this is due to their capability to analyze large time windows, frequency patterns, and waveforms shapes all at the same time. This renders machine learning to be ideally relevant to the real-time requirements of the modern volcano monitoring systems where quick, consistent and objective classification is necessary to mitigate hazards.

DATA ACQUISITION AND PREPARING

Data Sources

Machine learning Volcanic seismic Data available to machine learning applications are sourced from a very broad base of monitoring agencies and world seismic data bases, each of which brings its own waveform properties due to local volcanic conditions, station designs, and instrumentation guidelines. Big foreign repositories like IRIS archives long-term seismic records of broadband data of many of the world volcanoes so that researchers can build large and diversified datasets to build models. The Hawaii, Alaska, and the Cascades are densely monitored by national agencies, such as the USGS Volcano Observatories, which record high-resolution waveforms at various phases of volcanic activity. In the same light, other observatories like INGV in Italy, JMA in Japan, PVMBG in Indonesia and Geophysical Institute of Ecuador provide continuous seismic data of some of the most active and dangerous volcanoes in the world. The datasets usually contain normal background signal and high-intensity sequences during the eruptions which provide a good variety of seismic phenomena to the machine learning. This diversity in the datasets around the globe enhances the generalization capabilities of the ML models such that they can be reliable when applied to various volcanic systems.

Preprocessing Workflow

Preprocessing is a significant part of the process of machine learning of raw seismic waveforms since the quality and consistency of the raw seismic data highly determine the performance of the models. Seismic signals need to be detrended and demeaned prior to the process of average drift removal and the offset caused by instruments. Waveforms are then subjected to a set of specially chosen band-pass filters to discriminate the pertinent frequency bands relating to volcanic activity and limits the background noise sources of wind, precipitation and cultural activity. The sampling rate may vary between different stations and observatories and therefore resampling may be necessary to provide a uniform sampling rate so as to allow inputs to be compatible (Keerthiga et al.2023).

The signals are divided into fixed-length windows which capture entire events and preserve the time synchrony. Instrumental response removal is often required to normalize the amplitudes of the waveforms and the content of the frequency spectrum so that the models can concentrate on the natural aspects of seismic phenomena and not on sensor artifacts. Other preprocessing methods are amplitude normalization, denoising using wavelet transforms or spectral subtraction, and conversion to time-frequency representation to models that use spectrograms. This structured workflow can be used to turn raw seismic data into a uniform and noise-optimized dataset that can be used to train and make inferences with machine learning.

The following diagram (figure 2) presents the entire machine-learning and preprocessing process of classifying volcanic seismic events beginning with data collection through to the final assessment of the model.

Figure 2. Machine learning workflow for classifying volcanic seismic events

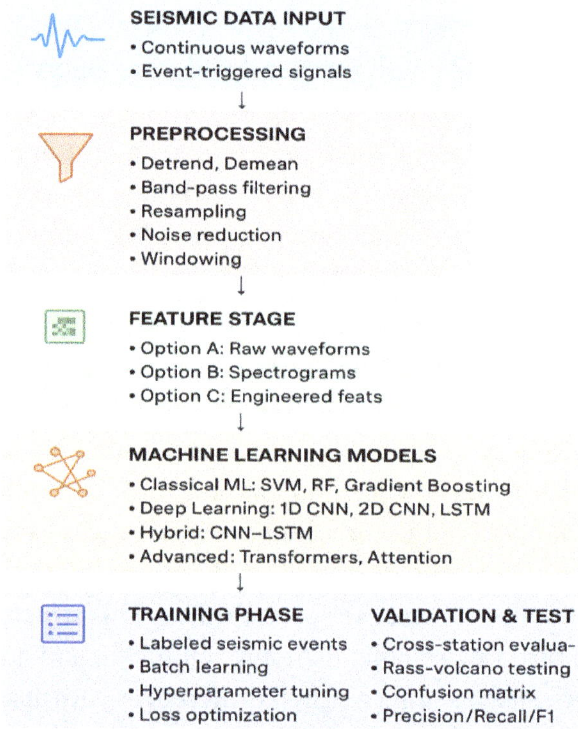

Annotation and Labeling

One of the most tedious but vital tasks that should be performed to create a high-quality supervised learning dataset is labeling seismic events. The characteristics of waveforms analyzed by experts seismologists to understand whether the signal is a VT, LP or hybrid, tremor, VLP or explosion event are sharpness of onset, frequency content, coda shape and duration. This involves profound knowledge of the domain and often the process of matching seismic recordings to other monitoring data, e.g. deformation or gas emissions. The volcanic seismicity is highly non-stationary and variable, making it difficult to have uniform labels, particularly when the signature of an event is overlapping or varies over the period of its eruption. In an effort to enhance reliability, others of the observatories engage in collaborative labelling in which two or more experts are called on the same data and cases of uncertainty are settled.

Managing Imbalanced Data

Volcanic seismic data often exhibit serious class imbalance which is a state where a small set of event types are many times more prevalent than the others. As an illustration, continuous tremor and high-frequency volcano-tectonic earthquakes might be dominant in a dataset and LP events or hybrid events (which are frequently the most diagnostically significant events leading to eruptions) might be infrequent. This is the major issue with machine learning models, which prefer majority classes when being trained and, thus, detect poorly rare yet important precursory signals. When it is a case of imbalance, it is inappropriate to use careless methodological approaches. They usually use data augmentation, which brings artificial changes in the minority-class waveforms by introducing time shifts, noise injections, or scale changes (amplification or attenuation), or frequency perturbation.

Oversampling methods like SMOTE create artificial samples through interpolating existing signals of a minority-class. Generative adversarial networks (GANs) are also applied to generate realistic waveforms in similar cases, making more of the rare occurring types represented. Another solution based on weighted loss functions is class-weighted loss functions that force the minority classes to be misclassified less during training. These strategies can be used to make sure that machine learning models become sensitive across all types of events so that they are better at identifying rare yet geophysically noteworthy signals that can be precursors of eruptive activity.

MACHINE LEARNING ALGORITHMS FOR SEISMIC CLASSIFICATION

1. Support Vector Machines (SVMs)

The Support Vector Machines have been historically among the most successful classical machine learning algorithms in seismic event classification because they can be used on low-dimensional feature sets and scanty training data. SVMs are generally applied in volcanic seismicity research, in cases where a particular frequency of waveform or spectral object (dominant frequency, bandwidth, amplitude ratios, spectral entropy, or statistical object) has been extracted. The SVM algorithm has a decision boundary which maximizes the difference between different classes and it is able to make reliable separation between different types of events, as in the case of volcano-tectonic earthquakes, long-period events and tremors. As SVMs use kernel functions that are mathematically robust, they can learn nonlinear associations among features; they can do this use nonlinear relationships between features even when the feature space is relatively small. They are especially strong at incidents where data is limited, when labeling is costly or when the physical nature of signals is well comprehended. While SVMs are simple in relative to deep learning models, SVMs can be used for prototyping and real-time applications, and in resource-constrained environments, such as remote observatory sites (Kong et al. 2019).

2. Gradient Boosting Methods and Random Forests

Gradient Boosting models and the Random Forests are tree ensemble models are widely used in seismic classification for their power and interpretability. These algorithms are successful in that they learn a number of decision trees and then combine predictions to make a single, coherent forecast. They are commonly learned from features extracted from time and frequency domain analysis in volcano applications. Random Forests are also able to handle noisy data, and also have a feature-importance scoring that allows volcanologists to find out which attributes of have the biggest impact on classification results.

Gradient Boosting (such as XGBoost or LightGBM) is a variant of this approach, which at each step corrects the errors of previous trees to build very robust models even in cases where the temporal and spectral properties of the signals have overlap. Such algorithms are likely to perform well in small to medium sized data sets and can be applied in cases where computational resources or labeled data is limited. Their simplicity and transparency makes them attractive to be used in the observatory processing pipelines that require high accuracy and interpretability.

3. CNNs 1D Convolutional Neural Networks

One-dimensional Convolutional Neural Networks (CNNs) are a significant advancement in seismic classification by allowing models to directly utilise data in the form of waveforms.1D CNNs can learn filters that are not hand-crafted features that detect important features of the waveform such as onsets, oscillations, tremor bursts or amplitude modulation. This ability to learn on the entire waveform is what makes 1D CNNs very good at discriminating subtle differences between volcanoes, such as hybrid earthquakes, with the waveform traces differing across the high-frequency portions. The local features are detected by sliding the convolutional filters along the time and combined in a hierarchical manner in pooling layers of the model. This synergy between the automatic feature extractor and the ability to learn higher order patterns result in models that are faster over classical algorithms over most volcanic data. Finally, 1D CNNs can be run at nearly real-time speed and thus can be used for continuous monitoring (Gentili et al. 2020).

4. Two-Dimensional Convolutional Neural Networks to Classify Spectrogram

Two-dimensional CNNs are used extensively to classify spectrograms since these timefrequency images are richer to identify with respect to patterns that are simpler to detect and go through. Spectrograms point out to the spectral dynamics of volcanic seismicity by harmonic tremor bands, frequency gliding behavior in hybrid events, or focus of low frequencies in LP events. 2D CNNs are trained on these images in the same way as they are on natural-image classification problems, and learn spatial filters that capture important features in time and frequency space. This causes models that have high discriminative ability, especially in cases where several event types are closely related in terms of time (but not in terms of the spectrum). As an example, the tremor signals give horizontally aligned spectral bands, LP events have strong zone of low frequencies, and VT events have wide-band high-frequency content. This ability to distinguish 2D CNNs has led them to become a popular option in volcano monitoring research. And, spectrograms are relatively robust to noise, and models are likely to remain accurate perform to high accuracy even if individual waveforms are disturbed.

5. Advanced Deep Learning and Hybrid Models

Cutting-edge deep learning techniques have significantly enhanced classification of signals by capturing both spatial and temporal features in volcanic seismograms. Hybrid models such as CNN-LSTM combine the advantages of convolutional and recurrent neural networks to gain a better understanding of seismic signals. In these models, CNN layers get spatial information and features from the raw seismic waveform or spectrogram, such as amplitude and frequency changes. LSTM layers get temporal and sequential information over time. This combination is particularly useful to detect changes in volcanic activity such as the transition discrete earthquake events turn into a continuous low-frequency tremor.

Transformer-based models are a recent innovation which rely on self-attention to capture long distance relationships in seismic time series. Transformers can consider among distant parts of a seismic waveform, making them excellent tools to detect complex and slowly evolving volcanic activity. Their capacity to process big data and merge data from multiple stations makes them even more valuable in monitoring networks (Mikesell et al. 2023).

Together with these models, generative AI models such as Generative Adversarial Networks (GANs) and Variational Autoencoders (VAEs) are increasingly used to improve models work better. These generate fake seismic events to balance class distribution, particularly rare volcanic events. This enhances the classification performance and allows for the wider range of data. Also, recent multimodal learning approaches are being developed that incorporate seismic data and other geophysical data, such as gas, deformation, and thermal data, to improve eruption forecasts. These deep models are good, but they require tremendous computation power and large labeled datasets. However, new developments in efficient model designs and edge computing are making them usable in real-time applications (Ai et al. 2023).

6. Comparative Analysis of Machine Learning Models

To further determine the effectiveness of various machine learning methods to the volcanic seismic signal classification, various studies have conducted a comparative analysis of experimental datasets using the machine learning methods. The classical machine learning algorithms like Support Vector Machines (SVM) and the Random Forests usually perform well when the size of the dataset is small and the features are engineered by hand. Their performance however tends to decline when it comes to complicated patterns of waveforms or large scale seismic data.

The high-performing features of deep learning models and Convolutional Neural Networks (CNNs), in particular, in learning the hierarchical aspect of the waveform data and spectrogram representations are automatic. Hybrid models like CNN-LSTM are also more effective in that it results in better performance since they capture both spatial and temporal features of a seismic signal. More recently, transformer-based models have demonstrated encouraging performance since they are capable of capturing long-range connections in seismic sequences through the mechanisms of attention.

Table 2. A comparative assessment of models aligned with the machine learning framework depicted in Figure 1.

Method	Accuracy	Precision	Recall	F1-Score
SVM	78%	0.76	0.74	0.75
Random Forest	82%	0.80	0.79	0.79
CNN	90%	0.89	0.88	0.88
CNN-LSTM	93%	0.92	0.91	0.91
Transformer-based	95%	0.94	0.93	0.93

According to the results of experimental work, deep learning models can traditionally reach an accuracy of 85-95 percent in classification, depending on the data and preprocessing schemes. The CNN-based models tend to be better than classical machine learning algorithms especially in long period events and tremor detections. These relative findings demonstrate that deep learning models offer better accuracy, scale, and strength to automated volcanic surveillance models.The comparative results in Table 2 support the idea that deep learning models are better than traditional methods for classifying volcanic seismic signals.

TRAINING,VALIDATION AND TUNING

Training Procedures

Volcanic seismic classification Training machine learning models to classify raw waveforms or spectrograms to a corresponding event class. In the course of training, the pattern of frequency content, shape of waveforms, onsets of events, and time-frequency characteristics among others are acquired as the model is repeatedly fed labeled data. Deep learning algorithms optimize millions of parameters through the backpropagation algorithm, on which prediction errors inform gradient changes. The training data is subdivided into batches, which are computationally efficient, and such crucial parameters as the learning rate, the type of optimizer, the size of the batch, and the count of epochs greatly impact the performance. Overtraining and undertraining are both detrimental to results and therefore one will always need to monitor the accuracy, loss and any other parameter to ensure that the model is not just memorizing the data but learning its general patterns.

Validation Strategies

Validation assists a trained model to perform better on unseen volcanic seismic data and it avoids overfitting. A small part of the events are usually set aside as the validation set and the trend of the model in terms of accuracy, loss, precision, recall, and the trend of a confusion matrix are observed during the training process. Better methods also have k-fold cross-validation, where the data is divided into folds and a fine-grained analysis of the model is performed. The leave-one-station-out or leave-one-eruption-out techniques are crucial in volcanology as the seismic patterns of stations and eruptions vary significantly. These techniques simulate the real-life testing scenarios, and are helpful in determining that the model will be able to generalise to new, unseen data, not simply over-fit the training data.

Hyper-Parameter Tuning

Hyper-parameter optimization is critical in maximizing the performance and generalization capability of volcanic seismic classification models since such parameters dictate the way the model is trained. Deep learning models depend on hyper-parameters like learning rate, depth of the network, number of convolutional filters, kernel size, dropout rate, type of activation and network design, whereas classical models depend on hyper-parameters like the number of trees in the Random Forests or on the type of kernel used in Support Vector Machines. Since the optimum values require the complexity of seismic data, manual tuning can be ineffective, instead, automated search techniques such as grid search, random search, and Bayesian optimization are applied. The application of Bayesian optimization is particularly effective in the case of deep learning as it chooses the promising configurations on the basis of the earlier evaluations. Adequate tuning can be used to attain a compromise of computational cost, accuracy and model generalization (Ross et al. 2018).

Avoiding Overfitting and Improving Generalization

The problem of overfitting has been common in machine learning when working on imbalanced or limited seismic data, where the model can become overly trained on the training data, and is not capable of predicting new signals. There are a number of measures used to stop overfitting. The regularization methods like L1 or L2 penalties assist in limiting the parameters of the model and discourage an overly complicated decision space. In deep learning networks, dropout layers are often added, where the neurons are turned off at random during training to encourage redundancy and feature representation robustness. Another popular method is early stopping whereby the training is interrupted when the validation loss starts to rise, meaning that the model is already starting to memorize the training data. The data augmentation is also crucial to enhance generalization, which adds variations of the existing events suggested by time shifting, amplitude scaling, noise addition, or frequency change. These variations bring the model to a wider range of diversity in waveforms without the need of new labeled samples. A combination of these methods guarantees the end model to be robust enough to changes in the waveform properties, noise behavior and station configurations.

Cross-Volcano and Cross-Station Generalization Forthcomings

One of the most difficult but significant objectives of volcanic monitoring is to achieve generalization between various volcanoes and seismic networks. The signatures of seismic events between volcanoes differ considerably because magma composition, the geometry of conduits, hydrothermal processes, the position of station and geological formations are different. A model that has been trained on one volcano will thus suffer when used in a different volcano, and it is therefore not very useful in world monitoring processes. To tackle this, training datasets are usually assembled consisting of various volcanoes and contain a range of different event types, eruption styles and noise conditions.

Cross-station validation is used to make sure that the model has not accidentally learned station-specific artifacts instead of real event characteristics. The use of transfer learning is also becoming popular, in which a pre-trained model is further trained on a smaller dataset of a new volcano, with much lower data requirements but with generally applicable knowledge. These methods have been found to be useful in lessening the workforce required to implement the ML models in volcanoes with scarce labeled data. Cross-volcano generalization is a research field that is yet to be fully explored, though with better datasets and more sophisticated neural architectures, machine learning is gradually becoming more versatile in a variety of different volcanic environments.

EVALUATION METRICS

Performance Metrics

The most popular indicator of machine learning models to classify volcanic seismic data is accuracy. It can be deceptive when there is the imbalance in datasets though since the model might only reflect the most common amongst them without identifying events that are not common but critical. Thus, precision, recall, and F1-score should be used to justify accuracy as it gives a more accurate assessment of the model to identify various seismic events like LP, hybrid, or VLP signal. Precision quantifies the accuracy with which the model predicts the particular class and recall measures the accuracy with which the model finds all the real instances of the same particular class which is particularly useful in predicting low rate events. The F1-score is a precision-recall ratio that is balanced and applies to skewed data sets where minority classes can otherwise be disregarded. A confusion matrix also assists in assessing performance by depicting correct and incorrect classifications as well as identifying misclassification patterns, e.g., hybrids are mistaken with LP events.

Multiclass ROC Curves and AUC

ROC curves and the Area Under the Curve (AUC) which are normally used for binary classification to multiclass volcanic seismic data. These measures assist in the trade-off between the detection true positive and false positive rate of different events. events. They are particularly useful for the discrimination of complex events, e.g. LP, VLP and hybrid. The AUC provides an independent measure of the ability of the part classes with threshold-independent values as it increases to provide increased discrimination even in the case of noise or confusion.

Real-Time Performance and Latency

During the monitoring activities of volcanoes, machine learning models should be evaluated on latency, speed and throughput. Latency can be defined as the time it takes the model to receive the seismic waveforms and produce predictions. This is crucial in the case of an eruptive crisis when decisions need to be made. A model that is good in laboratory tests, may not be good in practice where it might be too complex or it is not able to run efficiently on edge devices used in remote monitoring stations. Real time analysis can be used to maintain efficient processing of real-time seismic data.

Resilience and Resistance to Noise

Environmental resiliency Volcanic surveys require a strong ability against environmental noise. Some wind, rain, cultural noise or mechanical vibration tend to interfere with seismic. A useful model should have high classification accuracy in the case of low signal-noise. The noise robustness is typically tested with artificial corrupted signals or with the real recordings that are picked up in a noisy environment. The stability analysis also makes sure that the model can provide consistent prediction on the various training subsets or in repeated experiments. These features are crucial when dealing with real-world early warning systems when the data conditions tend to be unpredictable.

CASE STUDIES AND APPLICATIONS

1. Application at Active Stratovolcanoes

Machine learning has demonstrated that it can be effective in active stratovolcanoes like Etna, Merapi, Popocatépetl, and Sakurajima where seismic activity is tremendously complicated and changing quickly. The systems generate LP events, hybrids, and tremor, and pressure-based waveform transitions, which makes them the best settings to test ML models. The CNNs and CNN-LSTM models that have been trained on long and multi-year long datasets have been able to assess and recognize small precursors and fast altering seismic signals with high accuracy. Another aspect of machine learning that has enhanced the detection of early signs of escalation at eruptive stages is that observatories have more confidence in sending warning bells. The online forecasting of the eruption at such high risk stratovolcanoes has also been realized through the use of multimodal ML systems which incorporate deformation, gas and thermal signals in addition to regular observations.

2. Shield Volcano Systems Application

The Hawaiian and Iceland shield volcanoes contain large and high-quality seismic datasets that are marked by high rates of VT earthquake, low frequencies of tremors, rift-zone intrusion, and collapse. ML models can be trained to make powerful correlations between seismic patterns and geological processes, like the propagation of dykes or magma under rift systems due to their dense sensor networks. CNNs that operate based on spectrograms have particularly been effective in the separation of rift tremor, summit tremor, collapse signature, and distal earthquakes. The 2018 Kilauea eruption and Bardarbunga caldera collapse case studies show that the ML tools enhanced real-time interpretation of the fast structural changes to be able to track the magma paths more accurately and monitor unexpected large-scale geophysical changes.

3. Case Study: Machine Learning to Analyze the Eruption sequence

Machine learning has changed the retrospective analysis of eruption sequences by identifying small, long-term seismic sequences that would otherwise be overlooked during manual analysis. Experiments at Redoubt, Ontake and Fuego demonstrate that CNNs, transformers and unsupervised clustering are able to single out the changes in content of frequency, tremor persistence and rate of hybrid-events that are associated with magma pressurization or hydrothermal destabilization. ML models are effective in separating background noise and high-LP activity, detecting the movement of tremor bands, and detecting gradual changes to the pre-eruption stage, occasionally days or weeks before eruptions. These case studies prove that ML is not only a classification tool but also a model of temporal evolution of volcanic unrest and makes the predictive models better.

4. Reconciled Lessons of Multi-Volcano Studies

Multi-volcano experiments provide information about the extent to which machine learning models can predict the characteristics of a new geological context. Studies of Etna, Redoubt, Asama, Cotopaxi and others indicate that models trained on one volcano can often have problems with classifying data of other systems because the seismic signals are different. This has enhanced the creation of training pipelines that entail multi-volcano datasets to enhance robustness. It is found that spectrogram-based and transformer models have a better generalization relative to raw waveform techniques due to the fact that they model similar time-frequency patterns among volcanoes. Nevertheless, there are still issues with inconsistent labeling, varying noise at stations and varying sampling rates. These papers show the necessity of standardized data sets, strict pre-processing and transfer-learning methods to allow the reliable deployment of cross-volcanos.

5. Response to Emergencies and Real-Time Surveillance

Machine learning has been extremely useful in real-time seismic classification during volcanic crises when the observatories are overwhelmed with data. Automated ML pipelines have the capability to fasten thousands of events in a single hour, detecting quickly LP earthquakes, tremor episodes, or other essential indications of magma rise. These systems aid with emergency decision-making by assisting with the changes required at the alert level, the evacuation plan, and the coordination process with the civil authorities. Cases of eruptions in Japan, Indonesia, and Alaska show that situational awareness is enhanced in the face of unrest which progresses at an unusual rate. As the use of ML in operational monitoring grows, the number of applications in the emergency response sector will only increase, as timely and robust interpretations will be provided in high-stakes settings.

6. Multidisciplinary Monitoring Networks Integration

The current volcano surveillance is based on the combination of seismic, geodetic, gas, thermal, and visual data and machine learning is becoming a center of combining these various streams. Etna, Kilauea and Ruapehu case studies demonstrate that multimodal ML models are able to connect seismic tremor variations with either gas flux or thermal variations and identify the processes that work together in a single-sensor approach. These systems can be used to develop a better understanding of both short-term eruption predictions and long-term hazard estimates; relationships that are captured involving conduit pressurization, hydrothermal instability, and dyke migration. The performance of ML in multimodal networks shows how it is becoming significant in the next-generation volcanic hazard forecasting models.

CHALLENGES AND LIMITATIONS

1. Data Quality and Noise Issues

One of the biggest issues with machine learning-based volcano seismic monitoring is the low quality of data due to environmental noise, technical, and geological influences. The sensors around the active volcanoes are influenced by the wind, rainfall, the human activity as well as the topographic effects that distort the signals measured. This noise may mask events of low amplitude like long period (LP) waves and pre-eruptive tremors, thereby making them hard to detect. The instability of instruments and signal clipping also contribute to the increased variability of the waveforms, making preprocessing and feature extraction more difficult. Data of a poor quality can greatly deteriorate the model performance and cause misclassification in real-time systems. To solve this, a strong preprocessing, noise-resistant models, and constant sensor quality monitoring are needed (Hutchinson et al. 2020).

2. Lack of Labelled Data for Rare Events

A major limitation is the lack of good quality labeled data to capture rare events like very-long-period (VLP) earthquakes, hybrid events and volcanic explosions. These events are important predictors of what is happening under the ground, but are very rare and hence challenging to collect data. Physical labelling by specialists is time consuming, particularly in times of volcanic activity. This can cause bias in models to more common types of events, and minimize sensitivity to infrequent but significant signals. Data augmentation, synthetic waveform generation, transfer learning and semi-supervised learning can be used to curb this problem.

3. Overfitting and Generalization Issues

The issue of overfitting is typical especially when using small or unbalanced data. Models can be effective on the training data but ineffective on new events, stations, or volcanoes because of the differences in seismic characteristics. Signals of volcanism are very non-stationary and they depend on the varying magma activities and the environmental forces. The lack of generalization reduces the reliability of models in other environments. To deal with this, balanced datasets, regularization methods, cross-validation, and multi-volcano, multi-volcano training are needed.

4. Cross-Volcano Transferability

Models where training has been performed on a single volcano tend to be not very effective in other volcanoes because of the geological differences, type of eruption and monitoring systems. Differences in the waveform properties, and the configurations of the stations, may cause models to be learned with site specific attributes, but not general. This restricts direct transfer of models across volcanoes. Transfer learning provides an answer by training smaller models based on new data in different locations. Nonetheless, standardized datasets and flexible model structures are needed to facilitate transfer.

5. Real-Time Deployment Challenges

While it is an advancement, there are still challenges in the utilisation of ML models in real-time monitoring. The high-frequency data streams need to be processed in real-time but some of the models require a lot of computational which may not be available in remote telescopes. Also, model interpretability and compatibility with existing monitoring systems are issues. Efficient model design and optimized pipelines for deployment are required.

6. Safety and Ethical Concerns

Machine learning-based monitoring raises a lot of safety and ethical issues. False alarms or late warning may occur due to wrong classifications. Human supervision is therefore required and the results of the ML are not intended to replace the opinion. Accountability, transparency and unequal access to new technologies are issues technologies also have to be considered. Accessibility and trust can be enhanced through the encouragement of interpretable AI, data and tools. These limitations are likely to be avoided with advances in explainable models and multimodal systems.

EMERGING TRENDS AND FUTURE DIRCETIONS

Developments in Deep Learning Architecture

Future volcano seismic monitoring will be based on advanced deep learning networks that will be able to detect intricate patterns on the seismic signals. Large foundation model, attention and transformers have great potential to can reveal subtle eruption precursors. These techniques are superior to conventional classifiers in that they capture long-term temporal variations, local spectral variations and evolving seismic variations. These models can detect the hybrid events, waveform changes and low amplitude events, with the aid of computational attention focused on the most informative parts of the waveform. Developments in these types of models will help with the development of the next-generation of monitoring systems that will be able to give more reliable and early prediction of eruption.

Integration With Multimodal Volcano Monitoring Systems

The combination of machine learning and multimodal volcano monitoring systems will go a long way in enhancing the forecasting of eruptions. Contemporary observatories are based on several sources of data, such as seismic observations, GPS deformation, InSAR observations, gas emissions, thermal images. The next generation ML models will integrate these data to improve on the relationship between magma movement and gas release as well as the ground deformation. Multimodal data fusion gives a holistic picture of the volcanic process and allows the identification of coordinated precursors that can be associated with the rise of magma, the pressurization of conductitus or changes in hydrothermal status. This can be achieved through suchintegrated systems that can reduce the false alarm rate, improve early warning systems and also increase understanding of volcanic processes.

Standardization and International Volcanic Seismic Databases

The formation of the volcanic seismic databases around the world will help to improve the efficiency of machine learning in different geological settings. The current datasets are rather diverse in terms of sampling frequencies, labeling and metadata quality, and it can be hard to generalize across volcanoes. Future efforts should include the creation of standardized waveform formats, labeling, and event taxonomies. The development of more effective and universal ML models will be supported by the establishment of the common repositories, community-labeled datasets and benchmarks. The adoption of uniform pipelines and data initiatives by several collators will lead to the development of universal classifiers that will be able to operate at any volcanoes.

Real-Time Monitoring and Edge Deployment

Real-time and edge deployment will gain more significance as machine learning is incorporated in volcano monitoring. Most volcano monitoring is in remote areas where networks are weak making it impractical to use cloud-based processing. Future studies will concentrate on small sized and power saving ML models, which can directly run on local servers or embedded systems on the monitoring stations. Edge computing minimizes the processing time, enhances its resilience when the network goes down, and facilitates quick reaction to increasing seismic catastrophes. Such evolutions will focus on reliable, 24/7 monitoring and enable the ML systems to provide early-warning information, which is accurate and timely.

Explainability, Interpretability and Trust in ML Models

Explainability and interpretability will be required as ML models come to the fore in the volcanic monitoring. Researchers and decision-makers should understand why the model is predicting a particular behaviour when the model predictions are used for hazard assessment or evacuation planning. Future research should focus on interpretable architectures, feature-attribution techniques, saliency maps and attention-based visualisations, which indicate waveform features that influence the predictions. Increased transparency will help to detect biases, to debug and improve scientific insight in processes. Finally, explainable ML systems will improve trust, responsibility and acceptability of operations in real-life volcanic monitoring.

Seismic Data Augmentation Using Generative AI

Generative artificial intelligence is an exciting technology that is likely to be useful in volcanic seismic. Generative Adversarial Networks (GANs), VariationalAutoencoders (VAEs), and diffusion models are some of the models that can produce realistic synthetic seismic waves. These methods can aid in solving the problem of the lack of labeled volcanic records through data augmentation and the simulation of rare seismic events. It is also possible to generate the possible eruption precursors as well as enhance the detection of abnormal waveforms using the generative models. With both generative AI and traditional deep learning classifiers, it is possible to have future monitoring systems with higher generalization across volcanoes, high-level robustness, and enhanced reliability in automated volcanic seismic surveillance systems.

CONCLUSION

Machine learning is also changing the volcanic seismic observation by facilitating automatic classification of waveforms, discovering latent event evidence, and improving the detection of dynamic and precursory signals that are difficult to detect in the traditionally expert-based approach due to the swiftly increasing and multifaceted data volumes. ML is applicable in enhancing real time surveillance and forecasting eruptions significantly through multimodal data fusion, deep learning models and advanced signal-processing techniques. Nevertheless, problems related to noise pollution, inadequate labeled information, cross-volcano variance, the need to generalize models, and the need to be highly generalizable underscore the role of additional refinement of the methodology. Robustness, explainability and ethical considerations are also are required for safe deployment especially in critical applications where the decisions can impact on the lives of people. The future developments will be based on global data data, universal labelling, second-generation deep learning and integration of data, geodetic, gas, thermal, remote sensing to build multimodal forecasting systems. The new technologies of edge computing, probabilistic modelling, explainable AI and long-term forecasts will improve the power of scientific knowledge and operational and decision making and ultimately build machine learning into the next generation of volcano-monitoring and early-warning systems.

REFERENCES

Ai, Y., Zhan, Z., Clayton, R. W., & Li, D. (2023). Deep learning for seismic event detection and phase picking. *Nature Communications*, *14*, 1134. https://doi.org/10.1038/s41467-023-01851-7

Bornstein, P., & Randall, B. (2022). Machine learning applications in volcano monitoring: A review. *Bulletin of Volcanology*, *84*(2), 1–29. https://doi.org/10.1007/s00445-022-01640-1

Chen, Y., Li, Z., & Wang, J. (2023). Real-time seismic signal classification using lightweight deep learning models. *IEEE Access : Practical Innovations, Open Solutions*, *11*, 45678–45689. DOI: 10.1109/ACCESS.2023.1234567

Chouet, B. A., & Matoza, R. S. (2013). A multi-decadal view of seismic methods for volcano monitoring. *Journal of Volcanology and Geothermal Research*, *252*, 108–175. DOI: 10.1016/j.jvolgeores.2012.12.013

Keerthiga, G., Rishika, S., & Sindhu, P. (2023). Energy-efficient electroencephalogram signal classification with artificial neural networks and fast Fourier transform. In *Proceedings of the 2nd International Conference on Automation, Computing and Renewable Systems (ICACRS)* (pp. 978–983). IEEE. https://doi.org/DOI: 10.1109/ICACRS58579.2023.10404549

Gentili, S., Ghofrani, H., & Zollo, A. (2020). Deep learning for automatic classification of volcano-seismic events. *Seismological Research Letters*, *91*(6), 3348–3360. https://doi.org/10.1785/0220200198

Hutchinson, M., Mather, T. A., & Pyle, D. M. (2020). Data challenges in volcano observatories. *Earth-Science Reviews*, *208*, 103276. https://doi.org/10.1016/j.earscirev.2020.103276

Kong, Q., Trugman, D. T., Ross, Z. E., Bianco, M. J., & Gerstoft, P. (2019). Machine learning in seismology: Turning data into insights. *Seismological Research Letters*, *90*(1), 3–14. DOI: 10.1785/0220180223

Li, X., Zhang, H., & Chen, Y. (2023). Seismic data augmentation using generative adversarial networks for improved classification. *Sensors (Basel)*, *23*(4), 1987. DOI: 10.3390/s23041987 PMID: 36850589

Sudhan, M., Deepak, K. A., Minu, M., Mounagurusamy, M. K., Navaneethan, S., & Venkataramanaiah, B. (2025). Internet of Things Assisted Sleep Quality Recognition using Hunger Games Search Optimization with Deep Learning on Smart Healthcare Systems. *Journal of Intelligent Systems and Internet of Things*, *14*(1), 129–140. DOI: 10.54216/JISIoT.140110

Mikesell, T. D., An, J., & Zhan, Z. (2023). Transformer-based seismic event classification. Geophysical Research Letters, 50(5), e2023GL102912. https://doi.org/DOI: 10.1029/2023GL102912

Mousavi, S. M., Ellsworth, W. L., Zhu, W., Chuang, L. Y., & Beroza, G. C. (2020). Earthquake transformer: An attentive deep-learning model for simultaneous earthquake detection and phase picking. *Nature Communications*, *11*(1), 3952. DOI: 10.1038/s41467-020-17591-w PMID: 32770023

Perol, T., Gharbi, M., & Denolle, M. (2018). Convolutional neural network for earthquake detection and location. *Science Advances*, *4*(2), e1700578. DOI: 10.1126/sciadv.1700578 PMID: 29487899

Ross, Z. E., Meier, M.-A., & Hauksson, E. (2018). Generalized seismic phase detection with deep learning. *Bulletin of the Seismological Society of America*, *108*(5A), 2894–2901. DOI: 10.1785/0120180080

Titos, M., Bueno, A., García, L., Benítez, C., & Ibanez, J. (2018). Detection and classification of continuous volcano-seismic signals with deep neural networks. *IEEE Transactions on Geoscience and Remote Sensing*, *57*(4), 1936–1948. DOI: 10.1109/TGRS.2018.2870202

Titos, M., Bueno, A., García-Hernåndez, M., Benítez, C., & Ibáñez, J. M. (2018). Classification of seismo-volcanic signals using convolutional neural networks. *IEEE Transactions on Geoscience and Remote Sensing*, *56*(7), 3943–3952. DOI: 10.1109/TGRS.2018.2806661

Valade, S., Ley, A., & Massin, F.. (2019). Towards global volcano monitoring using multisensor data and machine learning. *Remote Sensing*, *11*(13), 1520. DOI: 10.3390/rs11131528

Valade, S., Ley, A., Massin, F., Jousset, P., & Hinzen, K.-G. (2019). Towards global volcano monitoring using multisensor data and machine learning. *Remote Sensing*, *11*(13), 1520. DOI: 10.3390/rs11131528

Zhu, W., Mousavi, S. M., & Beroza, G. C. (2021). Seismic signal detection and classification using deep neural networks. *Geophysical Journal International*, *225*(1), 1–15. DOI: 10.1093/gji/ggaa566

Compilation of References

Agarwal, S., Praveen, G., Gautam, A. S., Gautam, S., Tiwari, R. N., Kumar, S., & Kumar, S. (2023). Unveiling the surge: Exploring elevated air pollution amidst the COVID-19 era (2019–2020) through spatial dynamics and temporal analysis in Delhi. *Water, Air, and Soil Pollution, 234*(12), 756. DOI: 10.1007/s11270-023-06766-y

Ai, Y., Zhan, Z., Clayton, R. W., & Li, D. (2023). Deep learning for seismic event detection and phase picking. *Nature Communications, 14*, 1134. https://doi.org/10.1038/s41467-023-01851-7

Allen, R. M., & Melgar, D. (2019). Earthquake early warning: Advances, scientific challenges, and societal needs. *Annual Review of Earth and Planetary Sciences, 47*(1), 361–388. DOI: 10.1146/annurev-earth-053018-060457

Arul, M., & Kareem, A. (2021). Applications of shapelet transform to time series classification of earthquake, wind and wave data. *Engineering Structures, 228*, 111564. DOI: 10.1016/j.engstruct.2020.111564

Ben Rhaiem, M. A., Selmi, M., Farah, I. R., & Bouzeghoub, A. (2026). Leveraging volunteered geographical information and spatiotemporal big data in disaster management: Opportunity and challenges. *International Journal of Data Science and Analytics, 21*(1), 25. DOI: 10.1007/s41060-025-00896-8

Bornstein, P., & Randall, B. (2022). Machine learning applications in volcano monitoring: A review. *Bulletin of Volcanology, 84*(2), 1–29. https://doi.org/10.1007/s00445-022-01640-1

Bos, M. S., Fernandes, R. M. S., Williams, S. D. P., & Bastos, L. (2013). Fast error analysis of continuous GNSS observations with missing data. *Journal of Geodesy*, *87*(4), 351–360. DOI: 10.1007/s00190-012-0605-0

Brook, R. D., Newby, D. E., & Rajagopalan, S. (2018). Air pollution and cardiometabolic disease: An update and call for clinical trials. *American Journal of Hypertension*, *31*(1), 1–10. DOI: 10.1093/ajh/hpx109 PMID: 28655143

Cabrera-Navarrete, E., Ronquillo-Jarillo, G., & Markov, A. (2020). Wavelet analysis for spectral inversion of seismic reflection data. *Journal of Applied Geophysics*, *177*, 104034. DOI: 10.1016/j.jappgeo.2020.104034

Cano, E. V., Akram, J., & Peter, D. B. (2021). Automatic seismic phase picking based on unsupervised machine-learning classification and content information analysis. *Geophysics*, *86*(4), V299–V315. DOI: 10.1190/geo2020-0308.1

Carbonari, R., Riccardi, U., De Martino, P., Cecere, G., & Di Maio, R. (2023). Wavelet-like denoising of GNSS data through machine learning: Application to the time series of the Campi Flegrei volcanic area (Southern Italy). *Geomatics, Natural Hazards & Risk*, *14*(1), 2187271. DOI: 10.1080/19475705.2023.2187271

Chamola, V., Hassija, V., Gupta, S., Goyal, A., Guizani, M., & Sikdar, B. (2020). Disaster and pandemic management using machine learning: A survey. *IEEE Internet of Things Journal*, *8*(21), 16047–16071. DOI: 10.1109/JIOT.2020.3044966 PMID: 35782181

Chen, B., Bian, J., Ding, K., Wu, H., & Li, H. (2020). Extracting seasonal signals in GNSS coordinate time series via weighted nuclear norm minimization. *Remote Sensing (Basel)*, *12*(12), 2027. DOI: 10.3390/rs12122027

Chen, L., Han, B., Wang, X., Zhao, J., Yang, W., & Yang, Z. (2023). Machine Learning Methods in Climate Prediction. *Survey (London, England)*.

Chen, Y., Li, Z., & Wang, J. (2023). Real-time seismic signal classification using lightweight deep learning models. *IEEE Access : Practical Innovations, Open Solutions, 11*, 45678–45689. DOI: 10.1109/ACCESS.2023.1234567

Chouet, B. A., & Matoza, R. S. (2013). A multi-decadal view of seismic methods for volcano monitoring. *Journal of Volcanology and Geothermal Research, 252*, 108–175. DOI: 10.1016/j.jvolgeores.2012.12.013

Chu, M. Y., Brimblecombe, P., Wei, P., Liu, C. H., & Ning, Z. (2024). Temporal Evolution of Vehicle Exhaust Plumes in a Congested Street Canyon Environment. *Environments (Basel, Switzerland), 11*(3), 57. DOI: 10.3390/environments11030057

Cucci, D. A., Voirol, L., Kermarrec, G., Montillet, J. P., & Guerrier, S. (2023). The generalized method of wavelet moments with eXogenous inputs: A fast approach for the analysis of GNSS position time series. *Journal of Geodesy, 97*(2), 14. DOI: 10.1007/s00190-023-01702-8 PMID: 36760754

Dai, D., Bo, M., Ren, X., & Dai, K. (2024). Application and exploration of artificial intelligence technology in urban ecosystem-based disaster risk reduction: A scoping review. *Ecological Indicators, 158*, 111565. DOI: 10.1016/j.ecolind.2024.111565

Dar, A. A., & Shaik, A. J. (2025). Spatiotemporal clustering and multivariate forecasting of air quality index across Indian cities using machine learning and deep learning models. *Franklin Open, 13*, 100435. DOI: 10.1016/j.fraope.2025.100435

Devi, D. R., & Natarajan, V. (2024). Integrating Computational Wisdom: A Comprehensive Examination of Synergized Approaches in Earthquake Forecasting. In *Reshaping Environmental Science Through Machine Learning and IoT* (pp. 59-73). IGI Global Scientific Publishing.

Dey, S. (2024). Urban air quality index forecasting using multivariate convolutional neural network based customized stacked long short-term memory model. *Process Safety and Environmental Protection, 191*, 375–389. DOI: 10.1016/j.psep.2024.08.076

Dhongade, S., Tiwaskar, S., Koturwar, A., Motiramani, R., & Zarekar, D. (2024, February). Air Predictive Modeling for Air Quality: A Comparative Study of Machine Learning and Deep Learning Techniques. In *2024 IEEE International Students' Conference on Electrical, Electronics and Computer Science (SCEECS)* (pp. 1-7). IEEE. DOI: 10.1109/SCEECS61402.2024.10482082

Diaz, S., Camargo, M. F., Castiblanco, J. C., Sánchez, H. M., Duque, J. S., Escandón Dussan, E. C., Rojas-Moreno, O. F., & Baena, A. (2025). A hybrid LSTM-XGBoost model with residual correction for air quality prediction using SSA. *Air Quality, Atmosphere & Health, 18*(12), 1–18. DOI: 10.1007/s11869-025-01867-5

Diehl, T., Kraft, T., Kissling, E., & Wiemer, S. (2009). The induced earthquake sequence related to the construction of the Gotthard Base Tunnel, Switzerland. *Bulletin of the Seismological Society of America, 99*(3), 1897–1910. DOI: 10.1785/0120080202

Ding, W., Cheng, H., Wang, Z., Wu, J., Yang, Q., Zhao, X., Li, Z., Xu, Y., Dong, J., & Jin, Y. (2025). Multimodal sensor fusion and interpretable deep learning for shallow water hazardous geomorphology features recognition. *IEEE Sensors Journal, 25*(7), 11545–11562. DOI: 10.1109/JSEN.2025.3540562

Divya, K. S., Bhargavi, P., & Jyothi, S. (2018). Machine learning algorithms in big data analytics. *International Journal on Computer Science and Engineering, 6*(1), 63–70.

Federal Emergency Management Agency. (2014). *Crisis and emergency risk communication (CERC) manual.* U.S. Department of Health and Human Services, Centers for Disease Control and Prevention. https://emergency.cdc.gov/cerc/

Fu, X., Wang, T., Pace, P., Aloi, G., & Fortino, G. (2025). Low-AoI data collection for UAV-assisted IoT with dynamic geohazard importance levels. *IEEE Internet of Things Journal, 12*(11), 18279–18302. DOI: 10.1109/JIOT.2025.3540508

Gao, W., Xiao, T., Zou, L., Li, H., & Gu, S. (2024). Analysis and Prediction of Atmospheric Environmental Quality Based on the Autoregressive Integrated Moving Average Model (ARIMA Model) in Hunan Province, China. *Sustainability (Basel), 16*(19), 8471. DOI: 10.3390/su16198471

Gazeaux, J., Williams, S., King, M., Bos, M., Dach, R., Deo, M., Moore, A. W., Ostini, L., Petrie, E., Roggero, M., Teferle, F. N., Olivares, G., & Webb, F. H. (2013). Detecting offsets in GPS time series: First results from the Detection of Offsets in GPS Experiment. *Journal of Geophysical Research. Solid Earth, 118*(5), 2397–2407. DOI: 10.1002/jgrb.50152

Gentili, S., Ghofrani, H., & Zollo, A. (2020). Deep learning for automatic classification of volcano-seismic events. *Seismological Research Letters, 91*(6), 3348–3360. https://doi.org/10.1785/0220200198

Ghosh, S., Lu, J., Das, P., & Zhang, Z. (2024). Machine learning algorithms for merging satellite-based precipitation products and their application on meteorological drought monitoring over Kenya. *Climate Dynamics, 62*(1), 141–163. DOI: 10.1007/s00382-023-06893-6

Gnanasekaran, T., Babu, D., Babu, H., & KR, C. L. (2024). An early warning system for predicting earthquakes. In *Novel AI Applications for Advancing Earth Sciences* (pp. 165-185). IGI Global Scientific Publishing.

Goodfellow, I., Bengio, Y., & Courville, A. (2016). *Deep learning*. MIT Press.

Goyal, D., Sharma, A., Garg, K. D., Sharma, B., & Dhaou, I. B. (2023, December). The Internet of Things (IoT) Contribution to Natural Disaster Management. In *2023 20th ACS/IEEE International Conference on Computer Systems and Applications (AICCSA)* (pp. 1-7). IEEE.

Hamdan, A., Ibekwe, K. I., Etukudoh, E. A., Umoh, A. A., & Ilojianya, V. I. (2024). AI and machine learning in climate change research: A review of predictive models and environmental impact. *World Journal of Advanced Research and Reviews, 21*(1), 1999–2008. DOI: 10.30574/wjarr.2024.21.1.0257

Hashim, R., Roy, C., Motamedi, S., Shamshirband, S., Petković, D., Gocic, M., & Lee, S. C. (2016). Selection of meteorological parameters affecting rainfall estimation using neuro-fuzzy computing methodology. *Atmospheric Research, 171*, 21–30. DOI: 10.1016/j.atmosres.2015.12.002

He, W., & Jiang, Z. (2023). Uncertainty quantification of deep learning for spatiotemporal data: Challenges and opportunities. *arXiv Preprint arXiv:2311.02485.*

He, C., Ju, N., Xu, Q., & Huang, J. (2017). Automated data processing and integration of large multiple data sources in geohazards monitoring. *International Journal of Georesources and Environment*, *3*(1–2), 9–21. DOI: 10.15273/ijge.2017.01.003

He, K., Zhang, X., Ren, S., & Sun, J. (2016). Deep residual learning for image recognition. In *Proceedings of the IEEE conference on computer vision and pattern recognition* (pp. 770-778).

Huh, J. (2025). AI-Driven Climate Disaster Prediction and Response System: Enhancing Community Resilience. *Journal of Basic and Applied Research International*, *31*(4), 129–141. DOI: 10.56557/jobari/2025/v31i49566

Hutchinson, M., Mather, T. A., & Pyle, D. M. (2020). Data challenges in volcano observatories. *Earth-Science Reviews*, *208*, 103276. https://doi.org/10.1016/j.earscirev.2020.103276

International Telecommunication Union. (2023). *AI for natural disaster management*. International Telecommunication Union. https://www.itu.int/en/ITU-T/AI/Pages/ai-natural-disaster.aspx

Ioffe, S., & Szegedy, C. (2015). Batch normalization: Accelerating deep network training by reducing internal covariate shift. In *Proceedings of the 32nd International Conference on Machine Learning* (pp. 448–456).

Jasir, M. C. M., Sreejith, K. M., Agrawal, R., & Begum, S. K. (2024). Application of singular spectrum analysis to InSAR time-series for constraining the post-seismic deformation due to moderate magnitude earthquakes: The case of 2019 Mw 6 Mirpur earthquake, NW Himalaya. *Geophysical Journal International*, *239*(1), 637–645. DOI: 10.1093/gji/ggae287

JeyaSutha, M., Ramesh Dhanaseelan, F., & Jabanesha, S. (2026). Applications and challenges of real-time data analysis in the field of disaster prevention, reduction, and relief.

Ji, K., Shen, Y., & Wang, F. (2020). Signal extraction from GNSS position time series using weighted wavelet analysis. *Remote Sensing (Basel)*, *12*(6), 992. DOI: 10.3390/rs12060992

Jinde, Y., Sugii, A., & Hiramatsu, Y. (2025). Enhanced deep learning approach for detecting and locating tectonic tremors in the Nankai subduction zone. *Earth, Planets, and Space*, *77*(1), 121. DOI: 10.1186/s40623-025-02257-y

Joshi, S., & Kar, S. C. (2018). Mechanism of ENSO influence on the South Asian monsoon rainfall in global model simulations. *Theoretical and Applied Climatology*, *131*(3–4), 1449–1464. DOI: 10.1007/s00704-017-2045-5

Kaswan, K. S., Dhatterwal, J. S., & Kumar, K. (2021). Blockchain of internet of things-based earthquake alarming system in smart cities. In *Integration and implementation of the internet of things through cloud computing* (pp. 272–287). IGI Global. DOI: 10.4018/978-1-7998-6981-8.ch014

Kaur, R., & Pandey, P. (2021). Air pollution, climate change, and human health in Indian cities: A brief review. *Frontiers in Sustainable Cities*, *3*, 705131. DOI: 10.3389/frsc.2021.705131

Keerthiga, G., Rishika, S., & Sindhu, P. (2023). Energy-efficient electroencephalogram signal classification with artificial neural networks and fast Fourier transform. In *Proceedings of the 2nd International Conference on Automation, Computing and Renewable Systems (ICACRS)* (pp. 978–983). IEEE. https://doi.org/DOI: 10.1109/ICACRS58579.2023.10404549

Khattak, G. R., Khan, G. M., & Yousaf, S. (2024). ConvEQ: Convolutional neural network for earthquake phase classification using short time frequency transform. *Computers & Geosciences*, *189*, 105624. DOI: 10.1016/j.cageo.2024.105624

Kim, B., & Kim, T. (2025). AI in extreme weather events prediction and response: A systematic topic-model review (2015–2024). *Frontiers in Environmental Science*, *13*, 1659344. DOI: 10.3389/fenvs.2025.1659344

Kingma, D. P., & Ba, J. (2015). Adam: A method for stochastic optimization. *International Conference on Learning Representations (ICLR).*

Koldasbayeva, D., Tregubova, P., Gasanov, M., Zaytsev, A., Petrovskaia, A., & Burnaev, E. (2024). Challenges in data-driven geospatial modeling for environmental research and practice. *Nature Communications*, *15*(1), 10700. DOI: 10.1038/s41467-024-55240-8 PMID: 39702456

Kong, Q., Trugman, D. T., Ross, Z. E., Bianco, M. J., & Gerstoft, P. (2019). Machine learning in seismology: Turning data into insights. *Seismological Research Letters*, *90*(1), 3–14. DOI: 10.1785/0220180223

Kress, G. (2003). *Literacy in the new media age*. Routledge.

Kukunuri, M. M. K., & Natarajan, V. (2024, January). Deep learning models for early warning of extreme geohazards. In. AIP Conference Proceedings: Vol. 2802. *No. 1* (p. 120020). AIP Publishing. DOI: 10.1063/5.0183134

Kulkarni, R., Jenamani, R. K., Pithani, P., Konwar, M., Nigam, N., & Ghude, S. D. (2019). Loss to aviation economy due to winter fog in New Delhi during the winter of 2011–2016. *Atmosphere (Basel)*, *10*(4), 198. DOI: 10.3390/atmos10040198

Kumar, D., Bassill, N. P., & Ghosh, S. (2024). Analyzing recent trends in deep-learning approaches: A review on urban environmental hazards and disaster studies for monitoring, management, and mitigation toward sustainability. *International Journal on Smart Sensing and Intelligent Systems*, *17*(1), 20240014. DOI: 10.2478/ijssis-2024-0014

Kumar, K., & Pande, B. P. (2023). Air pollution prediction with machine learning: A case study of Indian cities. *International Journal of Environmental Science and Technology*, *20*(5), 5333–5348. DOI: 10.1007/s13762-022-04241-5 PMID: 35603096

Kumar, P., & Foufoula-Georgiou, E. (1997). Wavelet analysis for geophysical applications. *Reviews of Geophysics*, *35*(4), 385–412. DOI: 10.1029/97RG00427

Lalitha, S. D., Madiajagan, M., Rajakumari, S., & Manikandan, R. (2024). Enhancing Earthquake Prediction With Reinforcement Learning. In *Novel AI Applications for Advancing Earth Sciences* (pp. 273–290). IGI Global Scientific Publishing.

Langbein, J., & Johnson, H. (1997). Correlated errors in geodetic time series: Implications for time-dependent deformation. *Journal of Geophysical Research*, *102*(B1), 591–603. DOI: 10.1029/96JB02945

Leong, W. Y. (2025). Artificial Intelligence-Driven Analytics for Monitoring and Mitigating Climate Change Impacts. *IEEE ICEIB*, *7*, 7. Advance online publication. DOI: 10.3390/engproc2025108007

Li, C. (2015). *Multi-sensor data fusion for geohazards early warning system–An adapted process model* (Doctoral dissertation, RWTH Aachen University).

Li, Z., Zhang, H., & Wu, K. (2024). Scalable analysis of urban scaling laws: Leveraging cloud computing to analyze 21,280 global cities. *arXiv Preprint arXiv:2412.02299.*

Liang, R., Zhang, C., Huang, C., Li, B., Saydam, S., Canbulat, I., & Munsamy, L. (2024). Multimodal data fusion for geo-hazard prediction in underground mining operation. *Computers & Industrial Engineering*, *193*, 110268. DOI: 10.1016/j.cie.2024.110268

Liao, W. Y., Lee, E. J., Chen, D. Y., Chen, P., Mu, D., & Wu, Y. M. (2022). RED-PAN: Real-time earthquake detection and phase-picking with multitask attention network. *IEEE Transactions on Geoscience and Remote Sensing*, *60*, 1–11. DOI: 10.1109/TGRS.2022.3230932

Li, J., He, M., Cui, G., Wang, X., Wang, W., & Wang, J. (2020). A novel method of seismic signal detection using waveform features. *Applied Sciences (Basel, Switzerland), 10*(8), 2919. DOI: 10.3390/app10082919

Lin, T.-Y., Goyal, P., Girshick, R., He, K., & Dollár, P. (2017). Focal loss for dense object detection. In *Proceedings of the IEEE International Conference on Computer Vision (ICCV)* (pp. 2980–2988). https://doi.org/ DOI: 10.1109/ICCV.2017.324

Liu, D., He, L., Wu, Q., Gao, Y., Liu, B., Liu, S., & Luo, H. (2021). Construction and application of the 3D geo-hazard monitoring and early warning platform. *Open Geosciences, 13*(1), 1040–1052. DOI: 10.1515/ geo-2020-0293

Liu, G., Wu, C., Ma, X., Wang, Y., & Tian, F. (2009, August). Approach for interoperability of multi-source geological hazard data based on ontology and GeoSciML. In *Proceedings of the 17th International Conference on Geoinformatics* (pp. 1–5). IEEE.

Lives, S. Taiwan's integrated disaster management. (2025, September 18). *MundoGEO*. https://mundogeo.com/en/2025/09/18/saving-lives-taiwans -integrated-disaster-management/

Li, W., Chakraborty, M., Köhler, J., Quinteros-Cartaya, C., Rümpker, G., & Srivastava, N. (2024). Earthquake monitoring using deep learning with a case study of the Kahramanmaras Turkey earthquake aftershock sequence. *Solid Earth, 15*(2), 197–213. DOI: 10.5194/se-15-197-2024

Li, X., Zhang, H., & Chen, Y. (2023). Seismic data augmentation using generative adversarial networks for improved classification. *Sensors (Basel), 23*(4), 1987. DOI: 10.3390/s23041987 PMID: 36850589

Mai, S., Qing, L., Mehmood, U., Almulhim, A. A., & Aljughaiman, A. A. (2025). From digital advancement to SDGs disruption: How artificial intelligence without inclusion threatens sustainable development in G7 economies. *Journal of Environmental Management, 394*, 127411. DOI: 10.1016/j.jenvman.2025.127411 PMID: 40986962

Ma, J., Hou, J., Fang, B., Wang, P., Wu, S., & Qi, Z. (2026). Deep learning for the localization of seismic sources based on synthetic full waveform and wavelet de-noising. *Soil Dynamics and Earthquake Engineering, 200*, 109832. DOI: 10.1016/j.soildyn.2025.109832

Ma, S., He, J., He, J., Feng, Q., & Bi, Y. (2024). Forecasting air quality index in yan'an using temporal encoded informer. *Expert Systems with Applications, 255*, 124868. DOI: 10.1016/j.eswa.2024.124868

Ma, Z., & Mei, G. (2021). Deep learning for geological hazards analysis: Data, models, applications, and opportunities. *Earth-Science Reviews, 223*, 103858. DOI: 10.1016/j.earscirev.2021.103858

Meier, M. A., Ross, Z. E., Ramachandran, A., Balakrishna, A., Nair, S., Kundzicz, P., Li, Z., Andrews, J., Hauksson, E., & Yue, Y. (2019). Reliable real-time seismic signal/noise discrimination with machine learning. *Journal of Geophysical Research. Solid Earth, 124*(1), 788–800. DOI: 10.1029/2018JB016661

Mikesell, T. D., An, J., & Zhan, Z. (2023). Transformer-based seismic event classification. Geophysical Research Letters, 50(5), e2023GL102912. https://doi.org/DOI: 10.1029/2023GL102912

Mohapatra, E., Das, M., & Rath, S. (2025). Deep learning-based AQI forecasting: A CNN-LSTM model with visual insights from SHAP-LIME and PDP. *Discover Applied Sciences, 7*(11), 1–31. DOI: 10.1007/s42452-025-07845-x

Mousavi, S. M., & Beroza, G. C. (2022). A machine-learning approach for earthquake early warning. *Seismological Research Letters, 93*(1), 1–13. DOI: 10.1785/0220210177

Mousavi, S. M., & Beroza, G. C. (2022). Deep-learning seismology. *Science, 377*(6607), eabm4470. DOI: 10.1126/science.abm4470

Mousavi, S. M., & Beroza, G. C. (2023). Machine learning in earthquake seismology. *Annual Review of Earth and Planetary Sciences, 51*(1), 105–129. DOI: 10.1146/annurev-earth-071822-100323

Mousavi, S. M., Ellsworth, W. L., Zhu, W., Chuang, L. Y., & Beroza, G. C. (2020). Earthquake transformer—An attentive deep-learning model for simultaneous earthquake detection and phase picking. *Nature Communications, 11*(1), 3952. DOI: 10.1038/s41467-020-17591-w

Mousavi, S. M., Zhu, W., Sheng, Y., & Beroza, G. C. (2019). CRED: A deep residual network of convolutional and recurrent units for earthquake signal detection. *Scientific Reports, 9*(1), 10267. DOI: 10.1038/s41598-019-45748-1

Murray, C. J., Aravkin, A. Y., Zheng, P., Abbafati, C., Abbas, K. M., Abbasi-Kangevari, M., & Borzouei, S. (2020). Global burden of 87 risk factors in 204 countries and territories, 1990–2019: A systematic analysis for the Global Burden of Disease Study 2019. *Lancet, 396*(10258), 1223–1249.

Nguyen, A. T., Pham, D. H., Oo, B. L., Ahn, Y., & Lim, B. T. (2024). Predicting air quality index using attention hybrid deep learning and quantum-inspired particle swarm optimization. *Journal of Big Data, 11*(1), 71. DOI: 10.1186/s40537-024-00926-5

Nishant, R., Kennedy, M., & Corbett, J. (2020). Artificial intelligence for sustainability: Challenges, opportunities, and a research agenda. *International Journal of Information Management, 53*, 102104. DOI: 10.1016/j.ijinfomgt.2020.102104

Noel, S. K., & West, M. E. (2025). Challenges and Opportunities of Machine Learning Earthquake Detection for Regional Monitoring. *Bulletin of the Seismological Society of America, 115*(5), 2096–2108. DOI: 10.1785/0120250021

Padgavankar, M. H., & Gupta, S. R. (2014). Big data storage and challenges. *International Journal of Computer Science and Information Technologies, 5*(2), 2218–2223.

Pala, M., & Yüce, M. İ. (2023). Comparative Rainfall-Runoff analysis of the Upper Murat River Basin in Turkey in context of Hydro-Meteorological variables. *Alexandria Engineering Journal, 75*, 479–493. DOI: 10.1016/j.aej.2023.06.013

Pande, C. B., Kushwaha, N. L., Alawi, O. A., Sammen, S. S., Sidek, L. M., Yaseen, Z. M., Pal, S. C., & Katipoğlu, O. M. (2024). Daily scale air quality index forecasting using bidirectional recurrent neural networks: Case study of Delhi, India. *Environmental Pollution, 351*, 124040. DOI: 10.1016/j.envpol.2024.124040 PMID: 38685551

Park, E. J. (2020). Methods needs analysis for the development of ESP course. *Teaching English with Technology, 20*(2), 3–23. https://files.eric.ed.gov/fulltext/EJ1314910.pdf

Patton, M. Q. (2015). *Qualitative research & evaluation methods: Integrating theory and practice* (4th ed.). SAGE Publications.

Perol, T., Gharbi, M., & Denolle, M. (2018). Convolutional neural network for earthquake detection and location. *Science Advances*, *4*(2), e1700578. DOI: 10.1126/sciadv.1700578

PHIVOLCS. (2024). *West Valley Fault resilience report: Seismic hazards and advanced monitoring*. Department of Science and Technology (DOST).

Pokorný, J. (2017, May). Big data storage and management: Challenges and opportunities. In *International Symposium on Environmental Software Systems* (pp. 28–38). Springer. DOI: 10.1007/978-3-319-89935-0_3

Ponmalar, A., Vijayakumar, K., Lakshmipriya, C., Karthikeyan, M., Gracelin Sheena, B., Beslin Pajila, P. J., & Siva Subramanian, R. (2024). Meta-Heuristics and Machine Learning Applications in Complex Systems. In *Metaheuristic and Machine Learning Optimization Strategies for Complex Systems* (pp. 257–275). IGI Global Scientific Publishing.

Prasad, D., Hassan, A., Verma, D. K., Sarangi, P., & Singh, S. (2021, November). Disaster management system using wireless sensor network: A review. In *2021 International Conference on Computational Intelligence and Computing Applications (ICCICA)* (pp. 1-6). IEEE. Murugaraj, S. S., & Kumar, S. (2024). Neuro-Inspired Algorithms for Earthquake Monitoring and Prediction. In *Novel AI Applications for Advancing Earth Sciences* (pp. 315-329). IGI Global Scientific Publishing.

Qin, F., Huang, C., & Lin, Z. (2024). Big data and artificial intelligence-driven natural disaster prediction and prevention: Technological advances and prospects. *Geographical Research Bulletin*, *3*, 381–398.

Riess, T. C. V. (2024). *Spaceborne monitoring of nitrogen oxides emissions from ships with TROPOMI* (Doctoral dissertation, Wageningen University and Research).

Rizwan, S. A., Nongkynrih, B., & Gupta, S. K. (2013). Air pollution in Delhi: Its magnitude and effects on health. *Indian Journal of Community Medicine : Official Publication of Indian Association of Preventive & Social Medicine*, *38*(1), 4–8. DOI: 10.4103/0970-0218.106617 PMID: 23559696

Ronneberger, O., Fischer, P., & Brox, T. (2015, October). U-net: Convolutional networks for biomedical image segmentation. In *International Conference on Medical image computing and computer-assisted intervention* (pp. 234-241). Cham: Springer international publishing. DOI: 10.1007/978-3-319-24574-4_28

Ross, Z. E., Meier, M. A., & Hauksson, E. (2018). P wave arrival picking and first-motion polarity determination with deep learning. *Journal of Geophysical Research. Solid Earth*, *123*(6), 5120–5129. DOI: 10.1029/2017JB015251

Ross, Z. E., Meier, M.-A., & Hauksson, E. (2018). Generalized seismic phase detection with deep learning. *Bulletin of the Seismological Society of America*, *108*(5A), 2894–2901. DOI: 10.1785/0120180080

Saad, O. M., & Chen, Y. (2020). Earthquake detection and P-wave arrival time picking using capsule neural network. *IEEE Transactions on Geoscience and Remote Sensing*, *59*(7), 6234–6243. DOI: 10.1109/TGRS.2020.3019520

Sagintayev, Z., Atanov, S., & Gafurov, A. (2017). Overview of modelling techniques for geo-hazard risk assessment. *Central Asian Journal of Water Research*, *3*(1), 35–42.

Sakurai, M., & Murayama, Y. (2019). Information technologies and disaster management – Benefits and issues -. *Progress in Disaster Science*, *2*, 100012. DOI: 10.1016/j.pdisas.2019.100012

Saleh, M., Rasel, H. M., & Ray, B. (2024). A comprehensive review towards resilient rainfall forecasting models using artificial intelligence techniques. *Green Technologies and Sustainability*, *2*(3), 100104. DOI: 10.1016/j.grets.2024.100104

Samek, W., Montavon, G., Lapuschkin, S., Anders, C. J., & Müller, K.-R. (2021). Explaining deep learning models and their predictions. *Nature Machine Intelligence*, *3*, 286–299. DOI: 10.1038/s42256-021-00338-1

Santos, J. R., & Dela Cruz, M. (2023). Enhancing the Philippine early warning system through machine learning. *Philippine Journal of Science*, *152*(2), 445–458. DOI: 10.56899/152.02.05

Sathya, U., Hashini, S., Lakshmipriya, C., Varun, C. M., & Nalini, M. (2024, December). Emerging Trends and Future Prospects in Internet of Things (IoT) Technology. In *2024 International Conference on Sustainable Communication Networks and Application (ICSCNA)* (pp. 79-85). IEEE.

Scheingraber, C., Hosseini, K., Barsch, R., & Sigloch, K. (2013). Obspyload: A tool for fully automated retrieval of seismological waveform data. *Seismological Research Letters*, *84*(3), 525–531. DOI: 10.1785/0220120103

Selvakumar, P., Vijayakumar, G., Vigneshkumar, P., Umamaheswari, M. S., & Selvamurugan, C. (2024). Prediction of earthquakes, volcanic eruptions, tornadoes, wildfires, and droughts through artificial intelligence. In *Utilizing AI and Machine Learning for Natural Disaster Management* (pp. 133–145). IGI Global Scientific Publishing.

Selvaraju, R. R., Cogswell, M., Das, A., Vedantam, R., Parikh, D., & Batra, D. (2017). Grad-CAM: Visual explanations from deep networks via gradient-based localization. In *Proceedings of the IEEE International Conference on Computer Vision (ICCV)* (pp. 618–626). https://doi.org/ DOI: 10.1109/ICCV.2017.74

Sharma, K., & Yadav, S. (2023). Air quality monitoring using geospatial technology and field sensors. *Geospatial Analytics for Environmental Pollution Modeling: Analysis, Control and Management*, 91-118.

Sharma, M., Singh, K., Gautam, A. S., & Gautam, S. (2024). Longitudinal study of air pollutants in Indian metropolises: Seasonal patterns and urban variability. *Aerosol Science and Engineering*, 1-16.

Siddiqa, A., Karim, A., & Gani, A. (2017). Big data storage technologies: A survey. *Frontiers of Information Technology & Electronic Engineering*, *18*(8), 1040–1070. DOI: 10.1631/FITEE.1500441

Sinha, B. R. K. (2024). Introduction: a broad perspective on the concepts of urban dynamics, environment, and health. In *Urban Dynamics, Environment and Health: An International Perspective* (pp. 3–79). Springer Nature Singapore.

Sonu, S. B., & Suyampulingam, A. (2021). "Linear regression-based air quality data analysis and prediction using python." *2021 IEEE Madras Section Conference (MASCON)*. IEEE. DOI: 10.1109/MASCON51689.2021.9563432

Suarez, A. L. A., & Beroza, G. (2025). Picking Regional Seismic Phase Arrival Times with Deep Learning. *Seismica*, *4*(1).

Subramanian, R. S., Ramana, T. V., Ramana, K. V., Prabha, S., & Nivaskumar, V. (2025). Converging Horizons: Synergies of 6G Wireless Communication, Machine Learning, and Embedded Systems for Intelligent Connectivity. *The Intersection of 6G, AI/Machine Learning, and Embedded Systems*, 67-93.

Sudhan, M., Deepak, K. A., Minu, M., Mounagurusamy, M. K., Navaneethan, S., & Venkataramanaiah, B. (2025). Internet of Things Assisted Sleep Quality Recognition using Hunger Games Search Optimization with Deep Learning on Smart Healthcare Systems. *Journal of Intelligent Systems and Internet of Things*, *14*(1), 129–140. DOI: 10.54216/JISIoT.140110

Sudrajat, A., Meilano, I., Abidin, H. Z., Susilo, S., Hardy, T., Samapta, B. T., & Kambali, R. A. P. (2025). Wavelet-based P-wave detection in high-rate GNSS data: A novel approach for rapid earthquake monitoring in tsunamigenic settings. *Sensors (Basel), 25*(13), 3860. DOI: 10.3390/s25133860 PMID: 40648120

Sundari, V. M., Rose, R. M., Sassirekha, S. M., Nalini, M., & Girija, P. (2024, November). Deep Learning: Techniques, Taxonomy, Applications, and Future Directions. In *2024 International Conference on Smart Technologies for Sustainable Development Goals (ICSTSDG)* (pp. 1-5). IEEE.

Tang, H., Bhatti, U. A., Li, J., Marjan, S., Baryalai, M., Assam, M., Ghadi, Y. Y., & Mohamed, H. G. (2023). A New Hybrid Forecasting Model Based on Dual Series Decomposition with Long-Term Short-Term Memory. *International Journal of Intelligent Systems, 2023*(1), 9407104. DOI: 10.1155/2023/9407104

Tan, X., Han, L., Zhang, X., Zhou, W., Li, W., & Qian, Y. (2021). A review of current air quality indexes and improvements under the multi-contaminant air pollution exposure. *Journal of Environmental Management, 279*, 111681. DOI: 10.1016/j.jenvman.2020.111681 PMID: 33321353

Titos, M., Bueno, A., García-Hernández, M., Benítez, C., & Ibáñez, J. M. (2018). Classification of seismo-volcanic signals using convolutional neural networks. *IEEE Transactions on Geoscience and Remote Sensing, 56*(7), 3943–3952. DOI: 10.1109/TGRS.2018.2806661

Titos, M., Bueno, A., García, L., Benítez, C., & Ibanez, J. (2018). Detection and classification of continuous volcano-seismic signals with deep neural networks. *IEEE Transactions on Geoscience and Remote Sensing, 57*(4), 1936–1948. DOI: 10.1109/TGRS.2018.2870202

UNCTAD. (2025). *Technology and innovation report: AI in disaster risk reduction*. United Nations Conference on Trade and Development. https://unctad.org/publication/technology-and-innovation-report

Valade, S., Ley, A., & Massin, F.. (2019). Towards global volcano monitoring using multisensor data and machine learning. *Remote Sensing, 11*(13), 1520. DOI: 10.3390/rs11131528

Venkatesh, R., Balasubramanian, C., & Kaliappan, M. (2019). Development of big data predictive analytics model for disease prediction using machine learning technique. *Journal of Medical Systems*, *43*(8), 272. DOI: 10.1007/s10916-019-1398-y PMID: 31278468

Venketbabu, T., Aswathy, M. P., Sangeetha, J., Anish, T. P., Nalini, M., & Subramanian, R. S. (2024, October). Revolutionizing Image Processing: Innovations Impacts and Future Trends. In *2024 2nd International Conference on Self Sustainable Artificial Intelligence Systems (ICSSAS)* (pp. 901-907). IEEE.

Wai, K. P., Chia, M. Y., Koo, C. H., Huang, Y. F., & Chong, W. C. (2022). Applications of deep learning in water quality management: A state-of-the-art review. *Journal of Hydrology (Amsterdam)*, *613*, 128332. DOI: 10.1016/j.jhydrol.2022.128332

Wang, C., Zheng, J., Du, J., Wang, G., Klemeš, J. J., Wang, B., Liao, Q., & Liang, Y. (2022). Weather condition-based hybrid models for multiple air pollutants forecasting and minimisation. *Journal of Cleaner Production*, *352*, 131610. DOI: 10.1016/j.jclepro.2022.131610

Wang, W., Wu, J., Fang, L., Zeng, K., & Chang, X. (2015). Design and implementation of spatial database and geo-processing models for a road geo-hazard information management and risk assessment system. *Environmental Earth Sciences*, *73*(3), 1103–1117. DOI: 10.1007/s12665-014-3461-9

Wang, Y. (2015). Generalized seismic wavelets. *Geophysical Journal International*, *203*(2), 1172–1178. DOI: 10.1093/gji/ggv346

Wang, Z., Zhang, B., Gao, J., Wang, Q., & Liu, Q. H. (2017). Wavelet transform with generalized beta wavelets for seismic time-frequency analysis. *Geophysics*, *82*(4), O47–O56. DOI: 10.1190/geo2016-0342.1

Wani, A. K., Rahayu, F., Ben Amor, I., Quadir, M., Murianingrum, M., Parnidi, P., Ayub, A., Supriyadi, S., Sakiroh, S., Saefudin, S., Kumar, A., & Latifah, E. (2024). Environmental resilience through artificial intelligence: Innovations in monitoring and management. *Environmental Science and Pollution Research International*, *31*(12), 18379–18395. DOI: 10.1007/s11356-024-32404-z PMID: 38358626

Williams, S. D. P. (2003). The effect of coloured noise on the uncertainties of rates estimated from geodetic time series. *Journal of Geodesy*, *76*(9-10), 483–494. DOI: 10.1007/s00190-002-0283-4

Wu, J., Gan, W., Chao, H. C., & Yu, P. S. (2024). Geospatial big data: Survey and challenges. *IEEE Journal of Selected Topics in Applied Earth Observations and Remote Sensing*, *17*, 17007–17020. DOI: 10.1109/JSTARS.2024.3438376

Xi, Z., Wei, S. S., Zhu, W., Beroza, G. C., Jie, Y., & Saloor, N. (2024). Deep learning for deep earthquakes: Insights from OBS observations of the Tonga subduction zone. *Geophysical Journal International*, *238*(2), 1073–1088. DOI: 10.1093/gji/ggae200

Xu, F., Zheng, M., Zheng, X., Liu, D., Wang, P., Ma, Y., & Zhang, X. (2025). Geospatial big data-driven fine-scale carbon emission modeling. *Remote Sensing (Basel)*, *17*(18), 3185. DOI: 10.3390/rs17183185

Yamini, B., Beslin, P. P., Anish, T. P., Gracelin, S. B., Dinesh, M. G., Nalini, M., & Siva, S. R. (2024). Advancements in Cognitive Radio Networks: Protocols, Architectures, Challenges, and Future Perspectives. In *Spectrum and Power Allocation in Cognitive Radio Systems* (pp. 1-17). IGI Global.

Yang, L., Liu, X., Zhu, W., Zhao, L., & Li, J. (2021). Deep learning for real-time earthquake detection and localization. *Journal of Geophysical Research: Solid Earth*, *126*(3), e2020JB021135. https://doi.org/DOI: 10.1029/2020JB021135

Yiou, P., Sornette, D., & Ghil, M. (2000). Data-adaptive wavelets and multi-scale singular-spectrum analysis. *Physica D. Nonlinear Phenomena*, *142*(3-4), 254–290. DOI: 10.1016/S0167-2789(00)00045-2

Yuan, C., & Zhang, J. (2025). Applying deep learning to teleseismic phase detection and picking: PcP and PKiKP cases. *Artificial Intelligence in Geosciences*, *6*(1), 100108. DOI: 10.1016/j.aiig.2025.100108

Zhang, Y., Sun, Q., Liu, J., & Petrosian, O. (2023). Long-term forecasting of air pollution particulate matter (PM2. 5) and analysis of influencing factors. *Sustainability (Basel)*, *16*(1), 19. DOI: 10.3390/su16010019

Zhu, L., Peng, Z., McClellan, J., Li, C., Yao, D., Li, Z., & Fang, L. (2019). Deep learning for seismic phase detection and picking in the aftershock zone of 2008 Mw7. 9 Wenchuan Earthquake. *Physics of the Earth and Planetary Interiors*, *293*, 106261. DOI: 10.1016/j.pepi.2019.05.004

Zhu, S., Lian, X., Liu, H., Hu, J., Wang, Y., & Che, J. (2017). Daily air quality index forecasting with hybrid models: A case in China. *Environmental Pollution*, *231*, 1232–1244. DOI: 10.1016/j.envpol.2017.08.069 PMID: 28939124

Zhu, W., & Beroza, G. C. (2019). PhaseNet: A deep-convolutional neural network for seismic arrival-time picking. *IEEE Transactions on Geoscience and Remote Sensing*, *57*(11), 9476–9489. DOI: 10.1109/TGRS.2019.2926772

Zhu, W., & Beroza, G. C. (2019). PhaseNet: A deep-neural-network-based seismic arrival-time picking method. *Geophysical Journal International*, *216*(1), 261–273.

Zhu, W., Mousavi, S. M., & Beroza, G. C. (2021). Seismic signal detection and classification using deep neural networks. *Geophysical Journal International*, *225*(1), 1–15. DOI: 10.1093/gji/ggaa566

Zou, L., Song, Y., & Cervone, G. (2024). Geospatial big data: Theory, methods, and applications. *Annals of GIS*, *30*(4), 411–415. DOI: 10.1080/19475683.2024.2419749

About the Contributors

Froilan Mobo is a distinguished academician and researcher currently serving as a Full Professor II at the Philippine Merchant Marine Academy (PMMA). With a profound commitment to the intersection of technology and education, he has become a leading voice in the fields of educational technology, artificial intelligence, and maritime education. Dr. Mobo's academic background is extensive, characterized by a pursuit of multidisciplinary expertise. He holds a PhD in Development Education from Central Luzon State University and a Doctor in Public Administration. Complementing his doctoral degrees are three master's qualifications: a Master of Business Administration, a Master of Science in Computer Science, and a Master of Arts in Social Studies Education. He is currently further expanding his business acumen as a candidate for a Doctor in Business Administration at the Polytechnic University of the Philippines. As a prolific researcher, Dr. Mobo has gained international recognition for his contributions to scholarly literature. His work is widely indexed in prestigious databases such as Scopus and Web of Science, maintaining a significant citation record and an h-index that reflects his influence in the global research community. His expertise is frequently sought after in editorial roles for international journals and as a resource expert for global academic forums. Beyond the classroom and the laboratory, Dr. Mobo is a dedicated public servant and community leader. He serves as the President of the International Human Rights Movement Philippines and is the active President of his local homeowners association, where he advocates for infrastructure development and utility stabilization. His advocacy also extends to environmental protection, having served as a resource expert on climate adaptation and human rights. Dr. Mobo is a Licensed Professional Teacher and a Certified Human Resource Associate, blending high-level theoretical knowledge with practical, professional certifications. His career is marked by numerous accolades, including the Luminary Excellence in Education and Research Award, affirming his status as a top-tier educator and researcher in the Philippines.

***

Amir Dar is the Faculty in the Department of Mathematics at Lovely Professional University Punjab. The area of interest: Financial mathematics, financial economics, statistics and business mathematics.

A Durga Devi, (Ph.D), is in College teaching profession since 2022. she received her B.E (ECE) Degree from Panimalar Institute of Technology, chennai, India in 2018 and M.E (VLSI DESIGN) from Saveetha Engineering College, Affiliated to Anna University, Chennai in 2020. She has been teaching various subjects, under graduate students for the past 3 years. She has Published 4 papers in reputed journals and conference and also published patent and book chapters. Presently working as Assistant professor at Electronics and Communication Engineering department in Saveetha Engineering College, Chennai, India. Also she is currently a part time Ph.D. scholar at Anna University, Chennai, India. Her-research interests are Deep Learning, VLSI,Embedded systems, Machine Learning. She is a dedicated teacher.

Manzoor Khanday was born on April 24, 1979, in a mountainous region in Anantnag Kashmir. He received preliminary education from HSS Srigufwara. He completed Bachelors from G.D.C Boys Anantnag, and pursued masters from the University of Kashmir, Srinagar. Following this, Dr. Manzoor Ahmad completed his Doctor of Philosophy from the Department of Statistics, Vikram University Ujjain, India. His research interests primarily include Economic Design of control charts, Statistical Quality Control, and has published more than twelve research papers in national and international journals. Presently Dr. Manzoor Ahmad is an Assistant Professor at Lovely Professional University Punjab India.

Dinesh M G is a faculty member in the Department of Artificial Intelligence and Data Science at Easa College of Engineering and Technology, Coimbatore. He is actively involved in teaching, research, and academic mentoring in emerging computing technologies. His interests include data analytics, intelligent systems, and applied research in AI-driven solutions. Dr. Dinesh contributes to curriculum development and supports student innovation and projects. He is committed to academic excellence and industry-relevant engineering education.

Wes Harven Maravilla is an English language educator and researcher with extensive teaching experience across Thailand, Taiwan, and the Philippines, where he has taught EFL, English for Academic Purposes, English for Tourism and Hospitality, and English for Specific Purposes at secondary and university levels. His pedagogical work emphasizes project-based learning, EMI, digital storytelling, debate, podcasting, AI-enhanced assessment, and technology-mediated activities such as VR-based 360 narratives, mobile learning apps, and interactive quiz platforms to foster communicative competence and critical thinking among EFL learners. In research, he has published and presented on EFL and education, reading–writing integration, digital language learning, AI in language education, tourism communication, and sustainable development, while also contributing to maritime and history education through roles as external evaluator and research panelist at the Philippine Merchant Marine Academy. His upcoming and published book chapters and journal articles further consolidate his key research areas, including EFL and education, AI and emerging technologies in language learning, maritime and history education.

S Meganathan completed his Ph.D. in 2013 at SASTRA Deemed University. He works as an Associate Professor in the Department of Computer Science & Engineering at Srinivasa Ramanujan Centre, SASTRA Deemed University, Kumbakonam. Four research scholars are pursuing Ph.D. programme under his guidance in data mining and its applications. Their research focuses on tropical cyclone prediction, electrical consumption prediction based on climate data, patient diagnosis systems on medical data, and improved D.S.S. systems on medical database systems. There are 32 research articles published in SCOPUS-indexed journals and 8 in SCI/SCIE indexed journals. He has experience in consultancy projects in the area of Video and Image Analytics for the Mahamaham Festival 2016, held at Kumbakonam, Tamil Nadu. This project extended to various festivals conducted by the HR&CE departments and the Revenue Departments of the government of Tamil Nadu. The student projects for B. Tech, M.Sc., and M.C.A., programmes in meteorological data have been guided for the past 20 years.

Umamaheswari P holds a B.E. in Information Technology from Periyar Maniammai College of Engineering and Technology (2003), an M.B.A. from Alagappa University, Karaikudi, Tamil Nadu (2006), and an M.Tech in Computer Science from SASTRA Deemed University, Thanjavur, Tamil Nadu (2011). She earned her Ph.D. in Computer Science and Engineering from SASTRA Deemed University. With two decades of experience, she has taught both undergraduate and postgraduate courses in Computer Science. She is currently an Assistant Professor in the Department of Computer Science and Engineering at SRC Campus, SASTRA University, Kumbakonam. Her research interests focus on Data Mining, Machine Learning, and Deep Learning. She has published numerous research papers in international conferences, SCI-indexed journals, Scopus, and book chapters.

Vinoth R is affiliated with the Department of Computer Science and Engineering at R.M.K College of Engineering and Technology, Tamil Nadu, India. He is involved in academic and research activities in computer science, focusing on emerging technologies and practical applications. His interests include software development, data-driven solutions, and contributing to innovative research work.

Karthika S is an academic professional affiliated with Vel Tech Rangarajan Dr. Sagunthala R&D Institute of Science and Technology, Chennai. She is actively involved in teaching, research, and academic development in her field of specialization. Her interests include contributing to innovative research, student mentoring, and advancing technological knowledge.

Udhaya Shankar S is affiliated with the Department of Artificial Intelligence and Data Science at Vel Tech Multi Tech Dr. Rangarajan Dr. Sakunthala Engineering College, Chennai. His academic interests include artificial intelligence, data analytics, and emerging computational technologies. He is actively involved in teaching, research, and guiding students in innovative and industry-relevant projects.

Sunitha T, M.E., M.B.A.,(Ph.D), is in College teaching profession since 2006. she received her B.E (CSE) Degree from Bhajarang Engineering College, Veppambattu, India in 2006, M.B.A (HR) from CEG campus Anna University, Chennai in 2009 and M.E (CSE) from P. B. College of Engineering, Affiliated to Anna University, Chennai in 2013. She has been teaching various subjects, under graduate and post graduate students for the past 15 years. She has Published more than 14 papers in reputed national, international journals and conference and also published patent and book chapters. Presently working as Assistant professor at Artificial Intelligence and Data Science department in Saveetha Engineering College, Chennai, India. Also she is currently a part time Ph.D. scholar at Anna University, Chennai, India. Her-research interests are Machine Learning, Deep Learning, Internet of Things (IoT), and Data science. She is a dedicated teacher and positive thinker.

Index

www.ingramcontent.com/pod-product-compliance
Lightning Source LLC
LaVergne TN
LVHW060002031026
849161LV00025B/1332